# JOHNSON'S PREFACE TO SHAKESPEARE

A facsimile of the 1778 edition
with introduction and commentary by

## P.J. Smallwood
Lecturer in English, City of Birmingham Polytechnic

Published by Bristol Classical Press
English Editors: David Hopkins & Tom Mason
General Editor: John H. Betts

Cover illustration:  William Shakespeare, from an engraving in the 1778
edition of Johnson's *Preface*; Samuel Johnson, from an engraving by
E. Mitchell, from a painting by Sir Joshua Reynolds.

Printed in Great Britain

Published (1985) by

Bristol Classical Press
Department of Classics
University of Bristol
Wills Memorial Building
Queens Road
BRISTOL BS8 1RJ

Johnson, Samuel, *1709-1784*
  Johnson's Preface to Shakespeare: a facsimile
  of the 1778 edition.
  1. Shakespeare, William - Criticism and
  interpretation
  1. Title 11. Smallwood, P.J.
  822.3'3  PR2975

  ISBN 0-86292-179-1
  ISBN 0-86292-087-6 Pbk

Printed and Bound by Short Run Press Ltd., Exeter, Devon

CONTENTS


Introduction:

# INTRODUCTION

## I: *Samuel Johnson: The Man and his Works*

On its publication in 1765[1], the *Preface to Shakespeare*, which appeared with Johnson's edition of Shakespeare's plays, was the first extended and sustained attempt by Samuel Johnson at critical writing in prefatory form. Like the *Lives of the Poets* of some fifteen years later, the *Preface* was a critical essay on one writer's entire works (minus Shakespeare's poems). Yet, in the case of the *Preface*, Johnson had confronted a perhaps more difficult challenge than in any one of his *Lives*. The *Preface* to an edition of Shakespeare would by virtue of its subject call on the sum of his powers. It would present the supreme test of his talents and his abilities as a literary critic. It is generally agreed that Johnson rose to this challenge, and that the *Preface to Shakespeare* forms, along with the greatest of the *Lives*, the central corpus and vital focus of Johnson's literary criticism.

Yet the *Preface to Shakespeare* has at the same time always provoked adverse reactions, and inspired negative claims. Throughout its history, and even in recent years, the suggestion has been made that Johnson, in certain respects, was untrained, or unfitted, in his basic sensibilities for the criticism of Shakespeare. His fundamental preconceptions as a critic, were, it is

---

[1] The *Preface* is printed here in the version of 1778, the last issue of the second edition of the work to be supervised by Johnson before his death. The first edition, and the first issue of the second edition, were published in 1765. Minor authorial changes to the text were made in 1768, 1773, and 1778.

claimed, 'neoclassic' in nature, so that his mind was, for
that reason, alien to Shakespearean drama. As part of this
charge, it is sometimes implied that Johnson was temper-
amentally unsympathetic to Shakespeare; that his attitudes
were too narrow and his experience too limited. Justification for this view must of course rest on our general
conception of Johnson and the quality of his mind, and on
our idea of his experience of literature and of life. Particularly important is the kind of experience that Johnson
brought to the judgement of his author. So what we make
of Johnson's criticism of Shakespeare will be to some extent bound up with what we make of Johnson the man, and the
human qualities which infused and governed his critical
approach. For this reason, some brief comments on Johnson's life and works are perhaps useful at this stage.

Johnson was born in 1709, at Lichfield, in Staffordshire,
the son of Michael Johnson, a bookseller. He began to
gather his stores of learning in childhood, and while still
a boy he amassed, for later use, a wealth of literary knowledge from the volumes on the shelves of his father's shop.
In 1728, at the age of nineteen, he went to Oxford, as
a commoner at Pembroke College, where he distinguished
himself by writing verses in Latin; though it is said
that he was at this date depressed by poverty and plagued
by disease. Johnson was compelled through shortage of
money to leave Oxford after only one year and to return
to Lichfield, not knowing, says Boswell, "how he should
gain even a decent livelihood".

Among the various occupations of this stage of his life
was Johnson's first prose work, a translation from French
of Father Lobo's *Voyage to Abyssinia*, for which he received five guineas. About the same time, Johnson began
his correspondence with Edward Cave, editor of the famous

*Gentleman's Magazine*[2], and offered to undertake, for a
fee, sometimes "to fill a column".  He opened a small
academy at Edial, near Lichfield, but only three pupils
were put under his care, though one of them, a companion
of happier years, was David Garrick, later the celebrated
Shakespearean actor.  Johnson began in these years *The
Tragedy of Irene*, which was eventually produced on stage
with the assistance of Garrick.  But before long, Johnson
determined to leave Lichfield to test his fortune in
London, where he became a regular contributor to *The
Gentleman's Magazine*, and submitted a distinguished succession of poems and reviews, obtaining a "tolerable
livelihood" by assisting as editor.  In May 1738 Johnson's
poem, *London*, was published, and from that date his slow
but inexorable rise to eminence in the literary world
began.

Even from these early years, it would seem, Johnson's
singular character was apparent.  He had, from his youth,
exhibited a peculiar mixture of indolence and energy.
Johnson was ambitious to excel, though afflicted throughout his life by a morbid and melancholic disposition,
made worse by pain and sickness.  Yet even with these dis-
advantages, his talents as a writer were clear.  He was
extremely prolific, and in the years prior to the publication of the *Preface to Shakespeare* Johnson served a long
and varied apprenticeship in literature and criticism.
To the volumes of *The Gentleman's Magazine*, Johnson could
offer an unfailing supply of essays, translations and
lives.  Included with these were a succession of "Debates
in the Senate of Lilliput", or record of the orations
to be heard in the Houses of Parliament.  His abilities
as a biographical writer he revealed fully for the first

---

[2] *The Gentleman's Magazine*, appeared monthly, from 26 April 1731.

time in his *Life of Savage*, which appeared in 1744.  In
the following year, he published a pamphlet entitled
*Miscellaneous Observations on the Tragedy of Macbeth*,
attaching proposals for an edition of Shakespeare.  But
although further work on this edition was delayed,
Johnson's appetite for the arduous and extensive was
not satisfied: in 1747 he announced his plan for a
*Dictionary of the English Language*, a work which, though
it took a much greater period to complete than Johnson
had planned, secured him both immortality and a pension
for life.  The *Plan* was inscribed to the Earl of Chesterfield, who had at one time hinted his support.  In the
event, however, few favours were forthcoming.  When,
nearing the publication of the great work, the *Dictionary*
was recommended by Chesterfield, in two papers written
for *The World*, Johnson replied in his famous 'Letter',
in what has become a model of dignified contempt for a
proud and negligent patron.

The energy and the tenacity that Johnson brought to
the completion of many of his writings is clear from
his work on the *Dictionary*, a project which would have
overwhelmed any other spirit.  It is true that he was frequently fatigued, and sometimes distracted; but he was
never so weary that his efforts were abandoned in total des-
pair.  Johnson seems to have composed many works with more
effort than delight, professing little affection for his
task; so that they seem to be often sorrowfully conceived
and painfully completed.  He was not among those whose
labour is their pleasure, but seems rather to have been
driven to write by a mixture of penury and private com-
pulsion, or sometimes, perhaps, from "that hunger of
imagination which preys incessantly on life".  In his
later years, his pension secured him from the more menial
employments of the literary life, so that, to a

growing extent, he wrote as he wished.  But it seems
that the habit of drudgery remained when the need of it
had ceased.

Johnson illustrated the pages of his *Dictionary* with
quotations from English authors, chosen to elucidate
the meaning of the words.  These examples, he selected
from the vast field of his literary knowledge, and when
they were not already stored in his memory, he took pains
to seek them out.  In this connection, Johnson's habits
as a reader are worth a particular mention.  He read
rapidly, and with intense concentration.  As a youth,
it is said, he enlarged his literary knowledge by no
special plan, or scheme of study, but seized on whatever
came in his way.  He did not always read books through,
but would throw them aside, half-finished, perhaps eager
to pursue some new knowledge, having found what he required.

By the time of the *Preface to Shakespeare*, Johnson's crea-
tive reputation was firmly established.  In 1749, he turn-
ed aside from his work on the *Dictionary* to compose and
publish *The Vanity of Human Wishes*, for which, however,
he is said to have received only fifteen guineas.  In
the following year, on 20th March, Johnson began his
series of papers for *The Rambler*.  These papers, some
moral, some philosophical, and some literary, appeared
on two days of the week, without a break, till Saturday
17th March 1752.  They were hastily composed, with considerable reliance on Johnson's stores of learning and
his extensive reading.  At first, it seems, the public,
accustomed to the levity, facility and ease of Addison's
*Spectator*, did not receive very favourably the weighty morality and gravity of tone of the 'Ramblers'.  But with the
passage of time, Johnson's stern philosophy became in-

creasingly respected and learned readers acquired a
taste for the solemn and grand aspects of his style.

  With *The Rambler*, Johnson began his training in literary criticism: yet his tastes as a critic cannot be
securely determined from these essays alone.  Particular
authors are seldom considered, and the topics selected in
*The Rambler* are the more general issues of literary genre,
or matters of enduring critical debate, such as 'low
words', 'versification' and 'sound and sense'.  Johnson
appears at this stage in his critical writings to have no
very definite system for preferring one author to another.
The questions he discusses are frequently taken up only to
be dismissed, as if he were clearing from his mind the
redundancies and irrelevancies of contemporary opinion.
In the course of these papers, an occasional mention is
made of Shakespeare.  But though there is more on Shakespeare than on any other poet, there is still very little:
so the full extension of Johnson's powers as a critic
must, perhaps, first be sought in the *Preface to Shakespeare.*

  Johnson's experience as a writer of drama preceded his
practice as a critic.  In 1749, his own play, *Irene*,
was lavishly produced by David Garrick, now manager
of the theatre in Drury Lane.  *Irene* was acted for nine
nights, so that the profits of three nights were Johnson's.
The copyright was sold for one hundred pounds.  Garrick
himself, meanwhile, soon came to be numbered among the
eminent men of the age.  Johnson seems at different
times to have felt affection and amused contempt for
Garrick.  To repay Garrick for the promise of staging
*Irene*, Johnson had written a Prologue in 1747, containing
the following celebration of Shakespeare:

    When Learning's triumph o'er her barbarous foes
    First rear'd the stage, immortal SHAKESPEAR rose;

>     Each change of many-colour'd life he drew,
>     Exhausted worlds, and then imagined new:
>     Existence saw him spurn her bounded reign,
>     And panting Time toil'd after him in vain:
>     His pow'rful strokes presiding truth impress'd,
>     And unresisted passion storm'd the breast.

But in later years, Johnson became more and more irritated
with the acting profession, and his relations with Garrick
were occasionally strained.  It is sometimes said that
Johnson became jealous of Garrick, who certainly revelled
in the glitter of his fame.  Johnson's own reputation advanced only by laborious stages; Garrick's celebrity as
an actor was swiftly seized, with ready precocity.  But
if resentment was felt, it never evolved into malice.
Garrick's ludicrous pride made him a topic for humour,
and Johnson, on many occasions, delighted to tease and
deflate his old pupil.  He elevated the acting profession
to the position of a standing joke and named Garrick,
condescendingly, his "little David".  Reynolds, a friend
of both Johnson and Garrick, said that Johnson seemed to
regard Garrick as his private property, and would tolerate
criticism from no one but himself.

   Johnson's career as a writer was, of course, in part
shaped by his friends.  *The Adventurer*, begun in 1753,
was the joint project of Johnson, Hawkesworth and
Joseph Warton.  Two years later, in 1755, the *Dictionary*
was at last published, with a Preface.  The rewards, however, were few: much of the money received in subscriptions
had been spent in preparing the work for the press.  In
the following year, Johnson began his contributions to *The
Literary Magazine*, a monthly journal, gracing its pages
with a succession of essays and reviews on topics ranging
from the trivial to the profound.  Perhaps the most well
known of these is Johnson's review of Soame Jenyn's *Free*

*Enquiry into the Nature and Origin of Evil*, remarkable
for Johnson's acutely expressed scorn of complacent and
sophistical argument. At about this time, Johnson  turn-
ed again to his edition of Shakespeare, and collected subscriptions. But many more years were to pass before his
task was complete. In the meantime, Johnson produced a
new periodical paper, *The Idler*, begun in 1758. Johnson's
mother died in the following year. It is generally supposed that he wrote *Rasselas, Prince of Abyssinia* in the
evenings of one week to pay the costs of her funeral.

From this painful moment in his life, to the publication
of his edition, Johnson worked with increasing concentration
on the text of Shakespeare, returning as part of this work
to the Prefaces and notes of the earlier editors: Rowe,
Pope, Theobald, Hanmer and Warburton. Johnson's edition
was finally published in 1765, after many delays, and ac-
companied by the famous *Preface*. It was in general well
received, though Kenrick, a minor critic, occupied himself
with a violent attack on Johnson's opinions and learning,
but did not provoke a reply.

Johnson allowed his critical talents to lie dormant in
the years immediately following the publication of his
edition of Shakespeare. However, his opinions on authors
were affectionately recorded in the pages of Boswell's
*Life*, where they convey his character as a talker, and
leader of the Literary Club. Members of Johnson's Club
have sometimes complained that Johnson was occasionally
peevish in company, turning meetings of the Club into
disputes between rival contenders. But it seems from all
accounts that Johnson's kindness tempered his anger, and
that his satire of others was softened by a generous nature, devoid of meanness or cruelty.

The *Preface to Shakespeare* was the major critical work

of Johnson's early maturity; the *Lives of the Poets* the
masterpiece of his final years. In 1773, Johnson travelled
to Scotland with Boswell, and recorded his tour in his
*Journey to the Western Isles* (1775). He visited Paris
in these years, composed a series of political pamphlets,
and consolidated his friendship with the Thrales of
Streatham, with Dr. Burney and his daughter Fanny. The
first volume of his *Lives of the Poets* appeared in 1779.
The *Lives* were composed at the invitation of a committee
of London booksellers, who asked Johnson to name his terms.
The second volume of the *Lives* was published in 1781, and
was eagerly awaited by a public whose expectations had been
raised by the excellence of the first. But Johnson's habitual melancholy deepened after the publication of the
*Lives*. He busied himself with a final round of travels
and visits to friends, from which he gained some consolation. But the sickness of his body did not abate. He died
on 13th December 1784. Some days later his corpse was
interred in Westminster Abbey, near the foot of Shakespeare's
monument, and close to the remains of David Garrick.

* * * * * *

II: *The Publication of Johnson's Shakespeare Edition*

Johnson's discovery of Shakespeare can be traced to his
earliest years, when, according to the story he told of
himself, he was at the age of nine frightened by the ghost
in *Hamlet*, and rushed upstairs in his father's shop, to
have others around him. The *Observations on Macbeth* (1745),
with his *Proposals* for an edition, were Johnson's first
published works on Shakespeare. The *Observations* were
printed as a sample of the complete edition, with critical
reflections on notes and emendations by Theobald and Pope.

Johnson's own textual emendations, both in the *Observa-*
*tions* and in the finished edition, were made with considerable caution.  Johnson was the first editor of
Shakespeare to distinguish clearly between Shakespeare's
obscurity or difficulty as a writer, and the corruption
of his text.  Pope, in his edition of 1725, had exceed-
ed Rowe, the first eighteenth-century editor of Shakespeare, in conjectural freedom.  Theobald, provoked by
Pope, complained of Pope's indulgences in his *Shakespeare*
*Restored*, and published his own edition in 1734.  Pope,
in response, placed "Piddling Tibbald" among the heroes
of his satirical poem, *The Dunciad*.  With the *Observations*
*on Macbeth*, Johnson entered the contest, and gave, in this
work, not only a foretaste of his skills as an editor of
Shakespeare, but ample testimony to his powers as a critic
of poetry.  Even at this early date in his career, the *Ob-*
*servations* include one passage as striking as any to be found
in the breadth of Johnson's critical writings.  It is a comparison of two descriptions of night, one by Dryden, the
other by Shakespeare.  The relation of this comparison to
the feelings of the boy terrified by the ghost in *Hamlet* is
perhaps hard to resist.

> Night is described by two great poets,
> but one describes a night of quiet, the other
> of perturbation.  In the night of Dryden, all
> the disturbers of the world are laid asleep;
> in that of Shakespeare, nothing but sorcery,
> lust and murder is awake.  He that reads
> Dryden, finds himself lull'd with serenity,
> and disposed to solitude and contemplation.
> He that peruses Shakespeare, looks around
> alarmed, and starts to find himself alone.
> One is the night of a lover, the other that
> of a murderer[3].

---

[3] Dryden; *The Indian Emperour: being the sequel of the Indian Queen*,
III.ii; Shakespeare; *Macbeth*, II.i.

The complete edition appeared twenty years later.  There
is a story that Jacob Tonson, the bookseller, who claimed
to control the copyright of Shakespeare, threatened Cave,
who was to take subscriptions for Johnson's edition, with
a suit in Chancery, so that progress, for a time, was
delayed.  Johnson considered, but did not at that time
write, a 'Life' of Dryden, and only the growing demand of
the public for a new edition of Shakespeare persuaded him
to renew his original design, and publish a fresh *Proposal*
in 1756, with subscriptions now to be taken by J. and R.
Tonson *et al*.  Johnson had published his *Dictionary of
the English Language* in the previous year, and had
made extensive use of illustrations taken from Shakespeare.  He was now ready for a project hardly less great.
Some evidence of his critical feelings for Shakespeare
had been given in *The Rambler* (Nos. 156 and 168), and in
the Dedication to Mrs Lennox's *Shakespear Illustrated* of
1753.  But as in the case of the *Dictionary*, Johnson took
time to complete what had flourished in design.  The
subscribers were kept waiting.  One postponement followed
another and, in 1762, Charles Churchill, in Book III of
his poem *The Ghost*, included a satirical attack on Johnson
for cheating his friends of their money.  The list of subscribers had been lost, and although Churchill's satire,
according to Boswell, spurred Johnson on, Sir John Hawkins
reports that such a topor had seized his faculties "as
not all the remonstrances of his friends" could cure it.
He attests that Johnson "seemed to forget how many years
had passed since he had begun to take subscriptions for
his edition of Shakespeare", and he wrote that: "it was
by a wager, or some other pecuniary engagement" that he
was moved to finish the work[4].  Murphy allows that the

---

[4] *The Life of Samuel Johnson LL.D.*, ed. B.H. Davies (London: Cape,
1962), pp.192; 195.

editing of Shakespeare "was an office which he never
cordially embraced"[5]. Boswell describes the task as a
"Caesarean operation".

The *Preface* was composed last, when the labour of editing was over, and perhaps as a work more congenial to
Johnson's nature. Johnson once said to Reynolds that
there were two things he was confident he could do well:

> . . . one is the introduction to any literary
> work, stating what it is to contain, and how
> it should be executed in the most perfect manner;
> the other is a conclusion, showing from various
> causes why the execution has not been equal to
> what the author promised to himself and to the
> public

The edition was published in October 1765, and his critics
immediately compared what Johnson had proposed with what
he had performed. But he had clearly done enough to
ensure success; a second printing was soon needed, and, in
1773, the *Preface* and the edition were issued with re-
visions, and with additional notes, by George Steevens.
From that time on, many editions of Shakespeare adopted
Johnson's notes, and many reprinted the *Preface*, "The most
manly piece of criticism", wrote Adam Smith, "that was
ever published in any country"[6].

* * * * * *


III: *Johnson's Preface*

Not every reaction to the *Preface to Shakespeare* has been

---

[5] *Johnsonian Miscellanies*, ed. G.B. Hill (Oxford: Clarendon Press,
1907), I, 473.
[6] 'Anecdotes by William Seward', *Johnsonian Miscellanies*, II, 307

as positive as Smith's.  Today, Johnson's *Preface* is
generally regarded as his greatest single essay in
literary criticism, even his greatest single work.  Yet
it has tended to be thought of as interesting mainly in
the study of the history of criticism rather than the
study of Shakespeare's plays themselves.  The *Preface*,
nevertheless, holds a unique and permanent place in
Shakespearean criticism.  For not only was Johnson writing on the whole body of Shakespeare's drama, he seems to
have concentrated in his essay the whole force of his own
feelings and thoughts.  And this, perhaps, is one main
source of Johnson's enduring usefulness as a critic of
Shakespeare.  The crucial distinction of Johnson's
Shakespearean criticism is the very largeness and
freedom of his theme, unconfined to particular aspects of Shakespeare's work; whether tragedies, comedies, late plays, romances or any other species of drama.
In his *Preface*, Johnson was writing 'general criticism'.
General criticism, as practised by Johnson, is the art of
representing to readers the particular merits and principle
defects of a varied and fertile genius by a succession of
general views, just as a painter, in his study of nature,
might find form and shape in a scene from his distant pros-
pect.  No one feature is minutely examined at the expence of
the rest: critical power appears in the critic's summoning
to mind, and yoking together, the array of heterogeneous and
fugitive impressions that long and regular acquaintance with
an author will be likely to provide.

Within the wide scope of this general criticism, the various stages in Johnson's plan for the *Preface* are obvious
enough.  The opening sections are concerned with the general
and characteristic glories of Shakespeare; these are followed
by a passage on Shakespeare's faults, leading to an account
of the editorial wisdom that had, by Johnson's time, en-

crusted itself on Shakespeare's work.  Every section in-
volves some new approach; each part is skilfully woven
into the fabric of the whole work, as an unbroken train of
reason.  There are digressions and illustrations, some
expanded and some quickly curtailed.  In the earlier half,
Johnson's critical interest in his subject is more to the
fore; later, the interest shifts to the question of editing
Shakespeare, with a review of each editor's work.


   The broad similarity in structure between the Prefaces
of these previous editors, and Johnson's, have sometimes
led to the conclusion that there is little original in
the *Preface to Shakespeare*; that Johnson, trained in the
rules of 'neoclassical' criticism, borrowed almost all his
ideas.  It is true that there are abundant echoes of earlier
criticism in Johnson's *Preface*, and one function of the
notes to the present edition is to suggest something
of its range.  Johnson gathered a stock of critical
wisdom from his life-long engagement with literary ideas,
and applied it in his literary judgements. But Johnson's
*Preface* is more than a mere amalgam of thoughts plucked
from the writings of earlier critics, and cannot be
wholly explained by received standards and tastes.
The art of criticism had, by Johnson's time, been greatly
advanced by a body of eminent practitioners.  The principles
of poetical criticism had been debated, and settled, a
century before Johnson's *Preface*, in France.  Boileau's
*Art of Poetry* of 1674, and Rapin's *Reflections on Aristotle*,
of the same date, had been eagerly translated, and their
principles applied.  The English critics, in their turn,
adapted to their native conditions what they had learned
from the French, and in the generation before Johnson's,
Pope had expounded in inimitable manner the duties and
character of the true critic.  Johnson knew all these writings; he learnt from all of them some lesson in the pra-

tice and the theory of critical composition.

But while much in the *Preface* looks back to the past,
to Boileau, Rapin and Pope, as well as to Aristotle and
Horace, it re-appears with new life, and is invigorated
with fresh understanding. As Johnson says in the *Preface*
itself: "What mankind have long possessed they have often
examined and compared". A somewhat similar attitude
governed his approach to critical ideas: the old ideas,
as they were the products of repeated examination and
enquiry, had been tested by time. But it is when Johnson
is returning to the very oldest and fundamental critical ideas in the *Preface* that he appears to abandon
convention and seems out of step with his time; as in
his passage on 'mingled drama', or on the unities of time
and place. Sometimes, Johnson carries a conventional
aspect of Shakespearean commentary so much further than
any earlier critic that his criticism seems to have no
direct source, as in the section on Shakespeare's faults.
What Johnson borrowed from the past, he first made his
own. He distilled and united the ideas of the earlier
critics to bring them together in a new way, as old atoms
are united in new bodies.

There is freshness, too, in the style of the *Preface to
Shakespeare*. To many readers, Johnson, as he complained himself of Milton, formed his style by a perverse and pedantic
principle; so that the rhythms of his prose seem too grand
and rhetorical, his diction too frequently composed of
words having their origin in Latin, and his sentences too
long, with main and subordinate clauses too often reversed.
Perhaps, however, it would be juster to apply this criticism to
Johnson's earlier and lesser writings in prose than to his
*Preface to Shakespeare*. The style of the moral essays
is often tortured and involved: the moralist seems
sometimes entangled in subtleties, and chooses a lofty ex-

pression where simple language would serve, so hiding
his wisdom in a cumber of magnificent words.  But about
the time of the *Preface*, Johnson learnt the art of moder-
ating his style, and clarifying his sense.  Long and
short sentences are effectively juxtaposed, and the
cadence of sentences varied.  Tight compression of phrase
is more common than pomp, with a new simplicity and direct-
ness of diction.  Typical of the *Preface* is its succession
of pointed and resonant remarks, memorable long after the
work has been read, and having almost proverbial force,
like certain couplets by Pope: ". . . there is always an
appeal open from criticism to nature"; ". . . all pleasure
consists in variety"; ". . . he that thinks reasonably must
think morally";  "Notes are often necessary, but they are
necessary evils".

It was Johnson's habit in the *Preface*, to express abstract ideas in images and figures, and to sharpen and
enhance his critical remarks with frequent allusions and
comparisons.  The *Preface*, like the *Lives of the Poets*,
is regularly adorned with these flowers of imagination,
to assist rather than detract from the argument in
hand.  An elaborate instance is the comparison of Shakespeare first to a forest, and then to a mine, filled with
gold and diamonds, while other poets are compared to a
well-tended garden, and to a cabinet of precious rarities.
Johnson enlivens his criticism by a curious humour, half-
hidden, as it were, from the eye, as when he compares a
quibble by Shakespeare to the golden apple which lured
him from his course, whatever the seriousness of his purpose
or intent.  In the same place, he submits to the temptation he describes when he says that a quibble was the fatal
Cleopatra for which Shakespeare lost the world and was
content to lose it.

Not that the *Preface* is altogether free from difficulties

of style.  From time to time, in the course of his criticism, Johnson uses words familiar to modern readers in
one sense, in a sense of his own.  He displays, also, a
certain compactness of meaning; an effort, it so often seems,
to enclose in few words what might have been poured out
in many.  But the first source of obscurity is perhaps the
tendency of Johnson to assume in his reader what no writer
can afford to assume: earnest attention and vigorous comprehension.  For this reason, he is not always careful
fully to expand his thoughts, and to forestall the confu-
sions and mistakes of cursory attention.  The energy of
Johnson's mind made him impatient with the slow pace of
more studied and elaborated expression, and what he acknowledged in himself he was happy enough to attribute to others.
The *Lives of the Poets* were perhaps written in a
more measured and elegant style than the *Preface to Shakespeare*. But the brightness, sparkle and quickness of Johnson's
critical manner were never more effectively displayed than
in the *Preface* itself.

The stylistic compression of the *Preface to Shakespeare*
goes hand in hand with the density of thought, in the parts
of the *Preface*, and in the work as a whole.  The parts
which make up the whole of the *Preface* provided opportunities
for Johnson to expand his thoughts, in miniature essays,
contributing to, but in some respects separate from,
the general train of ideas.  One of these passages,
forming a set piece in its own right, is the digression
on the unities, and is worthy of particular mention.

At about the time of Corneille, as Johnson describes,
there arose in France a regular and systematic method for
examining drama.  This method, focussing upon the question
of credibility in dramatic representation, consisted of
a combination of greater and lesser decrees, supposed to be
sanctioned by the wisdom and authority of the Greek and

Roman critics.  The French critics, in fact, went far
beyond their Greek and Roman masters: they insisted that
a change of scene in a play should not involve any change
of place, and demanded that what passed on the stage should
in its progress consume no longer nor any shorter time
than that which would have expired in its passage in the
world.  The critics believed that credibility in drama was
thereby maintained, and illusion preserved.  Johnson, it
is true, was not the first writer to expose the flimsy
foundation of these rules, known as the unities of time
and place.  The early writings of Dryden amply display the
scepticism of the English critics, and the path which
Dryden followed was frequently re-trodden by his admirers.
Dryden, however, was by no means constant in his views:
he sometimes approves the unities and sometimes condemns
them.  It remained therefore to Johnson to consolidate
the arguments and to rectify the opinions of his countrymen.  The fallacy of the unities of time and place is so
skilfully explained in the *Preface*, and the practice of
Shakespeare so logically defended, that the digression
provides a model account of the workings and effect of
plays on the stage.  It transcends the occasion for which
it was composed; and though it may not be the first attack
on the unities by an English critic, it is, by general
consent, the best.

   But if Johnson's passage on the unities has always found admirers, it is a different matter with the passage on Shakespeare's faults.  Here, it is sometimes said, Johnson's
criticisms are too harsh, revealing his antipathy to Shakespeare, and the inappropriateness of his critical standards.
Yet Johnson's account of the defects is a natural consequence of his critical praise of Shakespeare as the poet
of nature, who succeeded regardless of literary rules.  In
his passage on the faults, Johnson reveals as part of his

account the curious features of Shakespeare's tempera-
ment as a writer. Some defects are produced by neglect;
some by over-ambition; some by affectation; others by
the irresistible power of temptation. Sometimes, Johnson
sees them as serious faults, sometimes as occasional and
trivial lapses. All are, however, regular faults, as
Johnson's notes to the plays reveal.

The most serious fault, described by Johnson as his
"first defect", was Shakespeare's neglect of moral purpose.
Johnson believed that Shakespeare, as he became bored or
tired, or as his imagination subsided, was too ready to
withdraw moral interest in the action and characters of
his plays. By abandoning right and wrong in their course,
Shakespeare, Johnson considered, diverted and destroyed
the emotions he had at the beginning of his plays so
successfully and dramatically aroused. This criticism
is levelled at some aspect of all the dramas: the remain-
ing defects are, however, presented as sometimes the faults
of particular modes of writing, and sometimes confined to
particular plays. Shakespeare's struggles with expression
are painstakingly described, in terms reminiscent of many
comments by Johnson on moments in the plays in his notes.
The most lively and perhaps good-natured passage is the
discourse on quibbles.

Johnson's criticism of the faults of Shakespeare is bal-
anced by his praise of the beauties: Shakespeare is the
poet of nature; his drama is the mirror of life; objections
to his Romans and kings are the petty cavils of petty minds.
There is little to suggest, in either the *Preface* or the *Lives
of the Poets*, that Johnson preferred the correct and 'polished'
dramas of his own age to the plays of Shakespeare. His
comparison, in the *Preface*, between *Othello*, and Addison's
*Cato*, is a vivid elaboration of the distinction to be

perpetually observed between Genuis and Art.  Its nearest
rival is perhaps the comparison between Homer and Virgil in
the Preface to the English translation of the *Iliad* by Pope,
to whom, it is possible to suspect, Johnson was somewhat indebted.

But Johnson did not stop short at praising the tragedy
of Shakespeare.  Some of the most striking passages in the
*Preface* are celebrations of Shakespearean comedy.  Tragedy,
according to Johnson, wherever it occured, (even in
comic plays), was an unwelcome effort for Shakespeare, a
mode of drama he toiled constantly to improve, but could
not perfect.  Shakespeare's scenes of tragedy were in
Johnson's opinion the products of studious attention:
those of comedy were relaxations of his art, natural and
instinctive displays of what at any moment flowed into his
mind.  Shakespeare, Johnson suggests, took pleasure to
repose in his scenes, speeches and strokes of comedy.  In
comedy, he seemed most evidently to delight in his powers,
and to give them free reign.

The power of comedy, Johnson described in two remarkable
paragraphs in the *Preface*, distinguishing the basis of
Shakespeare's comic scenes and comic dialogue from what
in the language of eighteenth-century criticism, he called
"manners".  In the course of this account, Johnson appealed
to the laws of matter, and to the physical principles which
determine the dissolution of mass.  The products of accidental and casual combination are subject to decay, he suggests,
as dyes, not being part of whatever they colour, lose their
brightness with the passage of years.  For Johnson, the
characters and language of Shakespeare were woven in the
colours of nature.  They therefore resisted decay, and
remained unfaded by time.  Johnson concludes his passage
on the comedy by giving to time the qualities of a stream,
to Shakespeare those of a rock, washed uninjured by water
which both heaps and scatters the sand.

Johnson, however, comes down on the side of neither
tragedy nor comedy: he did not prefer Shakespeare's comedies. Rather, it was in the mixture of comedy and tragedy
that for Johnson, Shakespeare expressed most fully his
sense of the variety of nature and the conflicts of life.
Johnson brings this out beautifully in his passage, early
in the *Preface*, on 'mingled drama'. Perhaps Johnson was
assisted in enjoying and understanding Shakespeare's
'mingled drama' because of his own experience of the vicissitudes of the world. Although Johnson regrets on many
occasions in his writings that happiness must, in human
experience, be tempered with pain, he also asserts that
all pleasure consists in variety, just as, in *Rasselas*,
written during his work on Shakespeare, he describes in
its early chapters the state of listless tedium that
accompanies unmingled delight. In other works, Johnson
showed no favour to shallow and ignorant optimism, though
he did in his own life find much to console him, and
relieved his sorrows by society and books. Johnson, with
these variations of comfort and wretchedness, seems to
have discovered in his reading of Shakespeare a mind congenial to his own. Tragedy was lightened by humour while
comedy was darkened by pain. Johnson dismisses with an appeal from criticism to nature the charge that Shakespeare
had polluted his tragedy with comic diversions and in-
decorous scenes. What is found in life, he suggests, will
also be found on the stage.

It is, perhaps, characteristic of Johnson that he should
apply his sense of the nature of human experience to his
account of the editing of Shakespeare's text, an account
which forms the entire final part of the *Preface*. The
faults of the earlier editions, he seems to suggest, were
the products of human weakness: Pope's pride; Theobald's
ostentation and ignorance; Hanmer's excess confidence both

in himself and in the earlier editors; Warburton's arrogance.
But in describing his own practice as an editor, Johnson
does not exempt himself from blame.  He stresses the
humility and caution necessary to an editor, condemning
the indulgence of editorial passion which is so often
directed to matters in themselves insignificant and minute.  Johnson's own policy as an editor was to prefer the
earliest copies of the text, however inelegant, and to
avoid needless conjecture, however seemingly warranted
by the improvement of sense.  He tells us of his decision
to confine conjecture to the "margin", or foot of the page,
instead of inserting it in the text.  He writes wittily
and satirically of the practice of composing notes of
great length, and charged with personal indignation at
others' folly, but laments with stoic calm his own imper-
manent emendations, as in the Preface to the *Dictionary* he
had regretted in a similar tone his faults and omissions.

   The *Preface to Shakespeare* is a literary criticism
conceived and expressed with the resources of art. Johnson
colours and heightens his ideas and perceptions by person-
ification, analogy, metaphor and simile, so that the effect
of his work resembles, and *is*, that of literature itself.
He brings such energy of attention to the judgement of his
author that throughout the whole course of the work, few,
if any, weak sentences are apparent.  Johnson's force as
a critic is bound up with his skill as a writer. Person-
ification, where emphasis is given to the discussion of
abstract qualities by showing them in allegorical form,
occurs in the description of the earlier editors of Shakespeare:

> I encountered in every page Wit strug-
> gling with its own sophistry, and Learning
> confined by the multiplicity of its views.

Simile, where one mode of activity is depicted by comparing

it with another, sometimes from a remote branch of nature,
Johnson exhibits in an adjacent passage, where he contrasts
the critical manner of two commentators on Shakespeare:

> . . . one stings like a fly, sucks a
> little blood, takes a gay flutter . . .
> the other bites like a viper.

Analogy, or the use of a logical parallel to strengthen
theoretical with physical truth, is a common element of
Johnson's style.  Here, an analogy from the observation
of geographical nature has been found for the judgement
of imaginative works:

> As among the works of nature no man can
> properly call a river deep, or a mountain
> high, without the knowledge of many moun-
> tains, and many rivers, so in the prod-
> uctions of genius . . .

Some of Johnson's comparisons are striking and memorable:
the pain felt while watching or reading a tragedy is like
that of a mother who weeps over her babe when she thinks
that death may take it from her.

As already observed, Johnson occasionally strikes a comic
or humorous note in his critical prose.  At times, there is no
more than the hint or suspicion of a smile on the writer's
face, as when, in the following remarks at the conclusion of
the passage on the unities, Johnson mocks himself, looking
with amusement on the heroic battles of literary criticism:

> I am almost frighted at my own temerity;
> and when I estimate the fame and strength
> of those that maintain the contrary opin-
> ion, am ready to sink down in reverential
> silence; as *Aeneas* withdrew from the de-
> fence of *Troy*, when he saw *Neptune* shak-
> ing the wall, and *Juno* heading the be-
> seigers.

Sometimes, however, the tone is stern, as when Dennis's
or Rymer's complaints concerning the Roman characters of
Shakespeare are despatched, after due consideration, as

"the petty cavils of petty minds".  On other occasions
Johnson is intimate and personal, and takes us inside
the world of doubt and uncertainty which is the lot of
an editor:

> As I practised conjecture more, I learn-
> ed to trust it less; and after I had
> printed a few plays, resolved to insert
> none of my own readings in the text.
> Upon this caution I now congratulate my-
> self, for every day increases my doubt
> of my own emendations.

It is typical of Johnson that he should, as here, mix his
private thoughts with the most general and impersonal truths.
He seems, at the end of his work, to be sitting in tranquil
contemplation of his author, detached, but not indifferent,
and musing on the irony of his own labours as an editor and
critic of Shakespeare's plays.  The *Preface*, like other
critical works by Johnson, exhibits his command of the
medium of prose: his characteristic and habitual manner
is continually modified by variety of tone and richness
of image.  Particular paragraphs, on the unities, 'mingled
drama', and the comic scenes, are especially fine.
Yet the *Preface* is more than a collection of splendid parts.
The particular passages, though beautiful, forceful or
elevated in themselves, are brought together by Johnson
as parts of the same overall thought about Shakespeare.
So Johnson's judgement, and his conception of
Shakespeare and the worth of his writings appear when
what is said in one place is taken with what is said in
another.  The impartiality of the *Preface* is perhaps its
most important and enduring quality as a criticism of
Shakespeare.  Johnson did not, like some critics, reserve
his adverse comments in servile reverence for Shakespeare:
servility, as we have seen, formed no part of his nature.
But what pleased him he thought might also please others,
and though Shakespeare's faults are honestly admitted, his

qualities are freely declared, without puerile extravagance, or exaggerated claims.

Criticism of particular moments, scenes, or passages in
Shakespeare can be found in Johnson's notes. His 'Observations' on particular plays contain the merits and defects of each work in summary form, memorably expressed,
and the notes in general record Johnson's singular skills
as an editor and textual critic. But the notes are no
more than notes. However impressive, they are written
without the formal rigour of an extended criticism. So
the reader returns to the general praise and general blame
of the *Preface* itself. Perhaps, in the end, the lasting
appeal of the *Preface* rests on the generous humanity of
its author, and on the understanding of life that Johnson
had gained from his own and others' experience, from his
reading both of Shakespeare and other poets, and had expressed in his own poems and prose by the time of the
*Preface*.

Walter Raleigh, whose popular edition of *Johnson on Shakespeare* appeared in 1905, wrote that:

> Those who approach the study of Shakes-
> peare under the sober and vigorous guid-
> ance of Johnson will meet with fewer
> exciting adventures [than when reading
> the romantic critics], but they will
> not see less of the subject. They will
> hear the greatness of Shakespeare dis-
> cussed in language so quiet and modest
> as to sound tame in ears accustomed to
> hyperbole, but they will not, unless
> they are very dull or very careless,
> fall into the error of supposing that
> Johnson's admiration for Shakespeare
> was cold or partial.

It is perhaps significant that Johnson, though he feared
madness, never gave way to it: the sanity of the *Preface to
Shakespeare*, uninfected by eccentricity or critical fashion,
continues to recommend it.

* * * * * *

# PREFACE.

THAT praifes are without reafon lavifhed on the dead, and that the honours due only to excellence are paid to antiquity, is a complaint likely to be always continued by thofe, who, being able to add nothing to truth, hope for eminence from the herefies of paradox; or thofe, who, being forced by difappointment upon confolatory expedients, are willing to hope from pofterity what the prefent age refufes, and flatter themfelves that the regard, which is yet denied by envy, will be at laft beftowed by time.

Antiquity, like every other quality that attracts the notice of mankind, has undoubtedly votaries that reverence it, not from reafon, but from prejudice. Some feem to admire indifcriminately whatever has been long preferved, without confidering that time has fometimes co-operated with chance; all perhaps are more willing to honour paft than prefent excellence; and the mind contemplates genius through the fhades of age, as the eye furveys the fun through artificial opacity. The great contention of criticifm is to find the faults of the moderns, and the beauties of the ancients. While an author is yet living, we eftimate his powers by his worft performance; and when he is dead, we rate them by his beft.

To works, however, of which the excellence is not abfolute and definite, but gradual and comparative; to works not raifed upon principles demonftrative and fcientifick, but appealing wholly to obfervation and experience, no other teft can be applied than length of duration and continuance of efteem. What mankind have long poffeffed they have often examined and compared, and if they perfift to value the poffeffion, it is becaufe frequent comparifons have confirmed opinion in its favour. As among the works of nature no man can properly call a river deep, or a mountain high, without the knowledge of many mountains, and many rivers; fo in the productions of genius, nothing can be ftiled excellent till it has been compared with other works of the fame kind. Demonftration immediately difplays its power, and has nothing to hope or fear from the flux of years; but works tentative and experimental muft be eftimated by their proportion to the general and collective ability of man, as it is difcovered in a long fucceffion of endeavours. Of the firft building that was raifed, it might be with certainty determined that it was round or fquare; but whether it was fpacious or lofty muft have been referred to time. The Pythagorean fcale of numbers was at once difcovered to be perfect; but the poems of Homer we yet know not to tranfcend the common limits of human intelligence, but by remarking, that nation after nation, and century after century, has been able to do little more than tranfpofe his incidents, new name his characters, and paraphrafe his fentiments.

The

The reverence due to writings that have long fub-
fifted arifes therefore not from any credulous confidence in the fuperior wifdom of paft ages, or gloomy
perfuafion of the degeneracy of mankind, but is the
confequence of acknowledged and indubitable pofitions, that what has been longeft known has been
moft confidered, and what is moft confidered is beft
underftood.

The poet, of whofe works I have undertaken the
revifion, may now begin to affume the dignity of an
ancient, and claim the privilege of eftablifhed fame
and prefcriptive veneration. He has long outlived
his century, the term commonly fixed as the teft of
literary merit. Whatever advantages he might once
derive from perfonal allufions, local cuftoms, or temporary opinions, have for many years been loft; and
every topick of merriment, or motive of forrow, which
the modes of artificial life afforded him, now only
obfcure the fcenes which they once illuminated. The
effects of favour and competition are at an end; the
tradition of his friendfhips and his enmities has pe-
rifhed; his works fupport no opinion with arguments,
nor fupply any faction with invectives; they can
neither indulge vanity, nor gratify malignity; but are
read without any other reafon than the defire of pleafure, and are therefore praifed only as pleafure is
obtained; yet, thus unaffifted by intereft or paffion,
they have paft through variations of tafte and changes
of manners, and, as they devolved from one generation
to another, have received new honours at every tranf-
miffion.

But

But becaufe human judgment, though it be gra-
dually gaining upon certainty, never becomes infallible; and approbation, though long continued, may
yet be only the approbation of prejudice or fafhion;
it is proper to inquire, by what peculiarities of excellence Shakefpeare has gained and kept the favour
of his countrymen.

Nothing can pleafe many, and pleafe long, but
juft reprefentations of general nature. Particular
manners can be known to few, and therefore few only
can judge how nearly they are copied. The irregular
combinations of fanciful invention may delight awhile,
by that novelty of which the common fatiety of life
fends us all in queft; but the pleafures of fudden
wonder are foon exhaufted, and the mind can only
repofe on the ftability of truth.

Shakefpeare is above all writers, at leaft above all
modern writers, the poet of nature; the poet that
holds up to his readers a faithful mirror of manners
and of life. His characters are not modified by the
cuftoms of particular places, unpractifed by the reft
of the world; by the peculiarities of ftudies or pro-
feffions, which can operate but upon fmall numbers;
or by the accidents of tranfient fafhions or temporary
opinions: they are the genuine progeny of common
humanity, fuch as the world will always fupply, and
obfervation will always find. His perfons act and
fpeak by the influence of thofe general paffions and
principles by which all minds are agitated, and the
whole fyftem of life is continued in motion. In the
writings of other poets a character is too often an
individual;

individual; in thofe of Shakefpeare it is commonly a fpecies.

It is from this wide extenfion of defign that fo much inftruction is derived. It is this which fills the plays of Shakefpeare with practical axioms and domeftick wifdom. It was faid of Euripides, that every verfe was a precept; and it may be faid of Shakefpeare, that from his works may be collected a fyftem of civil and oeconomical prudence. Yet his real power is not fhewn in the fplendor of particular paffages, but by the progrefs of his fable, and the tenor of his dialogue; and he that tries to recommend him by felect quotations, will fucceed like the pedant in Hierocles, who, when he offered his houfe to fale, carried a brick in his pocket as a fpecimen.

It will not eafily be imagined how much Shakefpeare excels in accommodating his fentiments to real life, but by comparing him with other authors. It was obferved of the ancient fchools of declamation, that the more diligently they were frequented, the more was the ftudent difqualified for the world, becaufe he found nothing there which he fhould ever meet in any other place. The fame remark may be applied to every ftage but that of Shakefpeare. The theatre, when it is under any other direction, is peopled by fuch characters as were never feen, converfing in a language which was never heard, upon topicks which will never arife in the commerce of mankind. But the dialogue of this author is often fo evidently determined by the incident which produces it, and is purfued with fo much eafe and fimplicity, that it

[A 3] feems

feems fcarcely to claim the merit of fiction, but to
have been gleaned by diligent felection out of common converfation, and common occurrences.

Upon every other ftage the univerfal agent is love,
by whofe power all good and evil is diftributed, and
every action quickened or retarded. To bring a lover,
a lady, and a rival into the fable; to entangle them
in contradictory obligations, perplex them with op-
pofitions of intereft, and harrafs them with violence
of defires inconfiftent with each other; to make them
meet in rapture, and part in agony; to fill their
mouths with hyperbolical joy and outrageous forrow;
to diflrefs them as nothing human ever was diftreffed;
to deliver them as nothing human ever was deivered,
is the bufinefs of a modern dramatift.  For this, probability is violated, life is mifreprefented, and language is depraved.  But love is only one of many
paffions, and as it has no great influence upon the
fum of life, it has little operation in the dramas of a
poet, who caught his ideas from the living world,
and exhibited only what he faw before him.  He
knew, that any other paffion, as it was regular or
exorbitant, was a caufe of happinefs or calamity.

Characters thus ample and general were not eafily
difcriminated and preferved, yet perhaps no poet ever
kept his perfonages more diftinct from each other.
I will not fay with Pope, that every fpeech may be
affigned to the proper fpeaker, becaufe many fpeeches
there are which have nothing characteriftical; but,
perhaps, though fome may be equally adapted to
every perfon, it will be difficult to find any that can
be

be properly transferred from the prefent poffeffor to another claimant. The choice is right, when there is reafon for choice.

Other dramatifts can only gain attention by hyperbolical or aggravated characters, by fabulous and unexampled excellence or depravity, as the writers of barbarous romances invigorated the reader by a giant and a dwarf; and he that fhould form his expectations of human affairs from the play, or from the tale, would be equally deceived. Shakefpeare has no heroes; his fcenes are occupied only by men, who act and fpeak as the reader thinks that he fhould himfelf have fpoken or acted on the fame occafion : even where the agency is fupernatural, the dialogue is level with life. Other writers difguife the moft natural paffions and moft frequent incidents; fo that he who contemplates them in the book will not know them in the world: Shakefpeare approximates the remote, and familiarizes the wonderful; the event which he reprefents will not happen, but if it were poffible, its effects would probably be fuch as he has affigned; and it may be faid, that he has not only fhewn human nature as it acts in real exigences, but as it would be found in trials, to which it cannot be expofed.

This therefore is the praife of Shakefpeare, that his drama is the mirror of life; that he who has mazed his imagination, in following the phantoms which other writers raife up before him, may here be cured of his delirious ecftafies, by reading human fentiments in human language; by fcenes from which a

[ A 4 ]                    hermit

hermit may eſtimate the tranſactions of the world, and a confeſſor predict the progreſs of the paſſions.

His adherence to general nature has expoſed him to the cenſure of criticks, who form their judgments upon narrower principles. Dennis and Rhymer think his Romans not ſufficiently Roman; and Voltaire cenſures his kings as not completely royal. Dennis is offended, that Menenius, a ſenator of Rome, ſhould play the buffoon; and Voltaire perhaps thinks decency violated when the Daniſh uſurper is repreſented as a drunkard. But Shakeſpeare always makes nature predominate over accident; and if he preſerves the eſſential character, is not very careful of diſtinctions ſuperinduced and adventitious. His ſtory requires Romans or kings, but he thinks only on men. He knew that Rome, like every other city, had men of all diſpoſitions; and wanting a buffoon, he went into the ſenate-houſe for that which the ſenate-houſe would certainly have afforded him. He was inclined to ſhew an uſurper and a murderer not only odious, but deſpicable; he therefore added drunkenneſs to his other qualities, knowing that kings love wine like other men, and that wine exerts its natural power upon kings. Theſe are the petty cavils of petty minds; a poet overlooks the caſual diſtinction of country and condition, as a painter, ſatisfied with the figure, neglects the drapery.

The cenſure which he has incurred by mixing comick and tragick ſcenes, as it extends to all his works, deſerves more conſideration. Let the fact be firſt ſtated, and then examined.

Shake-

Shakefpeare's plays are not in the rigorous and critical fenfe either tragedies or comedies, but compofitions of a diftinct kind; exhibiting the real ftate of
fublunary nature, which partakes of good and evil,
joy and forrow, mingled with endlefs variety of proportion and innumerable modes of combination; and
expreffing the courfe of the world, in which the lofs
of one is the gain of another; in which, at the fame
time, the reveller is hafting to his wine, and the
mourner burying his friend; in which the malignity
of one is fometimes defeated by the frolick of another; and many mifchiefs and many benefits are
done and hindered without defign.

Out of this chaos of mingled purpofes and cafu-
alties the ancient poets, according to the laws which
cuftom had prefcribed, felected fome the crimes of
men, and fome their abfurdities; fome the momen-
tous viciffitudes of life, and fome the lighter occurrences; fome the terrors of diftrefs, and fome the
gayeties of profperity. Thus rofe the two modes of
imitation, known by the names of *tragedy* and *comedy*,
compofitions intended to promote different ends by
contrary means, and confidered as fo little allied,
that I do not recollect among the Greeks or Romans
a fingle writer who attempted both.

Shakefpeare has united the powers of exciting
laughter and forrow not only in one mind, but in one
compofition. Almoft all his plays are divided between ferious and ludicrous characters, and, in the
fucceffive evolutions of the defign, fometimes produce

duce ferioufnefs and forrow, and fometimes levity and laughter.

That this is a practice contrary to the rules of criticifm will be readily allowed; but there is always an appeal open from criticifm to nature. The end of writing is to inftruct; the end of poetry is to inftruct by pleafing. That the mingled drama may convey all the inftruction of tragedy or comedy cannot be denied, becaufe it includes both in its alterations of exhibition, and approaches nearer than either to the appearance of life, by fhewing how great machinations and flender defigns may promote or obviate one another, and the high and the low co-operate in the general fyftem by unavoidable concatenation.

It is objected, that by this change of fcenes the paffions are interrupted in their progreffion, and that the principal event, being not advanced by a due gradation of preparatory incidents, wants at laft the power to move, which conftitutes the perfection of dramatick poetry. This reafoning is fo fpecious, that it is received as true even by thofe who in daily experience feel it to be falfe. The interchanges of mingled fcenes feldom fail to produce the intended viciffitudes of paffion. Fiction cannot move fo much, but that the attention may be eafily transferred; and though it muft be allowed that pleafing melancholy be fometimes interrupted by unwelcome levity, yet let it be confidered likewife, that melancholy is often not pleafing, and that the difturbance of one man may be the relief of another; that different auditors

have

have different habitudes; and that, upon the whole, all pleafure confifts in variety.

The players, who in their edition divided our author's works into comedies, hiftories, and tragedies, feem not to have diftinguifhed the three kinds, by any very exact or definite ideas.

An action which ended happily to the principal perfons, however ferious or diftrefsful through its intermediate incidents, in their opinion conftituted a comedy. This idea of a comedy continued long amongft us, and plays were written, which, by changing the cataftrophe, were tragedies to-day, and comedies to-morrow.

Tragedy was not in thofe times a poem of more general dignity or elevation than comedy; it required only a calamitous conclufion, with which the common criticifm of that age was fatisfied, whatever lighter pleafure it afforded in its progrefs.

Hiftory was a feries of actions, with no other than chronological fucceffion, independent on each other, and without any tendency to introduce or regulate the conclufion. It is not always very nicely diftinguifhed from tragedy. There is not much nearer approach to unity of action in the tragedy of *Antony and Cleopatra*, than in the hiftory of *Richard the Second*. But a hiftory might be continued through many plays; as it had no plan, it had no limits.

Through

Through all thefe denominations of the drama, Shakefpeare's mode of compofition is the fame; an interchange of ferioufnefs and merriment, by which the mind is foftened at one time, and exhilarated at another. But whatever be his purpofe, whether to gladden or deprefs, or to conduct the ftory, without vehemence or emotion, through tracts of eafy and familiar dialogue, he never fails to attain his purpofe; as he commands us, we laugh or mourn, or fit filent with quiet expectation, in tranquility without indifference.

When Shakefpeare's plan is underftood, moft of the criticifms of Rhymer and Voltaire vanifh away. The play of *Hamlet* is opened, without impropriety, by two centinels; Iago bellows at Brabantio's window, without injury to the fcheme of the play, though in terms which a modern audience would not eafily endure; the character of Polonius is feafonable and ufeful; and the Grave-diggers themfelves may be heard with applaufe.

Shakefpeare engaged in dramatick poetry with the world open before him; the rules of the ancients were yet known to few; the publick judgment was unformed; he had no example of fuch fame as might force him upon imitation, nor criticks of fuch authority as might reftrain his extravagance: he therefore indulged his natural difpofition, and his difpofition, as Rhymer has remarked, led him to comedy. In tragedy he often writes with great appearance of toil and ftudy, what is written at laft with little felicity; but in his comick fcenes, he feems to produce without labour,

labour, what no labour can improve. In tragedy he is always ſtruggling after ſome occaſion to be comick, but in comedy he ſeems to repoſe, or to luxuriate, as in a mode of thinking congenial to his nature. In his tragick ſcenes there is always ſomething wanting, but his comedy often ſurpaſſes expectation or deſire. His comedy pleaſes by the thoughts and the language, and his tragedy for the greater part by incident and action. His tragedy ſeems to be ſkill, his comedy to be inſtinct.

The force of his comick ſcenes has ſuffered little diminution from the changes made by a century and a half, in manners or in words. As his perſonages act upon principles ariſing from genuine paſſion, very little modified by particular forms, their pleaſures and vexations are communicable to all times and to all places; they are natural, and therefore durable; the adventitious peculiarities of perſonal habits, are only ſuperficial dies, bright and pleaſing for a little while, yet ſoon fading to a dim tinct, without any remains of former luſtre; but the diſcriminations of true paſſion are the colours of nature; they pervade the whole maſs, and can only periſh with the body that exhibits them. The accidental compoſitions of heterogeneous modes are diſſolved by the chance which combined them; but the uniform ſimplicity of primitive qualities neither admits increaſe, nor ſuffers decay. The ſand heaped by one flood is ſcattered by another, but the rock always continues in its place. The ſtream of time, which is continually waſhing the diſſoluble fabricks of other poets, paſſes without injury by the adamant of Shakeſpeare.

If

If there be, what I believe there is, in every nation, a ftile which never becomes obfolete, a certain mode of phrafeology fo confonant and congenial to the analogy and principles of its refpective language, as to remain fettled and unaltered; this ftyle is probably to be fought in the common intercourfe of life, among thofe who fpeak only to be underftood, without ambition of elegance. The polite are always catching modifh innovations, and the learned depart from eftablifhed forms of fpeech, in hope of finding or making better; thofe who wifh for diftinction forfake the vulgar, when the vulgar is right; but there is a converfation above groffnefs and below refinement, where propriety refides, and where this poet feems to have gathered his comick dialogue. He is therefore more agreeable to the ears of the prefent age than any other author equally remote, and among his other excellencies deferves to be ftudied as one of the original mafters of our language.

Thefe obfervations are to be confidered not as unexceptionably conftant, but as containing general and predominant truth. Shakefpeare's familiar dialogue is affirmed to be fmooth and clear, yet not wholly without ruggednefs or difficulty ; as a country may be eminently fruitful, though it has fpots unfit for cultivation : his characters are praifed as natural, though their fentiments are fometimes forced, and their actions improbable; as the earth upon the whole is fpherical, though its furface is varied with protuberances and cavities.

Shake-

Shakefpeare with his excellencies has likewife faults, and faults fufficient to obfcure and overwhelm any other merit. I fhall fhew them in the proportion in which they appear to me, without envious malignity or fuperftitious veneration. No queftion can be more innocently difcuffed than a dead poet's pretenfions to renown; and little regard is due to that bigotry which fets candour higher than truth.

His firft defect is that to which may be imputed moft of the evil in books or in men. He facrifices virtue to convenience, and is fo much more careful to pleafe than to inftruct, that he feems to write without any moral purpofe. From his writings indeed a fyftem of focial duty may be felected, for he that thinks reafonably muft think morally; but his precepts and axioms drop cafually from him; he makes no juft diftribution of good or evil, nor is always careful to fhew in the virtuous a difapprobation of the wicked; he carries his perfons indifferently through right and wrong, and at the clofe difmiffes them without further care, and leaves their examples to operate by chance. This fault the barbarity of his age cannot extenuate; for it is always a writer's duty to make the world better, and juftice is a virtue independent on time or place.

The plots are often fo loofely formed, that a very flight confideration may improve them, and fo carelefsly purfued, that he feems not always fully to comprehend his own defign. He omits opportunities of inftructing or delighting, which the train of his ftory feems to force upon him, and apparently rejects
thofe

thofe exhibitions which would be more affecting, for the fake of thofe which are more eafy.

It may be obferved, that in many of his plays the latter part is evidently neglected. When he found himfelf near the end of his work, and in view of his reward, he fhortened the labour to fnatch the profit. He therefore remits his efforts where he fhould moft vigoroufly exert them, and his cataftrophe is improbably produced or imperfectly reprefented.

He had no regard to diftinction of time or place, but gives to one age or nation, without fcruple, the cuftoms, inftitutions, and opinions of another, at the expence not only of likelihood, but of poffibility. Thefe faults Pope has endeavoured, with more zeal than judgment, to transfer to his imagined interpolators. We need not wonder to find Hector quoting Ariftotle, when we fee the loves of Thefeus and Hippolyta combined with the Gothick mythology of fairies. Shakefpeare, indeed, was not the only violator of chronology, for in the fame age Sidney, who wanted not the advantages of learning, has, in his *Arcadia,* confounded the paftoral with the feudal times, the days of innocence, quiet, and fecurity, with thofe of turbulence, violence, and adventure.

In his comick fcenes he is feldom very fuccefsful, when he engages his characters in reciprocations of fmartnefs and contefts of farcafm; their jefts are commonly grofs, and their pleafantry licentious; neither his gentlemen nor his ladies have much delicacy, nor are

are sufficiently diftinguifhed from his clowns by any appearance of refined manners. Whether he reprefented the real converfation of his time is not eafy to determine; the reign of Elizabeth is commonly fuppofed to have been a time of ftatelinefs, formality, and referve, yet perhaps the relaxations of that feverity were not very elegant. There muft, however, have been always fome modes of gaiety preferable to others, and a writer ought to chufe the beft.

In tragedy his performance feems conftantly to be worfe, as his labour is more. The effufions of paffion, which exigence forces out, are for the moft part ftriking and energetick; but whenever he folicits his invention, or ftrains his faculties, the offspring of his throes is tumour, meannefs, tedioufnefs, and obfcurity.

In narration he affects a difproportionate pomp of diction, and a wearifome train of circumlocution, and tells the incident imperfectly in many words, which might have been more plainly delivered in few. Narration in dramatick poetry is naturally tedious, as it is unanimated and inactive, and obftructs the progrefs of the action; it fhould therefore always be rapid, and enlivened by frequent interruption. Shakefpeare found it an encumbrance, and inftead of lightening it by brevity, endeavoured to recommend it by dignity and fplendor.

His declamations or fet fpeeches are commonly cold and weak, for his power was the power of nature; when he endeavoured, like other tragick

Vol. I.                [ B ]                writers,

writers, to catch opportunities of amplification, and instead of inquiring what the occasion demanded, to shew how much his stores of knowledge could supply, he seldom escapes without the pity or resentment of his reader.

It is incident to him to be now and then entangled with an unwieldy sentiment, which he cannot well express, and will not reject; he struggles with it a while, and if it continues stubborn, comprises it in words such as occur, and leaves it to be disentangled and evolved by those who have more leisure to bestow upon it.

Not that always where the language is intricate the thought is subtle, or the image always great where the line is bulky; the equality of words to things is very often neglected, and trivial sentiments and vulgar ideas disappoint the attention, to which they are recommended by sonorous epithets and swelling figures.

But the admirers of this great poet have most reason to complain when he approaches nearest to his highest excellence, and seems fully resolved to sink them in dejection, and mollify them with tender emotions by the fall of greatness, the danger of innocence, or the crosses of love. What he does best, he soon ceases to do. He is not long soft and pathetick without some idle conceit, or contemptible equivocation. He no sooner begins to move, than he counteracts himself; and terror and pity, as they are rising in the mind, are checked and blasted by sudden frigidity.

A quibble

A quibble is to Shakefpeare, what luminous vapours are to the traveller: he follows it at all adventures; it is fure to lead him out of his way, and fure to engulf him in the mire. It has fome malignant power over his mind, and its fafcinations are irrefiftible. Whatever be the dignity or profundity of his difquifition, whether he be enlarging knowledge or exalting affection, whether he be amufing attention with incidents, or enchaining it in fufpenfe, let but a quibble fpring up before him, and he leaves his work unfinifhed. A quibble is the golden apple for which he will always turn afide from his career, or ftoop from his elevation. A quibble, poor and barren as it is, gave him fuch delight, that he was content to purchafe it, by the facrifice of reafon, propriety, and truth. A quibble was to him the fatal Cleopatra for which he loft the world, and was content to lofe it.

It will be thought ftrange, that, in enumerating the defects of this writer, I have not yet mentioned his neglect of the unities; his violation of thofe laws which have been inftituted and eftablifhed by the joint authority of poets and of cricks.

For his other deviations from the art of writing, I refign him to critical juftice, without making any other demand in his favour, than that which muft be indulged to all human excellence; that his virtues be rated with his failings : but, from the cenfure which this irregularity may bring upon him, I fhall, with due reverence to that learning which I muft oppofe, adventure to try how I can defend him.

[ B 2 ]                    His

His histories, being neither tragedies nor comedies, are not subject to any of their laws; nothing more is necessary to all the praise which they expect, than that the changes of action be so prepared as to be understood, that the incidents be various and affecting, and the characters consistent, natural, and distinct. No other unity is intended, and therefore none is to be sought.

In his other works he has well enough preserved the unity of action. He has not, indeed, an intrigue regularly perplexed and regularly unravelled; he does not endeavour to hide his design only to discover it, for this is seldom the order of real events, and Shakespeare is the poet of nature: but his plan has commonly what Aristotle requires, a beginning, a middle, and an end; one event is concatenated with another, and the conclusion follows by easy consequence. There are perhaps some incidents that might be spared, as in other poets there is much talk that only fills up time upon the stage; but the general system makes gradual advances, and the end of the play is the end of expectation.

To the unities of time and place he has shewn no regard; and perhaps a nearer view of the principles on which they stand will diminish their value, and withdraw from them the veneration which, from the time of Corneille, they have very generally received, by discovering that they have given more trouble to the poet, than pleasure to the auditor.

The

The neceffity of obferving the unities of time and place arifes from the fuppofed neceffity of making the drama credible. The criticks hold it impoffible, that an action of months or years can be poffibly believed to pafs in three hours; or that the fpectator can fuppofe himfelf to fit in the theatre, while ambaffadors go and return between diftant kings, while armies are levied and towns befieged, while an exile wanders and returns, or till he whom they faw courting his miftrefs, fhall lament the untimely fall of his fon. The mind revolts from evident falfehood, and fiction lofes its force when it departs from the refemblance of reality.

From the narrow limitation of time neceffarily arifes the contraction of place. The fpectator, who knows that he faw the firft act at Alexandria, cannot fuppofe that he fees the next at Rome, at a diftance to which not the dragons of Medea could, in fo fhort a time, have tranfported him; he knows with certainty that he has not changed his place; and he knows that place cannot change itfelf; that what was a houfe cannot become a plain; that what was Thebes can never be Perfepolis.

Such is the triumphant language with which a critick exults over the mifery of an irregular poet, and exults commonly without refiftance or reply. It is time therefore to tell him, by the authority of Shakefpeare, that he affumes, as an unqueftionable principle, a pofition, which, while his breath is forming it into words, his underftanding pronounces to be falfe. It is falfe, that any reprefentation is miftaken for reality; that any dramatick fable in its materiality was ever credible, or, for a fingle moment, was ever credited.

The objection arifing from the impoffibility of paffing the firft hour at Alexandria, and the next at Rome, fuppofes, that when the play opens the fpectator really imagines himfelf at Alexandria, and believes that his walk to the theatre has been a voyage to Egypt, and that he lives in the days of Antony and Cleopatra. Surely he that imagines this may imagine more. He that can take the ftage at one time for the palace of the Ptolemies, may take it in half an hour for the promontory of Actium. Delufion, if delufion be admitted, has no certain limitation; if the fpectator can be once perfuaded, that his old acquaintance are Alexander and Cæfar, that a room illuminated with candles is the plain of Pharfalia, or the bank of Granicus, he is in a ftate of elevation above the reach of reafon, or of truth, and from the heights of empyrean poetry, may defpife the circumfcriptions of terreftrial nature. There is no reafon why a mind thus wandering in ecftafy fhould count the clock, or why an hour fhould not be a century in that calenture of the brains that can make the ftage a field.

The truth is, that the fpectators are always in their fenfes, and know, from the firft act to the laft, that the ftage is only a ftage, and that the players are only players. They come to hear a certain number of lines recited with juft gefture and elegant modulation. The lines relate to fome action, and an action muft
be

be in fome place; but the different actions that complete a ftory may be in places very remote from each other; and where is the abfurdity of allowing that fpace to reprefent firft Athens, and then Sicily, which was always known to be neither Sicily nor Athens, but a modern theatre.

By fuppofition, as place is introduced, time may be extended; the time required by the fable elapfes for the moft part between the acts; for, of fo much of the action as is reprefented, the real and poetical duration is the fame. If, in the firft act, preparations for war againft Mithridates are reprefented to be made in Rome, the event of the war may, without abfurdity, be reprefented, in the cataftrophe, as happening in Pontus; we know that there is neither war, nor preparation for war ; we know that we are neither in Rome nor Pontus; that neither Mithridates nor Lucullus are before us. The drama exhibits fucceffive imitations of fucceffive actions, and why may not the fecond imitation reprefent an action that happened years after the firft; if it be fo connected with it, that nothing but time can be fuppofed to intervene. Time is, of all modes of exiftence, moft obfequious to the imagination; a lapfe of years is as eafily conceived as a paffage of hours. In contemplation we eafily contract the time of real actions, and therefore willingly permit it to be contracted when we only fee their imitation.

It will be afked, how the drama moves, if it is not credited. It is credited with all the credit due to a drama. It is credited, whenever it moves, as a juft

picture

picture of a real original; as reprefenting to the auditor what he would himfelf feel, if he were to do or
fuffer what is there feigned to be fuffered or to be
done. The reflection that ftrikes the heart is not,
that the evils before us are real evils, but that they
are evils to which we ourfelves may be expofed. If
there be any fallacy, it is not that we fancy the players, but that we fancy ourfelves unhappy for a moment; but we rather lament the poffibility than fuppofe the prefence of mifery, as a mother weeps over
her babe, when fhe remembers that death may take
it from her. The delight of tragedy proceeds from
our confcioufnefs of fiction; if we thought murders
and treafons real, they would pleafe no more.

Imitations produce pain or pleafure, not becaufe
they are miftaken for realities, but becaufe they bring
realities to mind. When the imagination is recreated
by a painted landfcape, the trees are not fuppofed
capable to give us fhade, or the fountains coolnefs ;
but we confider, how we fhould be pleafed with fuch
fountains playing befide us, and fuch woods waving
over us. We are agitated in reading the hiftory of
*Henry the Fifth*, yet no man takes his book for the
field of Agincourt. A dramatick exhibition is a
book recited with concomitants that increafe or di-
minifh its effect. Familiar comedy is often more
powerful on the theatre, than in the page; imperial
tragedy is always lefs. The humour of Petruchio
may be heightened by grimace; but what voice or
what gefture can hope to add dignity or force to the
foliloquy of Cato ?

A play

A play read, affects the mind like a play acted.
It is therefore evident, that the action is not supposed to be real; and it follows, that between the acts
a longer or shorter time may be allowed to pass, and
that no more account of space or duration is to be
taken by the auditor of a drama, than by the reader
of a narrative, before whom may pass in an hour the
life of a hero, or the revolutions of an empire.

Whether Shakespeare knew the unities, and rejected them by design, or deviated from them by
happy ignorance, it is, I think, impossible to decide,
and useless to enquire. We may reasonably suppose,
that, when he rose to notice, he did not want the
counsels and admonitions of scholars and criticks,
and that he at last deliberately persisted in a practice,
which he might have begun by chance. As nothing
is essential to the fable, but unity of action, and as
the unities of time and place arise evidently from false
assumptions, and, by circumscribing the extent of
the drama, lessen its variety, I cannot think it much
to be lamented, that they were not known by him,
or not observed: nor, if such another poet could
arise, should I very vehemently reproach him, that
his first act passed at Venice, and his next in Cyprus.
Such violations of rules merely positive, become the
comprehensive genius of Shakespeare, and such cen-
sures are suitable to the minute and slender criticism
of Voltaire:

> *Non usque adeo permiscuit imis*
> *Longus summa dies, ut non, si voce Metelli*
> *Serventur leges, malint a Cæsare tolli.*

Yet

Yet when I speak thus slightly of dramatick rules, I cannot but recollect how much wit and learning may be produced against me; before such authorities I am afraid to stand, not that I think the present question one of those that are to be decided by mere authority, but because it is to be suspected, that these precepts have not been so easily received, but for better reasons than I have yet been able to find. The result of my enquiries, in which it would be ludicrous to boast of impartiality, is, that the unities of time and place are not essential to a just drama, that though they may sometimes conduce to pleasure, they are always to be sacrificed to the nobler beauties of variety and instruction ; and that a play, written with nice observation of critical rules, is to be contemplated as an elaborate curiosity, as the product of superfluous and ostentatious art, by which is shewn, rather what is possible, than what is necessary.

He that, without diminution of any other excellence, shall preserve all the unities unbroken, deserves the like applause with the architect, who shall display all the orders of architecture in a citadel, without any deduction from its strength; but the principal beauty of a citadel is to exclude the enemy ; and the greatest graces of a play are to copy nature, and instruct life.

Perhaps, what I have here not dogmatically but deliberately written, may recal the principles of the drama to a new examination. I am almost frighted at my own temerity; and when I estimate the fame and the strength of those that maintain the contrary opinion,

opinion, am ready to fink down in reverential filence; as Æneas withdrew from the defence of Troy, when he faw Neptune fhaking the wall, and Juno heading the befiegers.

Thofe whom my arguments cannot perfuade to give their approbation to the judgment of Shakefpeare, will eafily, if they confider the condition of his life, make fome allowance for his ignorance.

Every man's performances, to be rightly eftimated, muft be compared with the ftate of the age in which he lived, and with his own particular opportunities; and though to a reader a book be not worfe or better for the circumftances of the author, yet as there is always a filent reference of human works to human abilities, and as the enquiry, how far man may extend his defigns, or how high he may rate his native force, is of far greater dignity than in what rank we fhall place any particular performance, curiofity is always bufy to difcover the inftruments, as well as to furvey the workmanfhip, to know how much is to be afcribed to original powers, and how much to cafual and adventitious help. The palaces of Peru or Mexico were certainly mean and incommodious habitations, if compared to the houfes of European monarchs; yet who could forbear to view them with aftonifhment, who remembered that they were built without the ufe of iron?

The Englifh nation, in the time of Shakefpeare, was yet ftruggling to emerge from barbarity. The philology of Italy had been tranfplanted hither in the reign

reign of Henry the Eighth; and the learned languages had been fuccefsfully cultivated by Lilly, Linacre, and More; by Pole, Cheke, and Gardiner; and afterwards by Smith, Clerk, Haddon, and Afcham. Greek was now taught to boys in the principal fchools; and thofe who united elegance with learning, read, with great diligence, the Italian and Spanifh poets. But literature was yet confined to profeffed fcholars, or to men and women of high rank. The publick was grofs and dark; and to be able to read and write, was an accomplifhment ftill valued for its rarity.

Nations, like individuals, have their infancy. A people newly awakened to literary curiofity, being yet unacquainted with the true ftate of things, knows not how to judge of that which is propofed as its refemblance. Whatever is remote from common appearances is always welcome 'to vulgar, as to childifh credulity; and of a country unenlightened by learning, the whole people is the vulgar. The ftudy of thofe who then afpired to plebeian learning was laid out upon adventures, giants, dragons, and enchantments. *The Death of Arthur* was the favourite volume.

The mind, which has feafted on the luxurious wonders of fiction, has no tafte of the infipidity of truth. A play, which imitated only the common occurrences of the world, would, upon the admirers of *Palmerin* and *Guy of Warwick*, have made little impreffion; he that wrote for fuch an audience was under the neceffity of looking round for ftrange

events

events and fabulous tranfactions, and that incredibi-
lity, by which maturer knowledge is offended, was
the chief recommendation of writings, to unfkilful
curiofity.

Our author's plots are generally borrowed from
novels; and it is reafonable to fuppofe, that he chofe
the moft popular, fuch as were read by many, and
related by more; for his audience could not have
followed him through the intricacies of the drama,
had they not held the thread of the ftory in their
hands.

The ftories, which we now find only in remoter
authors, were in his time acceffible and familiar.
The fable of *As you like it*, which is fuppofed to be
copied from *Chaucer's Gamelyn*, was a little pamphlet
of thofe times; and old Mr. Cibber remembered the
tale of *Hamlet* in plain Englifh profe, which the
criticks have now to feek in *Saxo Grammaticus*.

His Englifh hiftories he took from Englifh chro-
nicles and Englifh ballads; and as the ancient writers
were made known to his countrymen by verfions,
they fupplied him with new fubjects; he dilated fome
of Plutarch's lives into plays, when they had been
tranflated by North.

His plots, whether hiftorical or fabulous, are always crouded with incidents, by which the attention
of a rude people was more eafily caught than by fentiment or argumentation; and fuch is the power of
the marvellous, even over thofe who defpife it, that
every

every man finds his mind more ftrongly feized by the tragedies of Shakefpeare than of any other writer; others pleafe us by particular fpeeches, but he always makes us anxious for the event, and has perhaps excelled all but Homer in fecuring the firft purpofe of a writer, by exciting reftlefs and unquenchable curiofity, and compelling him that reads his work to read it through.

The fhows and buftle with which his plays abound have the fame original. As knowledge advances, pleafure paffes from the eye to the ear, but returns, as it declines, from the ear to the eye. Thofe to whom our author's labours were exhibited had more fkill in pomps or proceffions than in poetical language, and perhaps wanted fome vifible and difcriminated events, as comments on the dialogue. He knew how he fhould moft pleafe; and whether his practice is more agreeable to nature, or whether his example has prejudiced the nation, we ftill find that on our ftage fomething muft be done as well as faid, and inactive declamation is very coldly heard, however mufical or elegant, paffionate or fublime.

Voltaire expreffes his wonder, that our author's extravagancies are endured by a nation, which has feen the tragedy of *Cato*. Let him be anfwered, that Addifon fpeaks the language of poets, and Shakefpeare, of men. We find in *Cato* innumerable beauties which enamour us of its author, but we fee nothing that acquaints us with human fentiments or human actions; we place it with the faireft and the nobleft progeny which judgment propagates by conjunction

junction with learning; but *Othello* is the vigorous
and vivacious offspring of observation impregnated
by genius. *Cato* affords a splendid exhibition of artificial and fictitious manners, and delivers juft and
noble fentiments, in diction eafy, elevated, and har-
monious, but its hopes and fears communicate no
vibration to the heart ; the compofition refers us only
to the writer; we pronounce the name of *Cato*, but
we think on *Addifon*.

The work of a correct and regular writer is a garden accurately formed and diligently planted, varied
with fhades, and fcented with flowers ; the compofition of Shakefpeare is a foreft, in which oaks extend
their branches, and pines tower in the air, inter-
fperfed fometimes with weeds and brambles, and
fometimes giving fhelter to myrtles and to rofes ; fill-
ing the eye with awful pomp, and gratifying the mind
with endlefs diverfity. Other poets difplay cabinets
of precious rarities, minutely finifhed, wrought into
fhape, and polifhed into brightnefs. Shakefpeare
opens a mine which contains gold and diamonds in
unexhauftible plenty, though clouded by incrufta-
tions, debafed by impurities, and mingled with a
mafs of meaner minerals.

It has been much difputed, whether Shakefpeare
owed his excellence to his own native force, or whether he had the common helps of fcholaftick education, the precepts of critical fcience, and the examples
of ancient authors.

There

There has always prevailed a tradition, that Shakefpeare wanted learning, that he had no regular education, nor much fkill in the dead languages. Jonfon, his friend, affirms, that *he had fmall Latin, and
lefs Greek*; who, befides that he had no imaginable
temptation to falfehood, wrote at a time when the
character and acquifitions of Shakefpeare were known
to multitudes. His evidence ought therefore to decide the controverfy, unlefs fome teftimony of equal
force could be oppofed.

Some have imagined, that they have difcovered
deep learning in many imitations of old writers; but
the examples which I have known urged, were drawn
from books tranflated in his time; or were fuch eafy
coincidences of thought, as will happen to all who
confider the fame fubjects; or fuch remarks on life
or axioms of morality as float in converfation, and
are tranfmitted through the world in proverbial fentences.

I have found it remarked, that, in this important
fentence, *Go before, I'll follow*, we read a tranflation
of, *I prae, fequar.* I have been told, that when Ca-
liban, after a pleafing dream, fays, *I cry'd to fleep
again*, the author imitates Anacreon, who had, like
every other man, the fame wifh on the fame occafion.

There are a few paffages which may pafs for imitations, but fo few, that the exception only confirms
the rule; he obtained them from accidental quotations, or by oral communication, and as he ufed what
he had, would have ufed more if he had obtained it.

The

The *Comedy of Errors* is confeffedly taken from the
*Menæchmi* of *Plautus*; from the only play of Plautus
wh.ch was then in Englifh. What can be more probable, than that he who copied that, would have
copied more; but that thofe which were not tranflated
were inacceffible?

Whether he knew the modern languages is un-
certain. That his plays have fome French fcenes
proves but little; he might eafily procure them to be
written, and probably, even though he had known
the language in the common degree, he could not
have written it without affiftance. In the ftory of
*Romeo* and *Juliet* he is obferved to have followed the
Englifh tranflation, where it deviates from the Italian; but this on the other part proves nothing againft
his knowledge of the original. He was to copy, not
what he knew himfelf, but what was known to his
audience.

It is moft likely that he had learned Latin fufficiently to make him acquainted with conftruction,
but that he never advanced to an eafy perufal of the
Roman authors. Concerning his fkill in modern
languages, I can find no fufficient ground of determination; but as no imitations of French or Italian
authors have been difcovered, though the Italian
poetry was then high in efteem, I am inclined to believe, that he read little more than Englifh, and chofe
for his fables only fuch tales as he found tranflated.

That much knowledge is fcattered over his works
is very juftly obferved by Pope, but it is often fuch

knowledge as books did not fupply. He that will underftand Shakefpeare, muft not be content to ftudy him in the clofet, he muft look for his meaning fometimes among the fports of the field, and fometimes among the manufactures of the fhop.

There is however proof enough that he was a very diligent reader, nor was our language then fo indigent of books, but that he might very liberally indulge his curiofity without excurfion into foreign literature. Many of the Roman authors were tranflated, and fome of the Greek; the Reformation had filled the kingdom with theological learning; moft of the topicks of human difquifition had found Englifh writers; and poetry had been cultivated, not only with diligence, but fuccefs. This was a ftock of knowledge fufficient for a mind fo capable of appropriating and improving it.

But the greater part of his excellence was the product of his own genius. He found the Englifh ftage in a ftate of the utmoft rudenefs; no effays either in tragedy or comedy had appeared, from which it could be difcovered to what degree of delight either one or other might be carried. Neither character nor dialogue were yet underftood. Shakefpeare may be truly faid to have introduced them both amongft us, and in fome of his happier fcenes to have carried them both to the utmoft height.

By what gradations of improvement he proceeded, is not eafily known; for the chronology of his works is yet unfettled. Rowe is of opinion, that *perhaps*
*we*

*we are not to look for his beginning, like thofe of other writers, in his leaft perfeÉt works; art had fo little, and nature fo large a fhare in what he did, that for ought I know,* fays he, *the performances of his youth, as they were the moft vigorous, were the beft.* But the power of nature is only the power of ufing to any certain purpofe the materials which diligence procures, or opportunity fupplies. Nature gives no man know-ledge, and when images are collected by ftudy and experience, can only affift in combining or applying them. Shakefpeare, however favoured by nature, could impart only what he had learned; and as he muft increafe his ideas, like other mortals, by gra-dual acquifition, he, like them, grew wifer as he grew older, could difplay life better, as he knew it more, and inftruct with more efficacy, as he was himfelf more amply inftructed.

There is a vigilance of obfervation and accuracy of diftinction which books and precepts cannot con-fer; from this almoft all original and native excel-lence proceeds. Shakefpeare muft have looked upon mankind with perfpicacity, in the higheft degree curious and attentive. Other writers borrow their characters from preceding writers, and diverfify them only by the accidental appendages of prefent man-ners; the drefs is a little varied, but the body is the fame. Our author had both matter and form to provide; for, except the characters of Chaucer, to whom I think he is not much indebted, there were no writers in Englifh, and perhaps not many in other modern languages, which fhewed life in its native colours.

[ C 2 ]                    The

The conteft about the original benevolence or malignity of man had not yet commenced. Speculation had not yet attempted to analyfe the mind, to trace the paffions to their fources, to unfold the feminal principles of vice and virtue, or found the depths of the heart for the motives of action. All thofe enquiries, which from that time that human nature became the fafhionable ftudy, have been made fometimes with nice difcernment, but often with idle fubtilty, were yet unattempted. The tales, with which the infancy of learning was fatisfied, exhibited only the fuperficial appearances of action, related the events, but omitted the caufes, and were formed for fuch as delighted in wonders rather than in truth. Mankind was not then to be ftudied in the clofet; he that would know the world, was under the neceffity of gleaning his own remarks, by mingling as he could in its bufinefs and amufements.

Boyle congratulated himfelf upon his high birth, becaufe it favoured his curiofity, by facilitating his accefs. Shakefpeare had no fuch advantage; he came to London a needy adventurer, and lived for a time by very mean employments. Many works of genius and learning have been performed in ftates of life that appear very little favourable to thought or to enquiry; fo many, that he who confiders them is inclined to think that he fees enterprize and perfeverance predominating over all external agency, and bidding help and hindrance vanifh before them. The genius of Shakefpeare was not to be depreffed by the weight of poverty, nor limited by the narrow converfation to which men in want are inevitably condemned;

demned; the incumbrances of his fortune were ſhaken from his mind, *as dew-drops from a lion's mane.*

Though he had ſo many difficulties to encounter, and ſo little aſſiſtance to ſurmount them, he has been able to obtain an exact knowledge of many modes of life, and many caſts of native diſpoſitions; to vary them with great multiplicity; to mark them by nice diſtinctions; and to ſhew them in full view by proper combinations. In this part of his performances he had none to imitate, but has been himſelf imitated by all ſucceeding writers; and it may be doubted, whether from all his ſucceſſors more maxims of theoretical knowledge, or more rules of practical prudence, can be collected, than he alone has given to his country.

Nor was his attention confined to the actions of men; he was an exact ſurveyor of the inanimate world; his deſcriptions have always ſome peculiarities, gathered by contemplating things as they really exiſt. It may be obſerved, that the oldeſt poets of many nations preſerve their reputation, and that the following generations of wit, after a ſhort celebrity, ſink into oblivion. The firſt, whoever they be, muſt take their ſentiments and deſcriptions immediately from knowledge; the reſemblance is therefore juſt, their deſcriptions are verified by every eye, and their ſentiments acknowledged by every breaſt. Thoſe whom their fame invites to the ſame ſtudies, copy partly them, and partly nature, till the books of one age gain ſuch authority, as to ſtand in

[ C 3 ]                                            the

the place of nature to another, and imitation, always deviating a little, becomes at laft capricious and cafual. Shakefpeare, whether life or nature be his fubject, fhews plainly, that he has feen with his own eyes; he gives the image which he receives, not weakened or diftorted by the intervention of any other mind ; the ignorant feel his reprefentations to be juft, and the learned fee that they are complete.

Perhaps it would not be eafy to find any author, except Homer, who invented fo much as Shakefpeare, who fo much advanced the ftudies which he cultivated, or effufed fo much novelty upon his age or country. The form, the characters, the language, and the fhows of the Englifh drama are his. *He feems,* fays Dennis, *to have been the very original of our Englifh tragical harmony, that is, the harmony of blank verfe, diverfified often by diffyllable and triffyllable terminations. For the diverfity diftinguifhes it from heroick harmony, and by bringing it nearer to common ufe makes it more proper to gain attention, and more fit for action and dialogue. Such verfe we make when we are writing profe; we make fuch verfe in common converfation.*

I know not whether this praife is rigoroufly juft. The diffyllable termination, which the critick rightly appropriates to the drama, is to be found, though, I think, not in *Gorboduc*, which is confeffedly before our author; yet in *Hieronymo* *, of which the date is not certain, but which there is reafon to believe at leaft as old as his earlieft plays. This however is cer-

* It appears from the induction of Ben Jonfon's *Bartholomew Fair* to have been acted before the year 1590.　Steevens.

tain.

tain, that he is the firſt who taught either tragedy or comedy to pleaſe, there being no theatrical piece of any older writer, of which the name is known, except to antiquaries and collectors of books, which are ſought becauſe they are ſcarce, and would not have been ſcarce, had they been much eſteemed.

To him we muſt aſcribe the praiſe, unleſs Spenſer may divide it with him, of having firſt diſcovered to how much ſmoothneſs and harmony the Engliſh language could be ſoftened. He has ſpeeches, perhaps ſometimes ſcenes, which have all the delicacy of Rowe, without his effeminacy. He endeavours indeed commonly to ſtrike by the force and vigour of his dialogue, but he never executes his purpoſe better, than when he tries to footh by ſoftneſs.

Yet it muſt be at laſt confeſſed, that as we owe every thing to him, he owes ſomething to us; that, if much of his praiſe is paid by perception and judgment, much is likewiſe given by cuſtom and veneration. We fix our eyes upon his graces, and turn them from his deformities, and endure in him what we ſhould in another loath or deſpiſe. If we endured without praiſing, reſpect for the father of our drama might excuſe us; but I have ſeen, in the book of ſome modern critick, a collection of anomalies, which ſhew that he has corrupted language by every mode of depravation, but which his admirer has accumulated as a monument of honour.

He has ſcenes of undoubted and perpetual excellence, but perhaps not one play, which, if it were

[C 4]                                              now

now exhibited as the work of a contemporary writer, would be heard to the conclusion. I am indeed far from thinking, that his works were wrought to his own ideas of perfection; when they were such as would satisfy the audience, they satisfied the writer. It is seldom that authors, though more studious of fame than Shakespeare, rise much above the standard of their own age; to add a little to what is best will always be sufficient for present praise, and those who find themselves exalted into fame, are willing to credit their encomiasts, and to spare the labour of contending with themselves.

It does not appear, that Shakespeare thought his works worthy of posterity, that he levied any ideal tribute upon future times, or had any further pro-spect, than of present popularity and present profit. When his plays had been acted, his hope was at an end; he solicited no addition of honour from the reader. He therefore made no scruple to repeat the same jests in many dialogues, or to entangle different plots by the same knot of perplexity, which may be at least forgiven him, by those who recollect, that of Congreve's four comedies, two are concluded by a marriage in a mask, by a deception, which perhaps never happened, and which, whether likely or not, he did not invent.

So careless was this great poet of future fame, that, though he retired to ease and plenty, while he was yet little *declined into the vale of years*, before he could be disgusted with fatigue, or disabled by infirmity, he made no collection of his works, nor desired to
rescue

rescue those that had been already published from the depravations that obscured them, or secure to the rest a better destiny, by giving them to the world in their genuine state.

Of the plays which bear the name of Shakespeare in the late editions, the greater part were not published till about seven years after his death, and the few which appeared in his life are apparently thrust into the world without the care of the author, and therefore probably without his knowledge.

Of all the publishers, clandestine or professed, their negligence and unskilfulness has by the late revisers been sufficiently shewn. The faults of all are indeed numerous and gross, and have not only corrupted many passages perhaps beyond recovery, but have brought others into suspicion, which are only obscured by obsolete phraseology, or by the writer's unskilfulness and affectation. To alter is more easy than to explain, and temerity is a more common quality than diligence. Those who saw that they must employ conjecture to a certain degree, were willing to indulge it a little further. Had the author published his own works, we should have sat quietly down to disentangle his intricacies, and clear his obscurities; but now we tear what we cannot loose, and eject what we happen not to understand.

The faults are more than could have happened without the concurrence of many causes. The style of Shakespeare was in itself ungrammatical, perplexed, and obscure; his works were transcribed for the

players

players by thofe who may be fuppofed to have feldom underftood them; they were tranfmitted by copiers equally unfkilful, who ftill multiplied errors ; they were perhaps fometimes mutilated by the actors, for the fake of fhortening the fpeeches ; and were at laft printed without correction of the prefs.

In this ftate they remained, not as Dr. Warburton fuppofes, becaufe they were unregarded, but becaufe the editor's art was not yet applied to modern languages, and our anceftors were accuftomed to fo much negligence of Englifh printers, that they could very patiently endure it. At laft an edition was undertaken by Rowe ; not becaufe a poet was to be publifhed by a poet, for Rowe feems to have thought very little on correction or explanation, but that our author's works might appear like thofe of his fraternity, with the appendages of a life and recommendatory preface. Rowe has been clamoroufly blamed for not performing what he did not undertake, and it is time that juftice be done him, by confeffing, that though he feems to have had no thought of corruption beyond the printer's errors, yet he has made many emendations, if they were not made before, which his fucceffors have received without acknowledgment, and which, if they had produced them, would have filled pages and pages with cenfures of the ftupidity by which the faults were committed, with difplays of the abfurdities which they involved, with oftentatious expofitions of the new reading, and felf-congratulations on the happinefs of difcovering it.

As

As of the other editors, I have preferved the prefaces, I have likewife borrowed the author's life from
Rowe, though not written with much elegance or
fpirit; it relates however what is now to be known,
and therefore deferves to pafs through all fucceeding
publications.

The nation had been for many years content enough
with Mr. Rowe's performance, when Mr. Pope made
them acquainted with the true ftate of Shakefpeare's
text, fhewed that it was extremely corrupt, and gave
reafon to hope that there were means of reforming
it. He collated the old copies, which none had
thought to examine before, and reftored many lines
to their integrity; but, by a very compendious criticifm, he rejeƈted whatever he difliked, and thought
more of amputation than of cure.

I know not why he is commended by Dr. War-
buton for diftinguifhing the genuine from the fpuri-
ous plays. In this choice he exerted no judgment
of his own; the plays which he received, were given
by Hemings and Condel, the firft editors; and thofe
which he rejeƈted, though, according to the licen-
tioufnefs of the prefs in thofe times, they were printed
during Shakefpeare's life, with his name, had been
omitted by his friends, and were never added to his
works before the edition of 1664, from which they
were copied by the later printers.

This is a work which Pope feems to have thought
unworthy of his abilities, being not able to fupprefs
his contempt of *the dull duty of an editor.* He underftood

ftood but half his undertaking. The duty of a collator is indeed dull, yet, like other tedious tafks, is very neceffary; but an emendatory critick would ill difcharge his duty, without qualities very different from dulnefs. In perufing a corrupted piece, he muft have before him all poffibilities of meaning, with all poffibilities of expreffion. Such muft be his comprehenfion of thought, and fuch his copioufnefs of language. Out of many readings poffible, he muft be able to felect that which beft fuits with the ftate, opinions, and modes of language prevailing in every age, and with his author's particular caft of thought, and turn of expreffion. Such muft be his knowledge, and fuch his tafte. Conjectural criticifm demands more than humanity poffeffes, and he that exercifes it with moft praife, has very frequent need of indulgence. Let us now be told no more of the dull duty of an editor.

Confidence is the common confequence of fuccefs. They whofe excellence of any kind has been loudly celebrated, are ready to conclude, that their powers are univerfal. Pope's edition fell below his own expectations, and he was fo much offended, when he was found to have left any thing for others to do, that he paffed the latter part of his life in a ftate of hoftility with verbal criticifm.

I have retained all his notes, that no fragment of fo great a writer may be loft; his preface, valuable alike for elegance of compofition and juftnefs of remark, and containing a general criticifm on his author,

thor, fo extenfive that little can be added, and fo
exact, that little can be difputed, every editor has an
intereft to fupprefs, but that every reader would demand its infertion.

Pope was fucceeded by Theobald, a man of narrow
comprehenfion, and fmall acquifitions, with no native
and intrinfic fplendor of genius, with little of the
artificial light of learning, but zealous for minute
accuracy, and not negligent in purfuing it. He collated the ancient copies, and rectified many errors.
A man fo anxioufly fcrupulous might have been expected to do more, but what little he did was commonly right.

In his reports of copies and editions he is not to
be trufted without examination. He fpeaks fometimes indefinitely of copies, when he has only one.
In his enumeration of editions, he mentions the two
firft folios as of high, and the third folio as of middle
authority ; but the truth is, that the firft is equivalent
to all others, and that the reft only deviate from it
by the printer's negligence. Whoever has any of
the folios has all, excepting thofe diverfities which
mere reiteration of editions will produce. I collated
them all at the beginning, but afterwards ufed only
the firft.

Of his notes I have generally retained thofe which
he retained himfelf in his fecond edition, except when
they were confuted by fubfequent annotators, or were
too minute to merit prefervation. I have fometimes
adopted his reftoration of a comma, without inferting
the

the panegyrick in which he celebrated himſelf for his atchievement. The exuberant excreſcence of his diƈtion I have often lopped, his triumphant exultations over Pope and Rowe I have ſometimes ſuppreſſed, and his contemptible oſtentation I have frequently concealed ; but I have in ſome places ſhewn him, as he would have ſhewn himſelf, for the reader's diverſion, that the inflated emptineſs of ſome notes may juſtify or excuſe the contraƈtion of the reſt.

Theobald, thus weak and ignorant, thus mean and faithleſs, thus petulant and oſtentatious, by the good luck of having Pope for his enemy, has eſcaped, and eſcaped alone, with reputation, from this undertaking. So willingly does the world ſupport thoſe who ſolicit favour, againſt thoſe who command reverence ; and ſo eaſily is he praiſed, whom no man can envy.

Our author fell then into the hands of Sir Thomas Hanmer, the Oxford editor, a man, in my opinion, eminently qualified by nature for ſuch ſtudies. He had, what is the firſt requiſite to emendatory criticiſm, that intuition by which the poet's intention is immediately diſcovered, and that dexterity of intelleƈt which diſpatches its work by the eaſieſt means. He had undoubtedly read much ; his acquaintance with cuſtoms, opinions, and traditions, ſeems to have been large ; and he is often learned without ſhew. He ſeldom paſſes what he does not underſtand, without an attempt to find or to make a meaning, and ſometimes haſtily makes what a little more attention would have found. He is ſolicitous to reduce to grammar, what he could not be ſure that his author intended

to

to be grammatical. Shakefpeare regarded more the feries of ideas, than of words ; and his language, not being defigned for the reader's defk, was all that he defired it to be, if it conveyed his meaning to the audience.

Hanmer's care of the metre has been too violently cenfured. He found the meafure reformed in fo many paffages, by the filent labours of fome editors, with the filent acquiefcence of the reft, that he thought himfelf allowed to extend a little further the licence, which had already been carried fo far without reprehenfion ; and of his corrections in general, it muft be confeffed, that they are often juft, and made commonly with the leaft poffible violation of the text.

But, by inferting his emendations, whether invented or borrowed, into the page, without any notice of varying copies, he has appropriated the labour of his predeceffors, and made his own edition of little authority. His confidence indeed, both in himfelf and others, was too great ; he fuppofes all to be right that was done by Pope and Theobald ; he feems not to fufpect a critick of fallibility, and it was but reafonable that he fhould claim what he fo liberally granted.

As he never writes without careful enquiry and diligent confideration, I have received all his notes, and believe that every reader will wifh for more.

Of

Of the laſt editor it is more difficult to ſpeak. Reſpeᵭt is due to high place, tenderneſs to living reputation, and veneration to genius and learning ; but he cannot be juſtly offended at that liberty of which he has himſelf ſo frequently given an example, nor very ſolicitous what is thought of notes, which he ought never to have conſidered as part of his ſerious employments, and which, I ſuppoſe, ſince the ardor of compoſition is remitted, he no longer num- bers among his happy effuſions.

The original and predominant error of his com- mentary, is acquieſcence in his firſt thoughts ; that precipitation which is produced by conſciouſneſs of quick diſcernment ; and that confidence which pre- ſumes to do, by ſurveying the ſurface, what labour only can perform, by penetrating the bottom. His notes exhibit ſometimes perverſe interpretations, and ſometimes improbable conjeᵭtures ; he at one time gives the author more profundity of meaning than the ſentence admits, and at another diſcovers abſurdi- ties, where the ſenſe is plain to every other reader. But his emendations are likewiſe often happy and juſt ; and his interpretation of obſcure paſſages learned and ſagacious.

Of his notes, I have commonly rejeᵭted thoſe, againſt which the general voice of the publick has exclaimed, or which their own incongruity imme- diately condemns, and which, I ſuppoſe the author himſelf would deſire to be forgotten. Of the reſt, to part I have given the higheſt approbation, by in-
ſerting

ferting the offered reading in the text; part I have
left to the judgment of the reader, as doubtful,
though fpecious; and part I have cenfured without
referve, but I am fure without bitternefs of malice,
and, I hope, without wantonnefs of infult.

It is no pleafure to me, in revifing my volumes,
to obferve how much paper is wafted in confutation.
Whoever confiders the revolutions of learning, and
the various queftions of greater or lefs importance,
upon which wit and reafon have exercifed their powers,
muft lament the unfuccefsfulnefs of enquiry, and the
flow advances of truth, when he reflects, that great
part of the labour of every writer is only the deftruc-
tion of thofe that went before him. The firft care
of the builder of a new fyftem, is to demolifh the
fabricks which are ftanding. The chief defire of him
that comments an author, is to fhew how much other
commentators have corrupted and obfcured him.
The opinions prevalent in one age, as truths above
the reach of controverfy, are confuted and rejected
in another, and rife again to reception in remoter
times. Thus the human mind is kept in motion
without progrefs. Thus fometimes truth and error,
and fometimes contrarieties of error, take each other's
place by reciprocal invafion. The tide of feeming
knowledge which is poured over one generation, re-
tires and leaves another naked and barren; the fudden
meteors of intelligence, which for a while appear to
fhoot their beams into the regions of obfcurity, on a
fudden withdraw their luftre, and leave mortals again
to grope their way.

These elevations and depreffions of renown, and the contradictions to which all improvers of knowledge muft for ever be expofed, fince they are not efcaped by the higheft and brighteft of mankind, may furely be endured with patience by criticks and annotators, who can rank themfelves but as the fatellites of their authors. How canft thou beg for life, fays Homer's hero to his captive, when thou knoweft that thou art now to fuffer only what muft another day be fuffered by Achilles?

Dr. Warburton had a name fufficient to confer celebrity on thofe who could exalt themfelves into antagonifts, and his notes have raifed a clamour too loud to be diftinct. His chief affailants are the authors of *The canons of criticifm*, and of *The revifal of Shakefpeare's text*; of whom one ridicules his errors with airy petulance, fuitable enough to the levity of the controverfy; the other attacks them with gloomy malignity, as if he were dragging to juftice an affaffin or incendiary. The one ftings like a fly, fucks a little blood, takes a gay flutter, and returns for more; the other bites like a viper, and would be glad to leave inflammations and gangrene behind him. When I think on one, with his confederates, I remember the danger of Coriolanus, who was afraid that *girls with fpits, and boys with ftones, fhould flay him in puny battle*; when the other croffes my imagination, I remember the prodigy in *Macbeth*:

*A falcon tow'ring in his pride of place,*
*Was by a moufing owl hawk'd at and kill'd.*

Let

Let me however do them juftice. One is a wit,
and one a fcholar *. They have both fhewn acute-
nefs fufficient in the difcovery of faults, and have
both advanced fome probable interpretations of obfcure paffages ; but when they afpire to conjecture
and emendation, it appears how falfely we all eftimate
our own abilities, and the little which they have been
able to perform might have taught them more candour
to the endeavours of others.

Before Dr. Warburton's edition, *Critical obfervations on Shakefpeare* had been publifhed by Mr. Upton†,
a man fkilled in languages, and acquainted with books,
but who feems to have had no great vigour of genius
or nicety of tafte. Many of his explanations are
curious and ufeful, but he likewife, though he profeffed to oppofe the licentious confidence of editors,
and adhere to the old copies, is unable to reftrain the
rage of emendation, though his ardour is ill feconded
by his fkill. Every cold empirick, when his heart
is expanded by a fuccefsful experiment, fwells into
a theorift, and the laborious collator at fome unlucky
moment frolicks in conjecture.

*Critical, hiftorical, and explanatory notes* have been
likewife publifhed upon Shakefpeare by Dr. Grey,

---

* It is extraordinary that this gentleman fhould attempt fo
voluminous a work, as the *Revifal of Shakefpeare's text*, when
he tells us in his preface, " he was not fo fortunate as to be
" furnifhed with either of the folio editions, much lefs any of
" the ancient quartos : and even Sir Thomas Hanmer's per-
" formance was known to him only by Dr. Warburton's repre-
" fentation." FARMER.
† Republifhed by him in 1748, after Dr. Warburton's edition,
with alterations, &c. STEEVENS.

whofe

whofe diligent perufal of the old Englifh writers has
enabled him to make fome ufeful obfervations. What
he undertook he has well enough performed, but as
he neither attempts judicial nor emendatory criticifm,
he employs rather his memory than his fagacity. It
were to be wifhed that all would endeavour to imitate
his modefty, who have not been able to furpafs his
knowledge.

I can fay with great fincerity of all my predeceffors,
what I hope will hereafter be faid of me, that not
one has left Shakefpeare without improvement, nor
is there one to whom I have not been indebted for
affiftance and information. Whatever I have taken
from them, it was my intention to refer to its original
author, and it is certain, that what I have not given
to another, I believed when I wrote it to be my own.
In fome perhaps I have been anticipated; but if I
am ever found to encroach upon the remarks of any
other commentator, I am willing that the honour, be
it more or lefs, fhould be transferred to the firft
claimant, for his right, and his alone, ftands above
difpute; the fecond can prove his pretenfions only to
himfelf, nor can himfelf always diftinguifh invention,
with fufficient certainty, from recollection.

They have all been treated by me with candour,
which they have not been careful of obferving to one
another. It is not eafy to difcover from what caufe
the acrimony of a fcholiaft can naturally proceed.
The fubjects to be difcuffed by him are of very fmall
importance; they involve neither property nor liberty; nor favour the intereft of fect or party. The
various

various readings of copies, and different interpretations of a paffage, feem to be queftions that might
exercife the wit, without engaging the paffions.    But
whether it be, that *fmall things make mean men proud*,
and vanity catches fmall occafions; or that all con-
trariety of opinion, even in thofe that can defend it
no longer, makes proud men angry ; there is often
found in commentaries a fpontaneous ftrain of invec-
tive and contempt, more eager and venomous than
is vented by the moft furious controvertift in politicks
againft thofe whom he is hired to defame.

Perhaps the lightnefs of the matter may conduce
to the vehemence of the agency ; when the truth to
be inveftigated is fo near to inexiftence, as to efcape
attention, its bulk is to be enlarged by rage and
exclamation: that to which all would be indifferent
in its original ftate, may attract notice when the fate
of a name is appended to it.    A commentator has
indeed great temptations to fupply by turbulence
what he wants of dignity, to beat his little gold to a
fpacious furface, to work that to foam which no art
or diligence can exalt to fpirit.

The notes which I have borrowed or written are
either illuftrative, by which difficulties are explained;
or judicial, by which faults and beauties are remarked ; or emendatory, by which depravations are
corrected.

The explanations tranfcribed from others, if I do
not fubjoin any other interpretation, I fuppofe commonly to be right, at leaft I intend by acquiefcence

to confefs, that I have nothing better to propofe,

After the labours of all the editors, I found many paffages which appeared to me likely to obftruct the greater number of readers, and thought it my duty to facilitate their paffage. It is impoffible for an expofitor not to write too little for fome, and too much for others. He can only judge what is neceffary by his own experience; and how long foever he may deliberate, will at laft explain many lines which the learned will think impoffible to be miftaken, and omit many for which the ignorant will want his help. Thefe are cenfures merely relative, and muft be quietly endured. I have endeavoured to be neither fuperfluoufly copious, nor fcrupuloufly referved, and hope that I have made my author's meaning acceffible to many, who before were frighted from perufing him, and contributed fomething to the publick, by diffufing innocent and rational pleafure.

The complete explanation of an author not fyftematick and confequential, but defultory and vagrant, abounding in cafual allufions and light hints, is not to be expected from any fingle fcholiaft. All perfonal reflections, when names are fuppreffed, muft be in a few years irrecoverably obliterated; and cuftoms, too minute to attract the notice of law, fuch as modes of drefs, formalities of converfation, rules of vifits, difpofition of furniture, and practices of ceremony, which naturally find places in familiar dialogue, are fo fugitive and unfubftantial, that they are not eafily retained or recovered. What can be known will be collected by chance, from the receffes of obfcure and
obfolete

obfolete papers, perufed commonly with fome other view. Of this knowledge every man has fome, and none has much; but when an author has engaged the publick attention, thofe who can add any thing to his illuftration, communicate their difcoveries, and time produces what had eluded diligence.

To time I have been obliged to refign many paffages, which, though I did not underftand them, will perhaps hereafter be explained, having, I hope, illuftrated fome, which others have neglected or miftaken, fometimes by fhort remarks, or marginal directions, fuch as every editor has added at his will, and often by comments more laborious than the matter will feem to deferve; but that which is moft difficult is not always moft important, and to an editor nothing is a trifle by which his author is obfcured.

The poetical beauties or defects I have not been very diligent to obferve. Some plays have more, and fome fewer judicial obfervations, not in proportion to their difference of merit, but becaufe I gave this part of my defign to chance and to caprice. The reader, I believe, is feldom pleafed to find his opinion anticipated; it is natural to delight more in what we find or make, than in what we receive. Judgment, like other faculties, is improved by practice, and its advancement is hindered by fubmiffion to dictatorial decifions, as the memory grows torpid by the ufe of a table-book. Some initiation is however neceffary; of all fkill, part is infufed by precept, and part is obtained by habit; I have therefore fhewn fo much

as

as may enable the candidate of criticifm to difcover the reft.

To the end of moft plays I have added fhort ftrictures, containing a general cenfure of faults, or praife of excellence; in which I know not how much I have concurred with the current opinion ; but I have not, by any affectation of fingularity, deviated from it. Nothing is minutely and particularly examined, and therefore it is to be fuppofed, that in the plays which are condemned there is much to be praifed, and in thefe which are praifed much to be condemned.

The part of criticifm in which the whole fucceffion of editors has laboured with the greateft diligence, which has occafioned the moft arrogant oftentation, and excited the keeneft acrimony, is the emendation of corrupted paffages, to which the publick attention having been firft drawn by the violence of the contention between Pope and Theobald, has been continued by the perfecution, which, with a kind of confpiracy, has been fince raifed againft all the publifhers of Shakefpeare.

That many paffages have paffed in a ftate of depravation through all the editions is indubitably certain ; of thefe the reftoration is only to be attempted by collation of copies, or fagacity of conjecture. The collator's province is fafe and eafy, the conjecturer's perilous and difficult. Yet as the greater part of the plays are extant only in one copy, the peril muft not be avoided, nor the difficulty refufed.

Of

Of the readings which this emulation of amend-
ment has hitherto produced, fome from the labours
of every publifher I have advanced into the text;
thcfe are to be confidered as in my opinion fufficiently
fupported; fome I have rejeéted without mention, as
evidently erroneous; fome I have left in the notes
without cenfure or approbation, as refting in equipoife
between objeétion and defence; and fome, which
feemed fpecious but not right, I have inferted with
a fubfequent animadverfion,

Having claffed the obfervations of others, I was at
laft to try what I could fubftitute for their miftakes,
and how I could fupply their omiffions. I collated
fuch copies as I could procure, and wifhed for more,
but have not found the colleétors of thefe rarities very
communicative. Of the editions which chance or
kindnefs put into my hands I have given an enumeration, that I may not be blamed for negleéting what
I had not the power to do.

By examining the old copies, I foon found that the
later publifhers, with all their boafts of diligence,
fuffered many paffages to ftand unauthorized, and
contented themfelves with Rowe's regulation of the
text, even where they knew it to be arbitrary, and
with a little confideration might have found it to be
wrong. Some of thefe alterations are only the ejeétion
of a word for one that appeared to him more elegant
or more intelligible. Thefe corruptions I have often
filently reétified; for the hiftory of our language,
and the true force of our words, can only be
preferved, by keeping the text of authors free
from

from adulteration. Others, and thofe very frequent, fmoothed the cadence, or regulated the meafure; on thefe I have not exercifed the fame rigour; if only a word was tranfpofed, or a particle inferted or omitted, I have fometimes fuffered the line to ftand; for the inconftancy of the copies is fuch, as that fome liberties may be eafily permitted. But this practice I have not fuffered to proceed far, having reftored the primitive diction wherever it could for any reafon be preferred.

The emendations, which comparifon of copies fupplied, I have inferted in the text; fometimes, where the improvement was flight, without notice, and fometimes with an account of the reafons of the change.

Conjecture, though it be fometimes unavoidable, I have not wantonly nor licentioufly indulged. It has been my fettled principle, that the reading of the ancient books is probably true, and therefore is not to be difturbed for the fake of elegance, perfpicuity, or mere improvement of the fenfe. For though much credit is not due to the fidelity, nor any to the judgment of the firft publifhers, yet they who had the copy before their eyes were more likely to read it right, than we who read it only by imagination. But it is evident that they have often made ftrange miftakes by ignorance or negligence, and that therefore fomething may be properly attempted by criticifm, keeping the middle way between prefumption and timidity.

Such

Such criticifm I have attempted to practife, and, where any paffage appeared inextricably perplexed, have endeavoured to difcover how it may be recalled to fenfe, with leaft violence. But my firft labour is, always to turn the old text on every fide, and try if there be any interftice, through which light can find its way; nor would Huetius himfelf condemn me, as refufing the trouble of refearch, for the ambition of alteration. In this modeft induftry I have not been unfuccefsful. I have refcued many lines from the violations of temerity, and fecured many fcenes from the inroads of correction. I have adopted the Roman fentiment, that it is more honourable to fave a citizen, than to kill an enemy, and have been more careful to protect than to attack.

I have preferved the common diftribution of the plays into acts, though I believe it to be in almoft all the plays void of authority. Some of thofe which are divided in the later editions have no divifion in the firft folio, and fome that are divided in the folio have no divifion in the preceding copies. The fettled mode of the theatre requires four intervals in the play, but few, if any, of our author's compoftions can be properly diftributed in that manner. An act is fo much of the drama as paffes without intervention of time, or change of place. A paufe makes a new act. In every real, and therefore in every imitative action, the intervals may be more or fewer, the reftriction of five acts being accidental and arbitrary. This Shakefpeare knew, and this he practifed; his plays were written, and at firft printed in one unbroken continuity, and ought now to be exhibited with

with fhort paufes, interpofed as often as the fcene is
changed, or any confiderable time is required to pafs.
This method would at once quell a thoufand abfurdities.

In reftoring the author's works to their integrity,
I have confidered the punctuation as wholly in my
power; for what could be their care of colons and
commas, who corrupted words and fentences. Whatever could be done by adjufting points, is therefore
filently performed, in fome plays, with much diligence, in others with lefs; it is hard to keep a bufy
eye fteadily fixed upon evanefcent atoms, or a dif-
curfive mind upon evanefcent truth.

The fame liberty has been taken with a few par-
ticles, or other words of flight effect. I have fometimes inferted or omitted them without notice. I have
done that fometimes, which the other editors have
done always, and which indeed the ftate of the text
may fufficiently juftify.

The greater part of readers, inftead of blaming
us for paffing trifles, will wonder that on mere trifles
fo much labour is expended, with fuch importance
of debate, and fuch folemnity of diction. To thefe
I anfwer with confidence, that they are judging of
an art which they do not underftand; yet cannot
much reproach them with their ignorance, nor pro-
mife that they would become in general, by learning
criticifm, more ufeful, happier, or wifer.

As

As I practised conjecture more, I learned to truft it lefs; and after I had printed a few plays, refolved to infert none of my own readings in the text. Upon this caution I now congratulate myfelf, for every day encreafes my doubt of my emendations.

Since I have confined my imagination to the margin, it muft not be confidered as very reprehenfible, if I have fuffered it to play fome freaks in its own dominion. There is no danger in conjecture, if it be propofed as conjecture; and while the text remains uninjured, thofe changes may be fafely offered, which are not confidered even by him that offers them as neceffary or fafe.

If my readings are of little value, they have not been oftentatioufly difplayed or importunately obtruded. I could have written longer notes, for the art of writing notes is not of difficult attainment. The work is performed, firft by railing at the ftupidity, negligence, ignorance, and afinine tafteleffnefs of the former editors, and fhewing, from all that goes before and all that follows, the inelegance and abfurdity of the old reading; then by propofing fomething, which to fuperficial readers would feem fpecious, but which the editor rejects with indignation; then by producing the true reading, with a long paraphrafe, and concluding with loud acclamations on the difcovery, and a fober wifh for the advancement and profperity of genuine criticifm.

All this may be done, and perhaps done fometimes without impropriety. But I have always fufpected that

that the reading is right, which requires many words
to prove it wrong; and the emendation wrong, that
cannot without fo much labour appear to be right.
The juftnefs of a happy reftoration ftrikes at once,
and the moral precept may be well applied to criticifm, *quod dubitas ne feceris.*

To dread the fhore which he fees fpread with
wrecks, is natural to the failor. I had before my
eye, fo many critical adventures ended in mifcarriage,
that caution was forced upon me. I encountered in
every page wit ftruggling with its own fophiftry, and
learning confufed by the multiplicity of its views.
I was forced to cenfure thofe whom I admired, and
could not but reflect, while I was difpoffeffing their
emendations, how foon the fame fate might happen
to my own, and how many of the readings which I
have corrected may be by fome other editor defended
and eftablifhed.

> *Criticks I faw, that other's names efface,*
> *And fix their own, with labour, in the place;*
> *Their own, like others, foon their place refign'd,*
> *Or difappear'd, and left the firft behind.* POPE.

That a conjectural critick fhould often be miftaken,
cannot be wonderful, either to others or himfelf, if
it be confidered, that in his art there is no fyftem,
no principal and axiomatical truth that regulates
fubordinate pofitions. His chance of error is renewed
at every attempt; an oblique view of the paffage,
a flight mifapprehenfion of a phrafe, a cafual inat-
tention to the parts connected, is fufficient to make
him

him not only fail, but fail ridiculoufly; and when
he fucceeds beft, he produces perhaps but one reading
of many probable, and he that fuggefts another will
always be able to difpute his claims.

It is an unhappy ftate, in which danger is hid
under pleafure. The allurements of emendation are
fcarcely refiftible. Conjecture has all the joy and all
the pride of invention, and he that has once ftarted
a happy change, is too much delighted to confider
what objections may rife againft it.

Yet conjectural criticifm has been of great ufe in
the learned world; nor is it my intention to depre-
ciate a ftudy, that has exercifed fo many mighty
minds, from the revival of learning to our own age,
from the bifhop of Aleria to Englifh Bentley. The
criticks on ancient authors have, in the exercife of
their fagacity, many affiftances, which the editor of
Shakefpeare is condemned to want. They are employed upon grammatical and fettled languages,
whofe conftruction contributes fo much to perfpicuity,
that Homer has fewer paffages unintelligible than
Chaucer. The words have not only a known regimen, but invariable quantities, which direct and confine the choice. There are commonly more manu-
fcripts than one; and they do not often confpire in the
fame miftakes. Yet Scaliger could confefs to Salma-
fius how little fatisfaction his emendations gave him.
*Illudant nobis conjecturæ noftræ, quarum nos pudet, pof-*
*teaquam in meliores codices incidimus.* And Lipfius
could complain, that criticks were making faults,
by trying to remove them, *Ut olim vitiis, ita nunc*
*remediis*

*remediis laboratur.* And indeed, where mere conjecture is to be ufed, the emendations of Scaliger and
Lipfius, notwithftanding their wonderful fagacity and
erudition, are often vague and difputable, like mine
or Theobald's.

Perhaps I may not be more cenfured for doing
wrong, than for doing little; for raifing in the publick expectations, which at laft I have not anfwered.
The expectation of ignorance is indefinite, and that
of knowledge is often tyrannical. It is hard to fatisfy
thofe who know not what to demand, or thofe who
demand by defign what they think impoffible to be
done. I have indeed difappointed no opinion more
than my own; yet I have endeavoured to perform
my tafk with no flight folicitude. Not a fingle paffage in the whole work has appeared to me corrupt,
which I have not attempted to reftore: or obfcure,
which I have not endeavoured to illuftrate. In
many I have failed like others; and from many,
after all my efforts, I have retreated, and confeffed
the repulfe. I have not paffed over, with affected
fuperiority, what is equally difficult to the reader
and to myfelf, but where I could not inftruct him,
have owned my ignorance. I might eafily have accumulated a mafs of feeming learning upon eafy
fcenes; but it ought not to be imputed to negligence,
that, where nothing was neceffary, nothing has been
done, or that, where others have faid enough, I have
faid no more.

Notes are often neceffary, but they are neceffary
evils. Let him, that is yet unacquainted with the
powers

powers of Shakefpeare, and who defires to feel the higheft pleafure that the drama can give, read every play, from the firft fcene to the laft, with utter negligence of all his commentators. When his fancy is once on the wing, let it not ftoop at correction or explanation. When his attention is ftrongly engaged, let it difdain alike to turn afide to the name of Theobald and of Pope. Let him read on through brightnefs and obfcurity, through integrity and corruption; let him preferve his comprehenfion of the dialogue and his intereft in the fable. And when the pleafures of novelty have ceafed, let him attempt exactnefs, and read the commentators.

Particular paffages are cleared by notes, but the general effect of the work is weakened. The mind is refrigerated by interruption; the thoughts are diverted from the principal fubject; the reader is weary, he fufpects not why; and at laft throws away the book which he has too diligently ftudied.

Parts are not to be examined till the whole has been furveyed; there is a kind of intellectual remotenefs neceffary for the comprehenfion of any great work in its full defign and in its true proportions; a clofe approach fhews the fmaller niceties, but the beauty of the whole is difcerned no longer.

It is not very grateful to confider how little the fucceffion of editors has added to this author's power of pleafing. He was read, admired, ftudied, and imitated, while he was yet deformed with all the improprieties which ignorance and neglect could accumulate upon him; while the reading was yet not rectified, nor his allusions understood; yet then did Dryden pronounce, " that Shakefpeare was the man, " who, of all modern and perhaps ancient poets, " had the largest and moft comprehenfive foul. All " the images of nature were ftill prefent to him, and " he drew them not laborioufly, but luckily: when " he defcribes any thing, you more than fee it, you " feel it too. Thofe, who accufe him to have wanted " learning, give him the greater commendation: he " was naturally learned: he needed not the fpectacles " of books to read nature; he looked inwards, and " found her there. I cannot fay he is every where " alike; were he fo, I fhould do him injury to com- " pare him with the greateft of mankind. He is " many times flat and infipid; his comick wit de- " generating into clenches, his ferious fwelling into " bombaft. But he is always great, when fome great " occafion is prefented to him: no man can fay, he " ever had a fit fubject for his wit, and did not then " raife himfelf as high above the reft of poets,

" *Quantum lenta folent inter viburna cupreſſi.*"

It is to be lamented, that fuch a writer fhould want a commentary; that his language fhould be- come obfolete, or his fentiments obfcure. But it is vain to carry wifhes beyond the condition of human things; that which muft happen to all, has happened to Shakefpeare, by accident and time; and more than has been fuffered by any other writer fince the ufe of types, has been fuffered by him through his own negligence of fame, or perhaps by that fupe- riority

riority of mind, which defpifed its own performances, when it compared them with its powers, and judged thofe works unworthy to be preferved, which the criticks of following ages were to contend for the fame of reftoring and explaining.

Among thefe candidates of inferior fame, I am now to ftand the judgment of the publick; and wifh that I could confidently produce my commentary as equal to the encouragement which I have had the honour of receiving. Every work of this kind is by its nature deficient, and I fhould feel little folicitude about the fentence, were it to be pronounced only by the fkilful and the learned.

Of what has been performed in this revifal, an account is given in the following pages by Mr. Steevens, who might have fpoken both of his own diligence and fagacity, in terms of greater felf-approbation, without deviating from modefty or truth.

JOHNSON.

[E 2]

# A NOTE ON THE COMMENTARY

*"It is impossible for an expositor not to write
too little for some, and too much for others"*

The following Commentary is intended to provide a set-
ting, or context, for Johnson's *Preface to Shakespeare*,
and to assist readers in understanding his language and
ideas. Where necessary, an attempt has been made to
clarify difficult or misleading terms. Sometimes Johnson's
own *Dictionary* has been used to elucidate obscurities;
sometimes interpretation has been aided by reference to
usage of the same word or term elsewhere in Johnson, or
by some other writer.

A primary purpose of the Commentary has been to link
the *Preface* with Johnson's annotations to Shakespeare in
his edition of the plays. His general remarks, it is
often the case, flow from a multiplicity of particular
judgements on moments in the plays, giving to his general
judgements the support of his detailed attention to
Shakespeare's text. Extracts from Johnson's annotations
to Shakespeare have therefore been printed as notes, or as
parts of notes, to the text of the *Preface* itself, the aim
being to help readers move more easily between Shakespeare
and Johnson. What, precisely, Johnson had in mind in his
general remarks, one can, of course, for much of the time
only guess. But the affinities between the *Preface* and the
notes are sometimes so clear that the annotations provide
a case in point, as it were, to support what, in general
terms, is observed in the *Preface*. By this method, it
may be that the *Preface* can be made more practically useful as literary criticism, as well as more enjoyable.

Quotations from Johnson's annotations to Shakespeare
in the following Commentary are taken from his second edition

of 1778.  Quotations from Shakespeare are made from the
same text and identified by Act and scene.  Line numbers
are not given as they do not appear in the original.
Wherever possible, references to Johnson's other writings
are to the Yale Edition of the Works of Samuel Johnson,
except in the case of the *Lives of the Poets*, quoted from
the edition of G.B. Hill.  Miscellaneous works not in
these standard editions are quoted from Arthur Murphy's
edition (1816).  Definitions from the *Dictionary* are
quoted from the first edition of 1755.

References to works by other writers in these notes
have been made to standard editions or, where no standard edition is available, from good contemporary editions.
Foreign authors are quoted in translation.  Current contemporary translations from French authors have been used
where these are appropriate, and available, as in the
case of Boileau's *Art Poétique* (1674), translated by
Dryden and Soame (1680), and Thomas Rymer's translation
of Rapin's *Réflexions sur la Poétique d'Aristote*, published in the same year as the original (1674).  The
'Loeb' version has been adopted for quotations from Greek
and Latin.  Line numbers are used to identify quotations
from verse, page numbers for quotations from prose.

Works cited once, or only occasionally, are fully identified in the Commentary itself.  The following standard
editions have been used for works quoted regularly in the
course of the Commentary.  Short titles, where used, are
signified below:

| | |
|---|---|
| ADDISON, Joseph:<br>  *The Spectator* | *The Spectator*, ed. D.F.<br>Bond (Oxford: Clarendon<br>Press, 1965). |
| BOILEAU-DESPREAUX,<br>  Nicolas: | *Epîtres, Art Poétique, Lutrin.*<br>*Dissertation sur la Joconde,*<br>*Arrest Burlesque, Traité du*<br>*Sublime.  Oeuvres Complètes,*<br>ed. Charles-H.  Boudhors |

BOSWELL, James:
*Life*

DENNIS, John:
*Critical Works*

DRYDEN, John:
*Essays*

DRYDEN, John:

HAZLITT, William:
*Works*

JOHNSON, Samuel:
*Yale*

JOHNSON, Samuel:

JOHNSON, Samuel:
*Lives*

JOHNSON, Samuel:
*Dict.*

POPE, Alexander:

RYMER, Thomas:
*Critical Works*

SCHLEGEL, A.W.:
*Lectures on Drama*

SHAKESPEARE, William:
*Shakespeare*

(Paris: Société Des Belles Lettres, 1939-52).
*The Life of Johnson*, ed. G. Birkbeck Hill, revised L.F. Powell (Oxford: Clarendon Press, 1934-50).
*The Critical Works of John Dennis*, ed. Edward Niles Hooker, 2 vols. (Baltimore: John Hopkins Press, 1939-43).
*Of Dramatic Poesie and Other Critical Essays*, ed. George Watson, 2 vols. (1962: repr. London: Everyman's Library, 1968).
*The Poems of John Dryden*, ed. James Kinsley, 4 vols. (Oxford: Clarendon Press, 1958).
*The Complete Works of William Hazlitt*, ed. P. Howe (Suffolk: Chaucer Press, 1930).
The Yale Edition of the Works of Samuel Johnson, gen. edd. A.T. Hazen *et al.* (New Haven Conn.: Yale University Press, 1958-).
*The Works of Samuel Johnson, LL.D.*, ed. Arthur Murphy (London, 1816).
*Lives of the English Poets*, ed. George Birkbeck Hill, 3 vols. (Oxford: Clarendon Press, 1905).
*A Dictionary of the English Language*, 2 vols. (London, 1755).
The Twickenham Edition of the Poems of Alexander Pope, gen. ed. John Butt (London: Methuen, 1961-1969).
*The Critical Works of Thomas Rymer*, ed. Curt A. Zimansky (New Haven: Oxford University Press, 1956).
*A Course of Lectures on Dramatic Art and Literature*, tr. John Black (revised ed. 1809; repr. London: Bohn's Standard Library, 1846).
*The Plays of William Shakespeare*, ed. Samuel Johnson and George Steevens, 10 vols. Second edition, revised and augmented:

VOLTAIRE:
*Oeuvres*

WORDSWORTH, William:
*Prose Works*

(London, 1778).
*Oeuvres Complètes de Voltaire*,
ed. Beuchot (Paris: Garnier,
1879).
*The Prose Works of William
Wordsworth*, ed. W.J.B. Owen
and J.W. Smyser, 3 vols.
(Oxford: Clarendon Press,
1974).

COMMENTARY

PAGE 1

That praises . . . etc.: Johnson is referring to the complaint common among living writers; that their merits
are neglected while respect is payed to the dead. Those
who complain, says Johnson, do so either because they
can themselves add nothing to that "truth" required by
all good writing, or because they attribute prejudice
to their first readers, a consolation for efforts in
literature attended with little success, and productive
of few rewards. Among this number, it seems possible to
suspect, Johnson at some time placed himself.

paid to antiquity: The Yale edition of the *Preface* cites
Boswell, *Life*, IV, 217: *I am always angry when I hear
ancient times praised at the expence of modern times.*

heresies of paradox: Johnson may mean unorthodox opinions
expressed, as here, in the form of paradox, or perhaps
the unorthodox views to which paradox, by its nature,
tends frequently to give birth.
     In his *Dictionary*, Johnson defined "heresy" as: *an
opinion of private men different from that of the
catholick and orthodox church.*
     Cf. Pope in the 1st ed. of his *Essay on Criticism*
(1711): . . . *if the Throng / By* Chance *go right,
they* purposely *go wrong: / So Schismatics the* dull
Believers *quit, / And are but damn'd for having* too
much Wit.
     Johnson defined "paradox" in his *Dictionary* as *a
tenet contrary to received opinion.*

posterity: In Ch. X of *Rasselas*, Johnson had Imlac assert
that the poet must *contemn the applause of his own time,
and commit his claims to the justice of posterity.*

denied by envy: Because living writers delude themselves
that it is only the envy of contemporaries that pre-
vents their work being valued at its true rate.

Antiquity: Both ancient literature and other artefacts
of the ancient world. Johnson is not thinking only
of classical antiquity.

votaries: I.e. worshippers.

73

time . . . cooperated with chance: Johnson means here
that the votaries of antiquity have failed to consider
that some old works survive more by good luck than by
inherent merit.

artificial opacity: Darkened, or smoked, glass produces
an artificial image of the sun when light passing through
it is viewed by the eye. In the same manner, the shades
of age produce an artificial image of past genius. In
each case, the sight of the object is more easily endured, and more readily admired.
      Johnson defined "opacity" in his *Dictionary* as
*Cloudiness; want of transparency.*

contention: *Dict.*: *strife; debate; contest; quarrel;
mutual opposition.*

faults of the moderns . . . beauties of the ancients:
Perhaps an allusion to the famous quarrel of the ancients
and the moderns. Participants in this debate about the
merits of ancient and modern writers included Boileau
and Swift.

rate them by his best: Johnson is a follower of Boileau in
this paragraph. Cf. *Réflexion VII, Réflexions critiques,*
p.98: . . . *l'antique at constante admiration qu'on a
toûjours euë pour ses Ouvrages est une preuve seure
et infaillable qu'on les doit admirer* (. . . the ancient
and unceasing admiration that has always been directed
towards his literary works is sure and infallible
evidence of the need to admire them).
      Cf. also René Rapin's *Reflections upon Ancient and
Modern Philosophy* (1678), pp.64-65:
      *There is therefore a mean to be observed bet-
      ween the Ancients and Moderns; these are to be
      respected without vilifying those. So let us
      endeavour to discover new Truth, and not ne-
      glect the Ancient. Let us not overthrow things
      established, to establish things that are un-
      certain: let us preserve our liberty, and let
      us not lose the use of our reason, by a blind
      adoration of the sentiments either of the
      Ancients or Moderns: let us do Justice to both;
      and let us value merit wherever it be, without
      minding whether it be old or new.*
One is reminded of Pope's lines from the *Essay on
Criticism,* ll. 406-07: *Regard not then if Wit be* Old *or*
New, */ But blame the* False *and value still the* True.

PAGE 2

definite: *Dict.*: 1. *Certain; limited; bounded.* 2. *Exact; precise.*

gradual: *Dict.*: *Proceeding by degree; advancing step by step; from one stage to another.* As part of his definition Johnson quoted the following lines from Milton: *Nobler birth / Of creatures animate with gradual life, / Of growth, sense, reason, all summ'd up in man.*

comparative: *Dict.*: *Estimated by comparison; not positive; not absolute.* Note that the opposition to "absolute" also occurs in this definition.

demonstrative: I.e. demonstrable; able to be demonstrated.

persist to: I.e. persist in valuing.

opinion in its favour: Cf. Boileau, *Réflexion VII, Réflexions critiques,* pp.93-98.
　In *The Rambler,* No.92 (2 Feb. 1751), Johnson had noted Boileau's comments with approval:
　　. . . *Boiléau justly remarks, that the books which have stood the test of time, and been admired through all the changes which the mind of man has suffered from the various revolutions of knowledge, and the prevalence of contrary customs, have a better claim to our regard than any modern can boast, because the long continuance of their reputation proves that they are adequate to our faculties, and agreeable to nature.*
　In the *Preface,* however, Johnson is concerned with the need to compare past with present excellence, an exercise that he was later to recommend to his readers in the course of his judgment on Pope's poetry in the *Life of Pope:*
　　*Let us look round upon the present time, and back upon the past; let us enquire to whom the voice of mankind has decreed the wreath of poetry; let their productions be examined and their claims stated, and the pretentions of Pope will be no more disputed (Lives,* III, 251).

stiled: Johnson defined "to style" in his *Dictionary* as *to call; to term; to name.*

**Demonstration:** I.e. scientific demonstration.

**works tentative and experimental:** I.e. works made according
to no known or fixed laws. Johnson defined "tentative"
in his *Dictionary* as: *Trying; essaying*, and "experimental" as: *Formed by observation*.

**discovered in:** I.e. found in.

**The Pythagorean scale of numbers . . . etc.:** Johnson
means that the poems of Homer are not *perfect*, and do
not *transcend the common limits of human intelligence*
except in the sense that their salient merits have
never been surpassed by the poems of later generations.
In *The Idler*, No.66 (21 July, 1759), he wrote:
> We see how little the united experience of
> mankind have been able to add to the heroic
> characters displayed by Homer, and how few
> incidents the fertile imagination of modern
> Italy has yet produced, which may not be
> found in the Iliad and the Odyssey.

D. Nichol Smith, in his notes to the *Preface* in
*Eighteenth Century Essays on Shakespeare* 2nd ed. (Oxford:
Clarendon Press, 1963), has drawn attention to Johnson's
praise of Homer in the *Diary of the Right Hon. William
Windham*, August 1784 (ed. 1866), p.17: *The source of
everything in or out of nature that can serve the purpose
of poetry to be found in Homer.* The thought is in essential respects that given by Johnson to Imlac in
*Rasselas*, Ch. X, where he wrote that *the first writers
took possession of the most striking objects for description, and the most probable occurences for fiction,
and left nothing to those that followed them, but trans-
cription of the same events, and new combinations of the
same images.*

Johnson mentions the Pythagorean scale of numbers
because Pythagoras, *the Samian sage*, who flourished in
the 6th century B.C. is supposed to have discovered
the mathematical basis of music. See Aristotle,
*Metaphysics*, I, v:
> . . . the so-called Pythagoreans applied them-
> selves to mathematics, and were the first to
> develop this science; and through studying
> it they came to believe that its principles
> are the principles of everything. And since
> numbers are by nature first among these prin-
> ciples, and they fancied that they could de-
> tect in numbers, to a greater extent than in
> fire and earth and water, many analogues of
> what is and comes into being - such and such
> a property of number being justice, and such
> and such soul or mind, another opportunity,

and similarly, more or less, with all the rest -
and since they saw further that the properties
and ratios of the musical scales are based on
numbers, and since it seemed clear that all
other things have their whole nature
modelled upon numbers, and that numbers are the
ultimate things in the whole physical universe,
they assumed the elements of numbers to be
the elements of everything, and the whole universe to be a proportion or number.

sentiments: Thoughts, notions, opinions.


PAGE 3


gloomy persuasion of the degeneracy of mankind: I.e. the
sense, common to all ages, that humankind is in a
state of perpetual degeneration.

The poet: Throughout his *Preface*, and elsewhere in his
criticism, Johnson refers to Shakespeare as a "poet".
The term seems to have had a wider meaning in Johnson's
day. Johnson's idea of the dramatist is included within his sense of the poet.

undertaken the revision: I.e. undertaken to edit.

personal allusions: I.e. allusions to actual people alive
in Shakespeare's time.

temporary opinions: I.e. opinions prevalent in the time
of Shakespeare.

for many years been lost: The Yale editor notes that
Adventurer *58 is devoted to this same subject.* Johnson
was concerned in this paper (26 May, 1753) with the
increasing incomprehensibility of literary works with
the passage of time:
    It often happens, that an author's reputation
    is endangered in succeeding times, by that
    which raised the loudest applause among his
    contemporaries: nothing is read with greater
    pleasure than allusions to recent facts,
    reigning opinions, or present controversies;
    but when facts are forgotten and controversies
    extinguished, these favourite touches lose all
    their grace; and the author in his descent to
    posterity must be left to the mercy of chance,
    without any power of ascertaining the memory
    of those things, to which he owed his luckiest
    thoughts, and his kindest reception.

artificial: In his *Dictionary* Johnson gives *Made by art;
not natural.*

once illuminated: For the same reason, Johnson had Imlac
insist that a poet *must divest himself of the prejudices
of his age or country; he must consider right and wrong
in their abstracted and invariable state; he must dis-
regard present laws and opinions, and rise to general
and transcendental truths, which will always be the
same.* In a note on *Love's Labour's Lost,* Act IV,
scene ii, Johnson took occasion to disagree with
Shakespeare's immediately previous editor, William
Warburton, that Shakespeare's satire was seldom personal. He remarked scathingly that: *It is the nature
of personal invectives to be soon unintelligible and
the author that gratifies private malice,* animam in
volnere penit, *destroys the future efficacy of his own
writings, and sacrifices the esteem of succeeding times
to the laughter of a day* (*Shakespeare,* II, 434).
    The context of these comments is the appearance of
the pedant, Holofernes. Johnson's use of a Latin
phrase may be a comic reminiscence of this character's
own ridiculously scholastic habit of expression.

veneration: Johnson defined "veneration" in his *Dictionary*
as: *Reverend regard; awful respect.* By *prescriptive
veneration* he means that respect which is prescribed
by critical custom, in opposition to that inspired by
a direct response to and feeling for the work or author
under discussion.
    Johnson distinguished those moments and scenes in
drama worthy of *prescriptive veneration* from those
which made an instantaneous and immediate appeal to
the heart. One of the latter is the bedchamber scene,
Act III, scene iii of *Henry VI Part II,* the death of
Cardinal Beaufort. The scene ends on a Biblical note:
*Forbear to judge, for we are sinners all. / Close up
his eyes, and draw the curtain close; / and let us
all to meditation.*
    Johnson's comment on the whole scene was:
    *This is one of the scenes which have been ap-
    plauded by the criticks, and which will continue
    to be admired when prejudice shall cease, and
    bigotry give way to impartial examination. These
    are beauties that rise out of nature and of truth;
    the superficial reader cannot miss them, and the
    profound can image nothing beyond them*
    (*Shakespeare,* VI, 376-77).
    The scene had been praised by an earlier editor of
Shakespeare, Nicholas Rowe, in his *Account of the Life
of Mr. William Shakespeare,* prefatory to his edition
(1709), where he wrote that the qualities of tenderness

and piety in the characters *must touch anyone who is capable either of fear or pity* (Shakespeare, I, 187-88).

**his century . . . the test of literary merit:** Both D. Nichol Smith and the Yale editor suggest that behind this statement stands Horace, *Epistles*, II, i, 39: *est vetus atque probus, centum qui perficit annos* (a writer who died a hundred years ago, is he to be reckoned among the perfect and ancient?). Smith suggests also Pope's *Epistle to Augustus* (1737), lines 49-60 and 69-72:

> If Time improve our Wit as well as Wine,
> Say at what age a Poet grows divine?
> Shall we, or shall we not, account him so,
> Who died, perhaps, an hundred years ago?
> End all dispute; and fix the year precise
> When British bards begin t'immortalize?
> 'Who lasts a century can have no flaw,
> I hold that Wit a Classic, good in law.'
> Suppose he wants a year, will you compound?
> And shall we deem him Ancient, right and sound,
> Or damn to all eternity at once,
> At ninety-nine, a Modern and a Dunce?
> 'We shall not quarrel for a year or two;
> By courtesy of England, he may do.'
>
> .  .  .  .  .  .  .  .  .  .  .  .  .  .  .  .  .  .  .  .  .  .
>
> Shakespeare (whom you and every Playhouse bill
> Style the divine, the matchless, what you will)
> For gain, not glory, winged his roving flight,
> And grew immortal in his own despite.

**the effects of favour and competition:** The eminence enjoyed by Shakespeare's works as a result of "favour" shown to them by contemporaries, and the qualities which would have appeared by virtue of Shakespeare's *competition* with lesser contemporaries. Johnson is referring to political and other interest such as assisted the success of Addison's *Cato*.

**the tradition of his friendships and his enmities:** The tradition whereby knowledge of Shakespeare's friendships and enmities was passed on.

**indulge vanity:** I.e. the vanity of those who look for approving or panegyrical references to themselves in contemporary works. Shakespeare's plays, Johnson is saying, do not have the appeal of works written to flatter a patron or recommend the opinions of a particular political party.

**interest:** As in vested interest.

**changes of manners:** Shifts in social and political convention.

**devolved:** I.e. rolled down.

**new honours at every transmission:** Cf. Pope, *Essay on
Criticism*, lines 189-92: *Hail* Bards Triumphant! *born
in* happier days: / Immortal *Heirs of Universal Praise! /
Whose Honours with Increase of Ages* grow, / As Streams
roll down, enlarging as they flow!*

PAGE 4

**approbation:** Cf. Boileau, *Réflexion VII, Réflexions
critiques,* p.93: *Il n'y a en effet que l'approbation de
la Posterité, qui puisse établir le vrai mérite des
Ouvrages.* (Nothing, in fact, but the approbation of
posterity can establish the true merit of literary
works.)  In the *Dictionary*, Johnson glosses "approbation"
as *the act of approving or expressing himself pleased.*

**peculiarities:** Not oddities, but distinctive qualities,
particularities.

**just representations of general nature:** I.e. just representations of the enduring pains, pleasures and facts of
existence.  In his phrase *general nature,* Johnson does
not mean only "human nature", but also that which is
experienced by humanity, including inanimate nature.  (For
praise of Shakespeare's descriptions of the inanimate
world, see p.37 of the *Preface*).  "General nature", for
Johnson, includes that elemental substance of nature,
independent of shifts in fashion, custom, law and society,
which yet expresses itself through change.

**Particular . . . .:** Cf. Imlac's discourse on poetry in
*Rasselas,* Ch. X, where he says that a poet must not
*number the streaks of the tulip, or describe the dif-
ferent shades in the verdure of the forest.*  For Johnson,
poetry could be merely general: Dryden's *Eleonora being
. . . general, fixes no impression upon the reader . . .*
(*Lives,* I, 441-42).  But he also thought that an ability
to rise to the general was a desirable quality in a poet.
The "metaphysical" poets, in pursuing the novelties of
nature, had missed generality, the common, enduring and
uniform experience which is always the same:
> *Great thoughts are always general, and consist
> in positions not limited by exceptions, and in
> descriptions not descending to minuteness . . .
> Those writers who lay on the watch for novelty*

> *could have little hope of greatness; for great*
> *things cannot have escaped former observation.*
> *Their attempts were always analytick . . .*
> ("Cowley", *Lives*, I, 21).

**manners:** In his *Dictionary*, Johnson defined "manners"
in the plural as *general way of life; morals; habits,*
but also, with reference to the artificial manners of
the world: *ceremonious behaviour; studied civility.*
"Manners" is a key term in seventeenth and eighteenth
century literary criticism. In the following passage
from Rymer's English version of René Rapin's *Reflections
on Aristotle* (1674), pp.35-36, it has been used by Rymer
to translate *moeurs*:

> *After the* Design *or* Fable, Aristotle *places the*
> Manners *for the second Part; he calls the*
> Manners *the cause of the* action, *for it is*
> *from these that a Man begins to* act . . .
> *so the* Manners *are, as it were, the first*
> *springs of all humane* actions. *The Painter*
> *draws Faces by their features; but the Poet*
> *represents the* minds *of Men by their* Manners:
> *and the most general Rule for painting* Manners,
> *is to exhibit every person in his proper Char-*
> acter. *A* Slave, *with base thoughts, and ser-*
> *vile inclinations. A* Prince, *with a liberal*
> *heart, and* air *of Majesty. A* Souldier, *fierce,*
> *insolent, surly, inconstant. An* old Man,
> *covetous, wary, jealous.*

**known to few, and . . . few only . . . etc:** Cf. Wordsworth's
criticism of Johnson's account of the epitaphs of Pope:
> *Let an Epitaph, then, contain at least these*
> *acknowledgements of our common nature; nor*
> *let the sense of their importance be sacrificed*
> *to a balance of opposite qualities or minute*
> *distinctions in individual character; which*
> *if they do not, (as will for the most part be*
> *the case) when examined, resolve themselves*
> *into a trick of words, will, even when they*
> *are true and just, for the most part be griev-*
> *ously out of place; for, as it is probable*
> *that few only have explored these intricacies*
> *of human nature, so can the tracing of them*
> *be interesting only to a few* (Essay upon
> *Epitaphs I* (1810), *Prose Works*, II, 59).

**nearly:** I.e. closely.

**irregular combinations of fanciful invention:** Though he uses
the word "irregular", Johnson is not invoking the rules
of drama. Shakespeare, as Johnson argues elsewhere in
his *Preface*, abandoned the rules to follow nature.

**pleasures of sudden wonder:** Cf. *The Rambler*, No. 137:
*That wonder is the effect of ignorance has often been
observed.*
Cf. also Wordsworth, *Essay Supplementary to the Preface* (1815): *Wonder is the natural product of Ignorance;
and as the soil was* in such good condition *at the time
of the publication of the Seasons* (*of Thomson*), *the crop
was doubtless abundant* (*Prose Works*, III, 75).

**the common satiety of life:** I.e. the state of weariness
produced by ordinary pleasures.

**stability of truth:** In *The Rambler*, No. 156, Johnson had
said that a writer should not *violate essential principles
by a desire of novelty*. In the *Preface*, he perhaps had
in mind the contrast between Shakespeare's dramas and
those of, say, Dryden, whose *Conquest of Granada* he
mentioned in his *Life of Dryden* as having been written
in its two parts *with a seeming determination to glut the
publick with dramatic wonders* (*Lives*, I, 349). As in all
his appeals to the Truth of great literature, Johnson here
again comes close to, and by his authority reinforces, the
conviction of Wordsworth. See Preface to the *Lyrical
Ballads* (1850):

> *Aristotle, I have been told, has said, that
> Poetry is the most philosophic of all writ-
> ings: it is so: its object is truth, not in-
> dividual and local, but general, and opera-
> tive; not standing upon external testimony,
> but carried alive into the heart by passion;
> truth which is its own testimony, which
> gives competence and confidence to the
> tribunal to which it appeals, and receives
> them from the same tribunal* (*Prose Works*,
> I, 139).

**modern writers:** I.e. modern as opposed to ancient. Not
necessarily eighteenth-century.

**poet of nature:** Cf. Dryden's paragraph on Shakespeare
from the *Essay on Dramatic Poesy* (1668), quoted by
Johnson in the conclusion to his *Preface*.

**mirror of manners:** See *Hamlet*, Act III, scene ii, where
Hamlet is advising the Players:
*Be not too tame neither, but let discretion
be your tutor: suit the action to the word,
the word to the action; with this special
observance, that you o'er-step not the
modesty of nature: For any thing so overdone is from the purpose of playing, whose*

*end, both at the first, and now, was, and is,*
*to hold as 'twere the mirror up to nature;*
*to shew virtue her own feature, scorn her*
*own image, and the very age and body of the*
*time his form and pressure* (Shakespeare, X,
287).
Hamlet's instructions are here in accord with the traditions of seventeenth and eighteenth century critical
thought on the creation and portrayal of character.

**of life:** In *The Rambler,* No. 156, Johnson had spent time
defending Shakespeare on the grounds that the stage
*pretends only to be the mirrour of life.*

**the peculiarities of studies or professions:** Johnson is
making a claim of general though not invariable truth in
this remark. Hotspur, in *Henry IV Part I,* he wrote,
*has only the soldier's virtues, generosity and courage*
(Shakespeare, V, 611).
In his *Life of Pope,* he wrote of Pope's *Epitaph on*
*Withers* that it affords an instance of commonplaces,
*though somewhat diversified by mingled qualities, and*
*the peculiarity of a profession* (Lives, III, 226).

**accidents:** For "accidental" Johnson gives in his *Dictionary:*
*Having the property of an accident, non essential.*

**temporary opinions:** The idea expressed here was later
applied by Johnson to *Hudibras* in his *Life of Butler:*
*But human works are not easily found without*
*a perishable part. Of the ancient poets every*
*reader feels the mythology tedious and oppres-*
*sive. Of Hudibras, the manners, being founded*
*on opinions, are temporary and local, and there-*
*fore become every day less intelligible, and*
*less striking. What Cicero says of philosophy*
*is true likewise of wit and humour, that 'time*
*effaces the fictions of opinion, and confirms*
*the determinations of Nature'* (Lives, I, 213-14).
Cf. also Johnson's comments upon Homer in his *Life*
*of Pope:*
*His positions are general, and his represent-*
*ations natural, with very little dependence on*
*local or temporary customs, on those change-*
*able scenes of artificial life which, by ming-*
*ling original with accidental notions, and*
*crowding the mind with images which time ef-*
*faces, produce ambiguity in diction, and ob-*
*scurity in books* (Lives, III, 114).

**genuine progeny:** I.e. legitimate offspring.

general passions and principles: I.e. modes of feeling
   common to all people.  Cf. Johnson's remark on the
   words of Queen Isabella to her manservant in Act II,
   scene ii of Richard II: *The involuntary and unaccount-*
   *able depression of the mind which every one has some*
   *time felt, is here very forcibly described* (*Shakes-*
   *peare*, V. 174).
      Cf. also his comment on King Henry's soliloquy in Act
   IV, scene i of *Henry V*, on the cares of kingship: *Some-*
   *thing like this, on less occasions, every breast has*
   *felt* (*Shakespeare*, VI, 113).
      Such general passions and principles were, of course,
   for Johnson, pervasively present in Shakespeare.


PAGE 5


individual: Almost a pejorative term in Johnson's day,
   meaning a mere individual; nothing but an individual;
   peculiar; exceptional, and therefore a distortion of
   truth.  Cf. Rymer/Rapin, *Reflections on Aristotle*,
   pp. 34-35:
      *Truth is well nigh always defective, by the*
      *mixture of particular conditions that compose*
      *it.  Nothing is brought into the world that*
      *is not remote from the perfection of its Idea*
      *from the very birth.  Originals and Models are*
      *to be search'd for in probability, and the*
      *universal principles of things, where noth-*
      *ing that is material and singular enters to*
      *corrupt them.*
      Johnson thought that Shakespeare had captured in his
   characters a sense of *the universal principles of things*,
   and that for this reason his plays would endure.  Perhaps
   the strength of the tradition behind Johnson's remark may
   be suggested by recalling the following lines from
   Chaucer's *The Knight's Tale*, here translated by Dryden
   (lines 1042-57);
      *Parts of the Whole are we; but God the whole;*
      *Who gives us Life, and animating Soul.*
      *For Nature cannot from a Part derive*
      *That Being, which the Whole can only give:*
      *He perfect, stable; but imperfect We,*
      *Subject to Change, and different in Degree.*
      *Plants, Beasts, and Man; and as our Organs are,*
      *We more or less of his Perfection share.*
      *But by a long Descent, th'Etherial Fire*
      *Corrupts; and Forms, the mortal Part, expire:*
      *As he withdraws his Vertue, so they pass,*
      *And the same Matter makes another Mass:*
      *This Law th'omniscient Pow'r was pleas'd to give,*

*That ev'ry Kind should by Succession live;*
*That Individuals die, his Will ordains;*
*The propagated Species still remains.*

commonly a species: Cf. Rasselas, Ch. X: *The business of*
*a poet . . . is to examine, not the individual, but the*
*species; to remark general properties and large appear-*
*ances.*

Johnson defined "species" in his *Dictionary* as a: *class*
*of nature; single order of beings.*

The point is not that Johnson ignored or disliked
Shakespeare's portraits of individuals in the plays, but
that within these individual portraits he found a representation of the species. The individual features
of Shakespeare's characters gave, for Johnson, outward
dramatic expression to the general, common and universal
principles of human nature, a continuous reality the same
in all times and in all places.

The subtlety of Johnson s thought at this point has
often been missed. The author of *The Critical Review*,
XX (Nov. 1765) 323 protested that Johnson's paragraph
was *by no means descriptive of Shakespeare*, since
*Shakespeare has succeeded better in representing the*
*oddities of nature than her general properties.* William
Hazlitt thought that Johnson had no interest in the individual traits in Shakespeare's characters:

. . . *he says of Shakespeare's characters, in*
*contradiction to what Pope had observed, and*
*to what every one else feels, that each char-*
*acter is a species, instead of being an in-*
*dividual. He in fact found the general species*
*or didactic form in Shakespeare's characters,*
*which was all he sought or cared for; he did not*
*find the individual traits, or the* dramatic dis-
*tinctions which Shakespeare has engrafted on this*
*general nature, because he felt no interest in*
*them* (Preface to *Characters of Shakespeare's*
*Plays, Works*, IV, 176).

The German critic, A.W. Schlegel, also took issue with
Johnson's remarks:

*A character which should be merely a person-*
*ification of a naked general idea, could neither*
*exhibit any great depth nor any great variety.*
*The names of genera and species are well known*
*to be merely auxiliaries for the understanding,*
*that we may embrace the infinite variety of*
*nature in a certain order* (See Lecture XXIII,
*Lectures on Drama*, tr. Black, p.363).

It is interesting, however, that both these nineteenth-
century critics come close to expressing very much what
Johnson meant in saying that the characters of other poets
are too often individuals, those of Shakespeare commonly
a species. Here is Hazlitt:

> *It is the business of poetry, and indeed of*
> *all works of imagination, to exhibit the species*
> *through the individual.  Otherwise there can*
> *be no opportunity for the exercise of the*
> *imagination, without which the descriptions*
> *of the painter or the poet are lifeless, un-*
> *substantial and vapid* (The Champion, 13 Nov.
> 1814, *A View of the English Stage, Works,* V,
> 204).

And here is Schlegel:

> *It is the power of endowing the creatures*
> *of his imagination with such self-existent*
> *energy, that they afterwards act in each con-*
> *juncture according to general laws of nature*
> *. . . The characters which Shakespeare has*
> *so thoroughly delineated have a number of in-*
> *dividual peculiarities, but at the same time*
> *they possess a significance which is not ap-*
> *plicable to them alone* (Lecture XXIII, *Lectures*
> *on Drama,* pp.362 and 363-64).

**extension:** for "extend" Johnson gives in his *Dictionary:*
*To widen to a large comprehension.*

**design:** In his *Dictionary* Johnson gives: *The idea which*
*an artist endeavours to execute or express* and cites
Pope's *Epistles: Thy hand strikes out some design /*
*Where life awakens and dawns at every line.*

**instruction:** *Dict.: Precepts conveying knowledge.*  But
Johnson is not referring exclusively to didactic instruction, or instruction comprised purely of precepts.
See *post* the remarks on Shakespeare's *real power.*  On
p.26 Johnson writes of the power of a play to *instruct*
*life.*

**practical axioms and domestick wisdom:** E.g. Polonius's
advice to Laertes, *Hamlet,* Act I, scene iii (*Shakespeare,*
X, 201): *Neither a borrower nor a lender be.*  The whole
speech is one long catalogue of axiomatic wisdom.
    In his *Dictionary,* Johnson defined "axiom" as *A pro-*
*position evident at first sight, that cannot be made plain-*
*er by demonstration.*  The practical axioms and domestic
wisdom of Shakespeare were remarked by Johnson, and for
the most part, approved, at innumerable moments in his
notes to the plays.  The kind of propositions, or axioms
and wisdom he had in mind might be exemplified by the
speech of Biron, from Act I, scene i of *Love's Labour's*
*Lost: Necessity will make us all forsworn / Three thousand*
*times within these three years' space; / For every man*
*with his affects is born, / Not by might master'd, but by*
*special grace.*
    These sentiments must have had a particular appeal to
Johnson the moralist, for he wrote that:

>Biron amidst his extravagances, speaks with
>great justness against the folly of vows.
>They are made without sufficient regard to
>the variations of life, and are therefore
>broken by some unforeseen necessity.  They
>proceed commonly from a presumptuous con-
>fidence, and a false estimate of human
>power (Shakespeare, II, 384).

Domestick wisdom is homely wisdom, not household hints.

**Euripides**: Greek tragic poet, born 480 B.C., author of
*Alcestis, Medea, Hippolytus, Andromache, Heracleidae,
Hecuba, Phoenissae, Orestes, Iphigeneia in Tauris,
Iphigeneia at Aulis, Baccae, Cyclops* etc.

**every verse was a precept**: See Cicero *Familiar Letters*,
XVI, 8.  Of Euripides, Cicero wrote: *Ego certe singulos
eius versus singula testimonia puto* (I, at any rate, regard all his lines, one after the other, as so many
declarations on oath).

**a system of civil and oeconomical prudence**: Aphoristic
wisdom.  But this is not all Johnson found in the plays,
or wanted from them.  For "oeconomics" Johnson gives in
his *Dictionary*: *Management of household affairs*.
     Later in the *Preface*, Johnson says that from Shakespeare
*a system of social duty may be selected*.

**the splendour of particular passages**: Johnson wrote of *The
Two Gentlemen of Verona*, in a note to Act I, scene i that
though *It is not indeed one of his most powerful effusions*,
there were, nevertheless, few plays which *have more lines
or passages which, singly considered, are eminently beautiful* (Shakespeare, I, 123).  Of *Julius Caesar*, likewise,
Johnson thought that *many particular passages deserve regard*, but admitted that he had *never been strongly agitated in perusing it* (Shakespeare, VIII, 119).

**fable**: A critical term in the seventeenth and eighteenth
century.  In the *Dictionary*, Johnson gives: *the contexture of events which constitute a poem epick or dramatick.*
     Cf. Rymer, *A Short View of Tragedy* (1692), Ch. VII,
*Critical Works*, p.13:
>The Fable is always accounted the Poets part.
>Because the other three parts of Tragedy, to
>wit the Characters are taken from the Moral
>Philosopher; the thoughts or sence, from them
>that teach Rhetorick; and the last part, which
>is the expression, we learn from the Grammar-
>ians.

See also Rowe, *Account of the Life of* . . . *Shakespeare*:

> *The fable is what is generally placed first,*
> *among those that are reckoned the constituent*
> *parts of a tragick or heroick poem; not, per-*
> *haps, as it is the most difficult or beautiful,*
> *but as it is the first properly to be thought*
> *of in the contrivance and course of the whole .*
> *. . (Shakespeare, I, 187).*

**tenor of his dialogue:** The holding power of the dialogue
to keep the attention of his reader or his audience.

**he that tries to recommend him:** See William Dodd, *The
Beauties of Shakespear* (1752). Dodd reprinted extracts
from each of Shakespeare's plays, arranged under various
heads. In his footnotes he drew attention to related
passages from other authors, English and classical.

**Hierocles:** Hierocles of Alexandria, *floruit* 5th. Cent. A.D.,
a Neoplatonist philosopher.

**a brick in his pocket as a specimen:** See *Hierocles Commentarius in Aurea Carmina*, ed. P. Needham (1709), p.462.
In a section entitled *Philosophi Facetiae* there is a long
list of jokes at the expense of pedants. Boswell, *Life*,
I, 150, claimed that Johnson wrote *A free translation of
the Jests of Hierocles, with an Introduction* for the
*Gentleman's Magazine*. See *The Jests of Hierocles, Gentleman's Magazine*, XI (Sept. 1741), 478, where the joke used
in the *Preface* is translated:
> *A Philosopher having an Inclination to see his*
> *House, was desired by the Person that proposed*
> *to buy it, to shew it him.* Sir, *says he,* You
> may spare yourself the Trouble of walking so
> far, for I always carry this Stone in my Pocket
> as a Specimen.

**sentiments:** Thoughts or feelings on or about life. In his
*Dictionary*, Johnson defined sentiment as *thought, notion;
opinion* and *the sense considered distinctly apart from the
language.*

**the ancient schools of declamation:** Schools or academies in
classical times, where the arts of oratory were taught.

**found nothing there . . . any other place:** The Yale editor
refers to Petronius, *Satyricon*, I, i:
> *No one would mind this claptrap if only it put*
> *our students on the road to real eloquence.*
> *But what with all these sham heroics and this*
> *stilted bombast you stuff their heads with,*
> *by the time your students set foot in court,*
> *they talk as though they were living in a-*
> *nother world.* *No, I tell you, we don't*

> *educate our children at school; we stultify*
> *them and then send them out into the world*
> *half-baked. And why? Because we keep them*
> *utterly ignorant of real life. The common*
> *experience is something they never see or*
> *hear.*

Cf. also Boileau, *L'Art poétique* (1674), tr. Dryden and
Soame, *The Art of Poetry* (1680 and 1683), Canto III, lines
562-71:

> *Make not your* Hecuba *with fury rage,*
> *And show a Ranting grief upon the Stage;*
> *Or tell in vain how the rough* Tanais *bore*
> *His sevenfold Waters to the Euxine Shore:*
> *These swoln expressions, this affected noise*
> *Shows like some Pedant, that declaims to Boys.*
> *In sorrow, you must softer methods keep;*
> *And, to excite our tears, your self must weep:*
> *Those noisie words with which ill Plays abound,*
> *Come not from hearts that are in sadness drown'd.*

**every stage but that of Shakespeare:** I.e. every modern stage;
the work of every dramatist still put on the stage.
Cf. Johnson's opinion of other stages in his *Lives of
the Poets.* Of Thomson, the author of *Tancred and Sigis-
munda,* he lamented that: *It may be doubted whether he was,
either by the bent of nature or habits of study, much
qualified for tragedy . . . his diffusive and descriptive
style produced declamation rather than dialogue.* Johnson's
experience of Shakespeare seems to have left him unsatis-
fied as a reader of dramas by anyone else. The speeches
in Milton's *Comus: . . . have not the spriteliness of a
dialogue animated by reciprocal contention, but seem
rather declamations deliberately composed, and formally
repeated, on a moral question.* Later in the *Preface,*
Johnson wrote that *inactive declamation is very coldly
heard, however musical or elegant, passionate or sublime,*
and in his *Life of Addison,* he regretted that *Cato* had,
by its success, *confirmed among us the use of dialogue
too declamatory, of unaffecting elegance, and chill
philosophy* (*Lives,* III, 293; I, 168; II, 133).

**commerce:** I.e. conversational exchanges.

**determined by the incident which produces it:** By comparison,
Johnson wrote of the dialogue of Congreve's *Old Bachelor*
as *one constant reciprocation of conceits, or clash of
wit, in which nothing flows necessarily from the occasion,
or is dictated by nature* (*Congreve, Lives,* II, 216).

**simplicity:** Great stress was placed on the value of simplicity in art by the great French and English critics of the
seventeenth and eighteenth century. Cf. Rymer/Rapin,

*Reflections on Aristotle*, p.56: . . . a simple *thought
in its proper place, is more worth than all the most
exquisite* words *and wit out of season.*

## PAGE 6

**seems scarcely to claim the merit of fiction:** Hardly seems
to have been invented at all by the poet, but to have
been collected and selected from conversations actually
heard in life.  The important word here is "seems".
Johnson is not denying fictional status to the plays of
Shakespeare but remarking upon their powerful and con-
vincing effect as fictions designed to portray Truth.

**gleaned by diligent selection:** "Selection" is a key term
for Johnson, as it is for Wordsworth.  Milton according
to Johnson: . . . *was master of his language in its full
extent; and has selected the melodious words with such
diligence, that from his book alone the Art of English
Poetry might be learned.*  Cowley, on the other hand,
*makes no selection of words nor seeks any neatness of
phrase* (*Milton* and *Cowley, Lives* I, 191, 59).
    Cf. also Wordsworth, Preface to *Lyrical Ballads* (1850):
. . . *the language of such poetry as is here recommended
is, as far as is possible, a selection of the language
really spoken by men.*  Wordsworth set himself: . . . *to
choose incidents and situations from common life, and to
relate or describe them throughout, as far as was possible
in a selection of language really used by men* (*Prose Works,*
I, 137, 123).

**Upon every other stage:** Of Dryden's *All for Love*, Johnson
wrote that it:
        . . . *has one fault equal to many, though rather
    moral than critical, that by admitting the rom-
    antick omnipotence of Love, he has recommended
    as laudable and worthy of imitation that con-
    duct which through all ages the good have
    censured as vicious, and the bad despised
    as foolish.*
    Cf. also Johnson's comments on Dryden's *Conquest of
Granada*, written, he explained, with a determination to:
        . . . *exhibit in its highest elevation a
    theatrical meteor of incredible love and
    impossible valour, and to leave no room for
    a wilder flight to the extravagance of post-
    erity.  All the rays of romantick heat,
    whether amorous or warlike, glow in Almanzor
    by a kind of concentration.  He is above all*

*laws; he is exempt from all restraints; he
ranges the world at will, and governs wherever he appears. He fights without enquiring
the cause, and loves in spite of the obligations of justice, of rejection by his mistress,
and of prohibition from the dead* (Lives, I, 361,
349).

**the universal agent**: I.e. the power which pervades everything.

**hypobolical joy and outrageous sorrow**: Johnson seems to have
found something of an anti-dote to these excesses in the
scene with Katharine on her sick-bed at Kimbolton in
*Henry VIII*, Act IV, scene ii, which he praised as *tender
and pathetick . . . without the help of romantick circumstances* (Shakespeare, VII, 283).

**to deliver them**: I.e. to save or rescue them.

**the business of a modern dramatist**: Cf. Addison, *The
Spectator*, No. 40 (1711):
> As our Heroes are generally Lovers, their
> Swelling and Blustering upon the Stage very
> much recommends them to the fair Part of
> their Audience. The Ladies are wonderfully
> pleased to see a Man insulting Kings, or
> affronting the Gods, in one Scene, and
> throwing himself at the Feet of his Mistress
> in another. Let him behave himself insolently
> towards the Men, and abjectly towards the
> Fair One, and it is ten to one but he proves
> a Favourite of the Boxes.

**any other passion**: Cf. Dryden, Preface to *Troilus and
Cressida* (1679):
> Shakespeare had an universal mind, which
> comprehended all characters and passions;
> Fletcher a more confin'd and limited: for
> though he treated love in perfection, yet
> honour, ambition, revenge, and generally all
> the stronger passions, he either touched not,
> or not masterly. To conclude all he was a
> limb of Shakespeare (Essays, I, 260).

**exorbitant**: Excessive; exceeding the common limits.

**. . . calamity**: Dick Minim, the semi-comical representative
of Johnson's own critical opinions and assumptions *often
hinted that love predominates too much upon the modern
stage* (The Idler, No. 60).

**ample:** Fully delineated.

**discriminated and preserved:** Properly distinguished and
  consistently maintained throughout a play. Johnson commented occasionally in his notes on Shakespeare's success
  or failure in preserving character. The character of
  Jaques, for example, in *As You Like It*, was in his opinion
  *natural and well preserved* (*Shakespeare*, III, 388).

**personages more distinct from each other:** The ability to
  keep characters distinct from each other was perhaps
  Johnson's most common item of praise for particular
  plays in his notes, as it had been Pope's. See his notes
  to *The Tempest, Troilus and Cressida, King Lear, Henry
  IV Part II* etc. Johnson sometimes makes a special point
  of commenting upon the dramatic advantages of this care of
  distinction, as in his note on Act II, scene i of *Henry
  VI Part III*: *The generous tenderness of Edward, and savage
  fortitude of Richard, are well distinguished by their
  different reception of their father's death* (See *Shakespeare*,
  I, 117; IX, 565; V, 611; VII, 458).
      But although Johnson thought that Shakespeare had given
  more attention to the distinction *between* characters than
  any other writer, he did not always think that the discrimination of character was essential to a good play.
  In *Antony and Cleopatra*, except for Cleopatra herself,
  *no character is very strongly discriminated*, while *Macbeth*
  has *no nice discriminations of character, the events are
  too great to admit the influence of particular dispositions*
  (See *Shakespeare*, VIII, 313- IV, 611).

**proper speaker:** Cf. Pope, *Preface to Shakespeare* (1725):
  *. . . had all the speeches been printed without the names
  of the persons, I believe one might have applied them
  with certainty to every speaker* (*Shakespeare*, I, 111).

**nothing characteristical:** Johnson applied this theory in
  his practice as an editor of the plays. Responding to
  the stage direction in *Macbeth*, Act III, scene vi, *Enter
  Lenox, and another Lord*, he wrote that it was not easy
  *to assign a reason why a nameless character should be
  introduced here, since nothing is said that might not
  with equal propriety have been put into the mouth of any
  other disaffected man.* The belief that there are many
  speeches which have *nothing characteristical* seems also
  to lie behind Johnson's rejection of Warburton's suggestion that a speech in *Coriolanus*, Act V, scene iii, should
  be given to Aufidius rather than Coriolanus, since the
  speech *suits Aufidius justly enough* (See *Shakespeare*, IV,
  549-50; VII, 490).

Page 7

aggravated characters: Overloaded, exaggerated, overdone.

fabulous: As in stories.

unexampled excellence or depravity: Of the hero of Edward
Young's *Busiris*, Johnson complained that his pride is
*such as no other man can have, and the whole is too
remote from known life to raise either grief, terror,
or indignation* (*Young, Lives*, III, 397).

barbarous romances: The Yale editor notes that Johnson read
and enjoyed those same romances he consigned to barbarians
and children.

invigorated: An unusual choice of word, meaning to animate,
or fill, with life and energy, but a striking usage that
is typical of Johnson.

probability: A sense of what is probable or likely, based
on one's experience of actual life.

language is depraved: For "deprave" Johnson gave in his
*Dictionary*: *to vitiate; to corrupt; to contaminate.*

love is only one of many passions: It is noteworthy that
Johnson does not complain that love is a weak passion.
But cf. Rymer/Rapin, *Reflections on Aristotle*, pp. 112-
13:
> . . . *'tis to degrade Tragedy from that* Majesty
> *which is proper to it, to mingle in it love,
> which is of a character always* light, *and
> little sutable to that* gravity *of which* Tragedy
> *makes profession. Hence it proceeds, that
> these* Tragedies *mixed with* gallantries *never
> make such admirable impressions on the spirit,
> as did those of* Sophocles *and* Euripides; *for
> all the bowels were moved by the great objects
> of* terrour *and* pity *which they proposed. 'Tis
> likewise for this, that the reputation of our
> modern* Tragedies *so soon decays, and yield but
> small delight at* two years *end; whereas the
> Greek pleases yet to those that have a good
> taste, after two thousand years; because what
> is not grave and serious on the Theatre, though
> it give delight at present, after a short time
> grows distasteful, and unpleasant; and because
> what is not proper for great thoughts and great
> figures in* Tragedy *cannot support it self. The
> Ancients who perceiv'd this, did not interweave
> their* gallantry *and love save in* Comedy. *For*

*love is of a character that always degenerates*
*from that* Heroick air, *of which* Tragedy *must*
*never divest it self.*
Charles Gildon, *Miscellaneous Letters and Essays* (1694),
p.151, had attempted to answer these strictures: . . .
*there is as much Wit required to the Just, and artificial*
*Management of the Passion of Love; as those of Fear and*
*Terror, and those other Species of Passions that are*
*subservient to the moving of them.*

**the sum of life:** The sum total of feelings and thoughts
which make up the whole of life. Johnson is not saying that love does not frequently make an appearance in
the dramas of Shakespeare. His concern is the falsi-
fication of human experience that is produced by ex-
clusive attention to love.

**equally deceived:** I.e. either by the plays of other drama-
tists or by the tales with which they share a distorted
view of life.

**Shakespeare has no heroes; his scenes are occupied only**
**by men . . . . :** I.e. Shakespeare does not have superhuman
figures as central characters in his plays.
   The principle underlying Johnson's praise is similar,
in very general terms, to that aired by other eighteenth-
century writers. See, for example, William Guthrie, *Essay*
*upon English Tragedy* (1747):
       *. . . though I have the prepossession of a*
       *whole age against me . . . there is not the*
       *least necessity of the chief personnage in a*
       *play to have either courage, wisdom, virtue,*
       *passion, or any other quality, above what is*
       *to be found in his real history, or in common*
       *life.*
   In the *Rambler*, No. 156 (1751) Johnson had written along
lines very much in accord with the prescriptions for
tragedy set out by Dryden in his *Essay on Dramatic Poesy*
(1668): *As the design of tragedy is to instruct by moving*
*the passions, it must always have a hero, a personage ap-*
*parently and incontestably superior to the rest, upon*
*whom the attention may be fixed, and the anxiety sus-*
*pended.* But by the time of the *Preface*, Johnson was no
longer thinking in terms of tragedy. As he shortly goes
on to say, Shakespeare's plays were not in the rigorous
and critical sense either tragedies or comedies, and so
were not subject to any of their laws.

**the agency:** Johnson means "the personage", but needs a more
general word to account for the non-human characters in
the plays, e.g. ghosts, witches, fairies etc.

level with life: I.e. on a level with the dialogue to be
found in life, not levelled down.  Thus, Johnson wrote
in his notes to *The Tempest*: *Ariel's lays, however season-*
*able and efficacious, must be allowed to be of no super-*
*natural dignity or elegance, they express nothing great,*
*nor reveal anything above mortal discovery* (*Shakespeare,*
I, 34).

approximates:  I.e. brings into proximity.


familiarizes the wonderful: Johnson is not saying that
Shakespeare in any way suppressed the remote and wonderful in his plays.  His stress is on the distinction and
skill Shakespeare shows in incorporating the supernatural
world.  What he admired in Shakespeare he was also to find
in Pope:  *In this work* (The Rape of the Lock) *are exhibited*
*in a very high degree the two most engaging powers of an*
*author: new things are made familiar, and familiar things*
*made new.* (*Life of Pope, Lives*, III, 233).
    The basis of Johnson's praise may perhaps in both in-
stances be found in Horace, *Ars Poetica*, 1.338: *ficta*
*voluptatis causa sint proxima veris* (*fictions meant to*
*please should be close to the real*).  But cf. Rymer/Rapin,
*Reflections on Aristotle*, pp.88-89:
        *But the importance is . . . that this* admirable
        *be* probable *. . . [Poets] by a false* Idea *they*
        *have of* Poesie *. . . place its beauty in the*
        *pleasant* surprises *of something extraordinary*
        *wonderful: whereas in truth it is not regularly*
        *to be found, but in what is natural and probable.*
        *For the sure way to the heart, is not by surpris-*
        *ing the spirit; and all becomes* incredible *in*
        *Poetry that appears* incomprehensible *. . . the*
        *necessity of* probability *is a great check to the*
        *Poets; who think to make the* incidents *the more*
        *heroick, by how much more* wonderful *and more*
        *surprizing they be, without regarding whether*
        *they be* natural.

exigences: States of pressing need.

if it were possible: Cf. Addison, *The Spectator*, No. 419
    (1712):
        *There is a kind of Writing, wherein the Poet*
        *quite loses sight of Nature, and entertains*
        *his Reader's Imagination with the Characters*
        *and Actions of such Persons as have many of*
        *them no Existence, but what he bestow on them.*
        *Such are Fairies, Witches, Magicians, Demons,*
        *and departed Spirits. This Mr.* Dryden *calls*
        *the Fairy way of Writing, which is, indeed,*

> *more difficult than any other that depends*
> *on the Poet's Fancy, because he has no Pattern*
> *to follow in it, and must work altogether out*
> *of his own Invention.*
>      *There is a very odd turn of Thought required*
> *for this sort of Writing, and it is impossible*
> *for a Poet to succeed in it, who has not a part-*
> *icular Cast of Fancy, and an Imagination natur-*
> *ally fruitful and superstitious* . . .
>      *Among the* English, Shakespear *has incomparably*
> *excelled all others. That noble Extravagance*
> *of Fancy, which he had in so great Perfection,*
> *thoroughly qualified him to touch this weak*
> *superstitious Part of his Reader's Imagination;*
> *to support him besides the Strength of his own*
> *Genius. There is something so wild and yet so*
> *solemn in the Speeches of his Ghosts, Fairies,*
> *Witches and the like Imaginary Persons, that we*
> *cannot forbear thinking them natural, tho' we*
> *have no Rule by which to judge them, and must*
> *confess, if there are such Beings in the World,*
> *it looks highly probable they should talk and*
> *act as he has represented them.*

A further resemblance may be found in Schlegel, *Lecture XXIII, Lectures on Drama*, p.363:

> *As he (Shakespeare) carries a bold and pregnant*
> *fancy into the kingdoms of nature, on the other*
> *hand, he carries nature into the regions of fancy*
> . . . *This Prometheus not merely forms men, he*
> *opens the gates of the magical world of spirits,*
> *calls up the midnight ghosts, exhibits before us*
> *the witches with their unhallowed rites, peoples*
> *the air with sportive fairies and sylphs; and*
> *these beings though existing only in the imagin-*
> *ation, nevertheless possess such truth and con-*
> *sistency, that even with such misshapen abortions*
> *as Caliban he extorts the assenting conviction,*
> *that were there such beings they would so conduct*
> *themselves.*

mazed his imagination: I.e. confused or bewildered his
  imagination.


PAGE 8


transactions: Goings on; business in the broad sense.

hermit . . . confessor . . . passions: These are examples
  of people remote from society, who therefore know nothing
  of life. The confessor, or priest who takes confession,
  acquires only from others his experience of the world.

**not completely royal:** Not entirely living up to the regal
character and refined behaviour that might be expected
of a king.

**play the buffoon:** Cf. John Dennis, *On the Genius and Writings of Shakespear, Critical Works,* II, 5:
> *If* Shakespear *had these great Qualities by*
> *Nature, what would he not have been, if he*
> *had join'd to so happy a Genius Learning*
> *and the Poetical Art. For want of the*
> *latter, our Author has sometimes made gross*
> *Mistakes in the Characters which he has*
> *drawn from History, against the Equality*
> *and Conveniency of Manners of his Dramatical*
> *Persons. Witness* Menenius *in the following*
> *Tragedy, whom he has made an errant Buffoon,*
> *which is a great Absurdity. For he might as*
> *well have imagin'd a grave majestick* Jack-
> Pudding, *as a Buffoon in a* Roman *Senator.*

    D. Nichol Smith quotes George Colman's response to
Johnson's reference to Dennis from the *St. James's Chronicle*
(Oct. 1765):
> *Has not Mr. Johnson here made too liberal a*
> *concession to Dennis? and on examination of*
> *the play of Coriolanus, would it not appear*
> *that the character of Menenius, though mark-*
> *ed with the peculiarities of an hearty old*
> *gentleman, is by no means that of a buffoon?*
> *Many have defended Polonius, who is much less*
> *respectable than Menenius.*

**as a drunkard:** Voltaire, *Dissertation sur la tragedie*
*ancienne et moderne,* prefixed to *Semiramis* (1749),
*Oeuvres,* IV, *Théâtre,* III, 502: *Hamlet, sa mère et son*
*beau-père, boivent ensemble sur le théâtre: on chante à*
*table, on s'y querelle, on se bat, on se tue* (Hamlet,
*his mother and his step-father, are drinking together on*
*stage: they sing during dinner, they quarrel, they fight,*
*they get killed*). See *Hamlet,* Act I, scene iv (*Shakes-*
*peare,* X, 207-08):
> Ham. *The king doth wake to-night, and takes his rouse,*
> *Keeps wassel, and the swaggering up-spring reels;*
> *And, as he drains his draughts of Rhenish down,*
> *The kettle-drum, and trumpet, thus bray out*
> *The triumph of his pledge.*
>
> Hor. *Is it a custom?*
> Ham. *Ay, marry, is't:*
> *But, to my mind, - though I am native here,*
> *And to the manner born, - it is a custom*
> *More honour'd in the breach, than the observance.*
> *This heavy-headed revel, east and west,*
> *Makes us traduc'd, and tax'd of other nations:*
> *They clepe us, drunkards, and with swinish phrase*
> *Soil our addition*

**Dennis:** John Dennis (1657-1734), best known as a cantank-
erous old critic, immortalized by Pope's satire of him
in the *Essay on Criticism* and *The Dunciad*. Dennis had
published his *Three Letters on the Genius and Writings
of Shakespear* in 1711. His criticism is cited later in
the *Preface* (p.38), on the subject of Shakespeare's
verse.

**Rhymer:** Thomas Rhymer, or Rymer (1641-1713), a respected
antiquary and critic, whose criticism, Johnson wrote
in his *Life of Dryden* has *the ferocity of a tyrant*
(*Lives*, I, 413). In 1674 Rymer published a translation
of *Réflexions sur la Poétique d'Aristote* (1674), by
René Rapin. Rymer's Shakespearean criticism is contained
in his notorious *Short View of Tragedy* (1692), consisting
of an attack on the tragedy of *Othello*, with some comments
on *Julius Caesar*. His play, *Edgar, or the English Monarch:
an Heroick Tragedy* (1678), was written in order to demon-
strate the rules. Rymer's *Foedera*, the collection of
historical documents made by Rymer as historiographer
to the king, is still used by historians.
    Pope, in conversation with Spence, called Rymer *on the
whole, one of the best critics we ever had*. See *Anecdotes,
Observations, and Characters of Books and Men*, ed. S.
Weller Singer (1858), p.130.

**not sufficiently Roman:** Dennis thinks this in *On the Genius
and Writings of Shakespear*. See *Critical Works*, II, 5.
For Rymer's opinion, see his *Short View of Tragedy*, Ch.
VIII, *Reflections on the* Julius Caesar, in *Critical
Works*, p.165:
    *In the former play* (Othello), *our poet might
    be bolder, the persons being all his own Crea-
    tures, and meer fiction. But here he sins not
    against nature and Philosophy only, but against
    the most known History, and the memory of the
    Noblest Romans, that ought to be sacred to all
    Posterity.*
    Johnson believed that *Julius Caesar* was too straight-
forwardly, and simply, a "Roman" play: . . . *his adherence
to the real story, and to Roman manners, seems to have im-
peded the natural vigour of his genius* (*Shakespeare*, VIII,
119).

**Voltaire:** Johnson seems to be replying to various remarks
in Voltaire's *Appel à toutes les nations de l'Europe*
(1761). The *Appel* was composed in reply to two articles
in the *Journal encyclopédique*, 15 Oct. 1760, *Parallèle
entre Shakespeare et Corneille, traduit de l'anglais*
and 1 Nov. 1760, *Parallèle entre Otwai et Racine, traduit
litteralement de l'anglais*. The *Appel* was retitled *Du
Théâtre anglais, par Jérôme Carré* in 1764. A criticism
of the whole play *Hamlet* forms a substantial section of
the *Appel*. See *Oeuvres* XXIV, *Mélanges* III, 191-221.

neglects the drapery: I.e. neglects to represent position,
rank, and historical period by the clothing of the person he paints; or perhaps meaning that he gives less detailed attention to the clothes in order to give prom-
inence to the figure.
    Voltaire was not silenced by Johnson. See *Du Théâtre
Anglais*, in *Art Dramatique* (1770), *Oeuvres*, XVII,
*Dictionnaire Philosophique*, I, 397-98:

> *J'ai jeté les yieux sur une édition de Shakespeare,*
> *donné par le sieur Samuel Johnson. J'y ai vu*
> *qu'on traite de petits esprits les étrangers*
> *qui sont étonnés que dans les pièces de ce grand*
> *Shakespeare, "un senateur romain fasse le bouffon,*
> *et qu'un roi paraisse sur le théâtre en ivrogne."*
>
> *Je ne veux point soupçonner le sieur Johnson*
> *d'être un mauvais plaisant, et d'aimer trop le*
> *vin; mais je trouve un peu extraordinaire qu'il*
> *compte la bouffonnerie et l'ivrognerie parmi les*
> *beautés du théâtre tragique; la raison qu'il en*
> *donne n'est pas moins singulière. "Le poète, dit*
> *il, dédaigne ces distinctions accidentales de*
> *conditions et de pays, comme un peintre qui,*
> *content d'avoir peint la figure, néglige la drap-*
> *erie". La comparaison serait plus justes s'il*
> *parlait d'un peintre qui, dans sujet noble, intro-*
> *duirait des grotesques ridicules, peindrait dans*
> *la bataille d'Arbelles Alexandre le Grand monté*
> *sur un âne, et la femme de Darius buvant avec des*
> *goujats dans un cabaret.*
>
> (*I've just been looking at an edition of Shakespeare,*
> *done by Mr Samuel Johnson. There, I saw treated*
> *as 'little wits' the foreign writers who have*
> *expressed surprise that in the dramas of this so-*
> *called great Shakespeare a Roman Senator plays the*
> *buffoon, and a king appears drunk on the stage.*
> *I'm not in any way wanting to raise the sus-*
> *picion that Johnson is a practical joker, or likes*
> *wine rather too much himself; but I do find it a*
> *little extraordinary that he counts buffoonery and*
> *inebriation among the beauties of tragic drama;*
> *the reason he gives is no less noteworthy. 'The*
> *poet,' he says, 'disdains the accidental distinct-*
> *ions of condition and country, as a painter, happy*
> *with the figure, neglects the drapery.' The com-*
> *parison would have been more just if he had spoken*
> *of an artist who, in treating a noble subject, had*
> *introduced grotesque absurdities, and had depicted*
> *Alexander the Great at the Battle of Arbelles*
> *mounted on a donkey, and the wife of Darius drink-*
> *ing with the louts in a tavern.*)

makes nature predominate over accident: Shows the
essential distinctions of human character and disposition as opposed to the accidents of social and
professional distinction.

superinduced: Johnson defined "superinduce" in his
*Dictionary* as: *To bring on as a thing not originally
belonging to that on which it is brought.*

adventitious: *Dict.: Extrinsically added, not essential-
ly inherent.*

Romans: Cf. Rowe, *Account of the Life of* . . . *Shakespeare:*
*Nor are the manners, proper to the persons
represented, less justly observed, in those
characters taken from Roman history; and of
this, the fierceness and impatience of
Coriolanus, his courage and disdain of the
common people, and virtue and philosophical
temper of Brutus, and the irregular greatness of mind in M. Antony, are beautiful
proofs* (*Shakespeare*, I, 188).

kings: Johnson was of course conscious that in Shakespeare's
plays regal decorum was sometimes necessary, though sometimes overlooked.  See his notes on *Henry V*, Act III,
scene vi: *This phrase* ("upon our cue") *the author learned
among players, and has imparted* . . . *to kings*, and Act IV,
scene i: *This conceit* ("twenty French crowns") (is)
*rather too low for a king* . . . *alluding to the venereal
desease* (*Shakespeare*, VI, 91, 112).

thinks only on men: Cf. Hazlitt, *Characters, Works*, IV,
273, on *Richard II*:
*He* (Richard) *is, however, human in his distresses; for to feel pain, and sorrow, weakness, disappointment, remorse and anguish, is
the lot of humanity, and we sympathise with
him accordingly.  The sufferings of the man
make us forget that he ever was a king.*

cavils: I.e. false or frivolous objections.


Page 9


in the rigorous and critical sense either tragedies or
comedies: Schlegel complained that Johnson had confused
art with life in this passage.  See *Lecture XXIII,*

Lectures on Drama, p.371:
> While in real life the vulgar is found close
> to the sublime . . . the merry and the sad
> usually accompany one another . . . it does
> not follow that because both are found to-
> gether, therefore, they must not be separ-
> able in the compositions of Art.

But cf. Lecture XII, Lectures on Drama, pp.340-42 and
344:
> We may safely admit that the most of the
> English and the Spanish dramatic works are
> neither tragedies nor comedies in the sense
> of the ancients: they are romantic dramas.
> While the ancient art and poetry rigorously
> separate things which are dissimilar; the
> romantic delights in indissoluble mixtures;
> all contrarieties, nature and art, poetry
> and prose, seriousness and mirth, recollect-
> ion and anticipation, spirituality and sensual-
> ity, terrestrial and celestial, life and death,
> are by it blended together in the most inti-
> mate combination.
>     . . . It does not (like the Old Tragedy)
> separate seriousness and action, in a rigid
> manner, from among the whole ingredients of
> life; it embraces at once the whole of the
> chequered drama of life with all its circum-
> stances.

Cf. also S.T. Coleridge, Lecture on Classical and
Romantic Drama (1810), Coleridge's Shakespearean Criticism, ed. T.M. Raysor, I, 197-98: Shakespeare's plays,
Coleridge had said: . . . are in the ancient sense neither
tragedies nor comedies, nor both in one, but a different
genus, diverse in kind, nor merely different in degree, -
romantic dramas, or dramatic romances.

distinct kind: I.e. different kind.

sublunary: I.e. under the moon; on earth, as opposed to the
nature described by, say, Milton, in Paradise Lost.
Johnson had used the phrase "sublunary nature" in his
Preface to the Dictionary (1755). In the Dictionary itself, he defined "sublunary" as: Situated beneath the
moon; earthly; terrestrial; of this world, and quoted
Donne: Dull sublunary lovers, love, / Whose soul is sense,
cannot admit / Of absence, 'cause it doth remove / The
thing which elemented it.

partakes of good and evil, joy and sorrow: Cf. Henry Crabbe
Robinson's account of Coleridge's definition of Shakespearean drama, Diary, 1811-12, in Coleridge's Shakespearean Criticism, I, 211-12:

> *The ancient drama, exhibits a sort of abstract-*
> *ion, not of character, but of idea. A certain*
> *sentiment or passion was exhibited in all its*
> *purity, unmixed with anything that could inter-*
> *fere with its effect. Shakespeare imitates*
> *life, mingled as we find it with joy and*
> *sorrow.*

the reveller . . . burying his friend: Possibly a reference
to *Hamlet*, though Johnson may not be thinking of any
particular scene in Shakespeare, or in any other dramatist.   See, however, Steeven's note to Malone's *Shakes-*
*peare* (1821), I, 66, where he quotes Thomas Twining's
commentary on Aristotle:

> *The unlearned reader will understand me to*
> *allude particularly to the scene (in the*
> *Alcestis of Euripides), in which the dome-*
> *stick describes the behaviour of Hercules:*
> *and to the speech of Hercules himself, which*
> *follows.   Nothing can well be of a more*
> *comick cast than the servant's complaint.*
> *He describes the hero as the most greedy*
> *and ill-mannered guest he had ever attend-*
> *ed, under his master's hospitable roof;*
> *calling about him, eating, drinking, and*
> *singing, in a room by himself, while the*
> *master and all the family were in the height*
> *of funereal lamentation.*

This is quoted in a note to the succeeding paragraph,
where Johnson states that he does not recall any Greek or
Roman writer who attempted both tragedy and comedy.
    In the *Alcestis*, the servant berates Heracles for getting
drunk while Admetus mourns Alcestis, and reminds him of
the impermanence of mortal life.

frolick: I.e. the prank, as in *Midsummer Night's Dream*, or
in *Much Ado About Nothing*, where Dogberry hinders the
malignity of Bastard John.

casualties: Chance occurences.

vicissitudes: For "vicissitude" Johnson gave in his *Diction-*
*ary*: *Regular change, return of the same things in the same*
*succession.*

imitation: Cf. *Life of Cowley, Lives*, I, 19:

> *If the father of criticism has rightly denom-*
> *inated poetry* τέχνη μιμητικὴ, *an imitative art,*
> *these writers will, without great wrong, lose*
> *their right to the name of poets; for they can-*
> *not be said to have imitated any thing; they*
> *neither copied nature nor life; neither*
> *painted the forms of matter, nor represented*
> *the operations of intellect.*

*tragedy* and *comedy*: Placed in italics in Johnson's text,
  to signify his detachment from the concepts he mentions,
  or his implicit criticism of them.

a single writer who attempted both: Johnson may have forgotten the Satyr plays, or perhaps is not thinking of
  them as comedies.  Isaac Reed, *The Plays of William
  Shakespeare* (1803) noted that it appeared from this remark that Johnson had forgotton the *Cyclops* of Euripides.
  Johnson had first stated his view that no man amongst the
  ancients *is recorded to have undertaken more than one
  kind of dramatick poetry* in *The Rambler*, No. 169.  Cf.
  Dryden, *Essay on Dramatic Poesy* (*Essays*, I, 38):
  *Aristophanes, Plautus, Terence, never any of them writ
  a tragedy; Aeschylus, Euripides, Sophocles and Seneca,
  never meddled with comedy: the sock and buskin were not
  worn by the same poet.*

ludicrous characters: I.e. humorous characters.


PAGE 10


an appeal open from criticism to nature: Nature was the
  central criterion of Johnson's mature critical judgement.
  Cf. his comment in *The Rambler*, No. 23:
        *. . . though the rule of Pliny be judiciously
        laid down, it is not applicable to the writer's
        cause, because there is always an appeal from
        domestick criticism to a higher judicature,
        and the publick, which is never corrupted,
        nor often deceived, is to pass the last sen-
        tence upon literary claims.*
  By the time of the *Preface* "nature" has replaced "the
  publick".

instruct by pleasing: Cf. Horace, *Ars Poetica*, lines 333-
  34: *Aut prodesse volunt aut delectare poetae / aut simul
  et iucunda et idonea dicere vitae* (poets aim either to
  benefit, or to amuse, or to utter words at once both
  pleasing and helpful to life).

alterations: All editions published in Johnson's lifetime
  have "alterations" and correction to "alternations" was
  made in 1785 by Isaac Reed.
     In *The Rambler*, No. 156, Johnson had defined not mingled
  drama, but tragi-comedy:
        *. . . is it not certain that the tragic and
        comic affections have been moved alternately
        with equal force, and that no plays*

> *have oftner filled the eye with tears, and*
> *the breast with palpitation, than those which*
> *are variegated with interludes of mirth?*

At this stage, Johnson's position was close to that of
Dryden, who, he recorded in his *Life of Dryden*, maintained
in the Dedication to *The Spanish Fryar* that: . . . *the*
*drama required an alternation of comick and tragick scenes,*
*and that it is necessary to mitigate by alleviations of*
*merriment the pressure of ponderous events, and the fatigue*
*of toilsome passions* (*Lives*, I, 357).

obviate: I.e. prevent.

concatenation: Chaining together.

It is objected . . .: By a long procession of renaissance,
seventeenth-century and eighteenth-century critics.

passions are interrupted: Perhaps the passions of the
characters rather than the passions of the audience.
But see *post* Johnson's discussion of Shakespeare's
quibbles, and his notes on this subject in the edition,
where the progress of the audience's passions is concerned.

principal event . . . poetry: Throughout this part of his
argument, Johnson mockingly adopts the excessively grave
tone of an imagined objector to Shakespeare's practice,
as he later does when discussing Shakespeare's neglect
of the unities of time and place.

move: I.e. move us.

specious: *Dict.*: *Plausible; superficial* (?); *not solidly*
*right; striking at first view.*

Fiction cannot move so much . . .: The question of how drama
moves is raised later in the *Preface* (pp.23-24), in connection with the unities of time and place.


PAGE 11.


habitudes: Dispositions; mental constitutions.

all pleasure consists in variety: In his criticism of Butler's
*Hudibras*, where *the scenes are too seldom changed*, Johnson
proclaimed with similar force that: *The great source of*
*pleasure is variety* (*Butler, Lives*, I, 211-12). Cf. also
Johnson's comment upon *Hamlet*:
> *If the dramas of Shakespeare were to be*
> *characterised, each by the particular ex-*
> *cellence which distinguishes it from the*

> *rest, we must allow to the tragedy of Hamlet*
> *the praise of variety. The incidents are so*
> *numerous, that the argument of the play would*
> *make a long tale* (See *Shakespeare*, X, 415).

**definite ideas:** Johnson is referring to the division of
the plays by Shakespeare's actors, and first editors,
John Heming, or Hemings, and Henry Condel, in 1623.
They are mentioned by name on p.43 of the *Preface*.

**catastrophe:** Not, as in modern usage, an awful or terrible
event. In his *Dictionary*, Johnson gives: *The change or
revolution, which produces the conclusion or final
event of a dramatick piece.*

**and comedies to-morrow:** The Yale editor gives as examples
Suckling's *Aglaura* (1637), and Howard's *Vestal Virgin*
(1665). Nichol Smith cites Downes, *Roscius Anglicanus*
(1708), p.22 for an account of an altered version of
*Romeo and Juliet*, where, by preserving Romeo and Juliet
alive, *twas play'd alternately, tragical one day and
tragicomical another; for several days together.*

**the common criticism:** I.e. the criticism commonly made,
*not* the common or routine criticism of professional
critics.

**nicely:** I.e. finely.

**the tragedy of** *Antony* **and** *Cleopatra*: Johnson wrote in his
final note to this play: *The events, of which the principle
are described according to history, are produced without
any art of connexion or care of disposition* (*Shakespeare*,
VIII, 313).


PAGE 12


**denominations:** "Denomination" is defined in Johnson's
*Dictionary* as: *A name given to a thing, which commonly
marks some principal quality of it.*

**composition is the same:** Cf. Rowe: *Account of the Life of
. . . Shakespeare*: The Merry Wives of Windsor, The
Comedy of Errors, *and* The Taming of the Shrew, *are all
pure comedy; the rest, however they are called, have something of both kinds* (*Shakespeare*, I, 182-83).

interchange of seriousness and merriment: Of *Hamlet*,
Johnson wrote that: *The scenes are interchangeably
diversified with merriment and solemnity* (*Shakespeare*,
X, 415).

easy: Unstrained, natural.  See Johnson's paper on *Easy
Poetry* in *The Idler*, No. 77.

familiar dialogue: As between familiars, or people well
acquainted with each other.

as he commands us, we laugh or mourn: Johnson's remarks on
the pleasures and pains of reading a great author provide
some of the most pleasing moments in his criticism.  Cf.
his comment on Milton that *such is the power of his poetry
that his call is obeyed without resistance, the reader
feels himself in captivity to a higher and nobler mind,
and criticism sinks in admiration* (*Milton*, *Lives*, I, 190).
Johnson later applied this image of the mind in captiva-
tion to Shakespeare in his *Life of Dryden*:
> *Works of imagination excel by their allurment
> and delight; by their power of attracting and
> detaining the attention.  That book is good in
> vain which the reader throws away.  He only is
> the master who keeps the mind in pleasing cap-
> tivity; whose pages are perused with eagerness,
> and in hope of new pleasure are perused again;
> and whose conclusion is perceived with an eye
> of sorrow, such as the traveller casts upon
> departing day.
>      By his proportion of this predomination I
> will consent that Dryden should be tried . .
> . of this, which, in defiance of criticism,
> continues Shakespeare the sovereign of the
> drama* (*Lives*, I, 454).

not easily endure: Because of the offensive language used
by Iago in this scene.  The affront to Brabantio's office
would offend a "modern audience's" sense of decorum.  But
Rymer complained that humanity itself was offended in the
scene.  See *Short View of Tragedy*, Ch. VII, *Critical
Works*, p.138: *But besides the Manners to a* Magnifico,
*humanity cannot bear that an old Gentleman in his mis-
fortune should be insulted over with such a rabble of
Skoundrel language, when no cause or provocation.*

Polonius . . . seasonable and useful: Suitable to his position as a senior minister of state, and useful for the
performance of his duties in that office.  Warburton had
criticized the character of Polonius in his notes on
*Hamlet*.  In a note on Act II, scene ii (*Shakespeare*, X,
240-41), Johnson responded as follows:

*This account of the character of Polonius,*
*though it sufficiently reconciles the seeming*
*inconsistency of so much wisdom with so much*
*folly, does not perhaps correspond exactly to*
*the ideas of our author.  The commentator makes*
*the character of Polonius a character only of*
*manners, discriminated by properties super-*
*ficial, accidental, and acquired.  The poet*
*intended a nobler delineation of a mixed char-*
*acter of manners and of nature.  Polonius is*
*a man bred in courts, exercised in business,*
*stored with observation, confident in his*
*knowledge, proud of his eloquence, and de-*
*clining into dotage.  His mode of oratory is*
*truly represented as designed to ridicule the*
*practice of those times, of prefaces that made*
*no introduction, and of method that embarrassed*
*rather than explained.  This part of his char-*
*acter is accidental, the rest is natural.*
*Such a man is positive and confident, because*
*he knows that his mind was once strong, and*
*knows not that it is become weak.  Such a man*
*excels in general principles but fails in the*
*particular application.  He is knowing in retro-*
*spect, and ignorant in foresight.  While he de-*
*pends upon his memory, and can draw from his*
*repositories of knowledge, he utters weighty*
*sentences, and gives useful counsel; but as the*
*mind in its enfeebled state cannot be kept long*
*busy and intent, the old man is subject to sud-*
*den dereliction of his faculties, he loses the*
*order of his ideas, and entangles himself in his*
*own thoughts, till he recovers the leading prin-*
*ciple, and falls again into his former train.*
*This idea of dotage encroaching upon wisdom,*
*will solve all the phaenomena of the character*
*of Polonius.*

. . . **heard with applause:** All the scenes and characters
mentioned in this paragraph were criticized by Voltaire,
*Appel à toutes les nations de l'Europe, Oeuvres,* XXIV,
*Mélanges,* III, 191-221.  Iago's bellowings had been
criticized by Rymer, *Short View of Tragedy,* Ch. VII,
*Critical Works,* pp.135-38, and by Voltaire, *Avertisement*
*du Traducteur* (1764), *Oeuvres,* VII, *Théâtre,* VI, 436.
   Criticisms of the grave-diggers occur in various other
places in Voltaire's writings.  See, for example, *Oeuvres,*
XX, *Mélanges,* I, *Lettres Philosophiques, Lettre* XVIII,
149, where he wrote of *ses Farces monstrueuses qu'on*
*appelle Tragédies* (these monstrous farces they call tragedies), and of the grave-diggers that they *creusent une*
*fosse en buvant, en chantant des vaudevilles, et en*
*faisant sur les têtes des morts qu'ils recontrent des*

*plaisanteries convenable à gens de leur metier* ( . . .
*dig a grave while drinking, while singing popular songs,
and while cracking the sort of jokes over the heads of
the dead that are typical of people of their profession*).
See also *Dissertation sur la tragédie ancienne et moderne* (1749), *Oeuvres*, IV, *Théâtre*, III, 502.

**world open before him:** Cf. *Rasselas*, Ch. XVI: *I am pleased
to think, said the prince, that my birth has given me
at least, one advantage over others, by enabling me to
determine for myself.  I have here the world before me;
I will review it at leisure* . . . Cf. also Milton,
*Paradise Lost*, Bk. XII, 645-49:
> *Some natural tears they dropped, but wiped them soon;
> The world was all before them, where to choose
> Their place of rest, and providence their guide:
> They hand in hand with wandering steps and slow,
> Through Eden took their solitary way.*

**led him to comedy:** Johnson is probably thinking of the
following passage from Rymer's *Short View of Tragedy*
(See *Critical Works*, p.169):
> *Everyone must be content to wear a Fools Coat,
> who comes to be dressed by him.  Nor is he more
> civil to the Ladies.  Portia, in good manners,
> might have challeng'd more respect: she that
> shines, a glory of the first magnitude in the
> Gallery of Heroick Dames, is with our Poet,
> scarce one remove from a Natural: She is the
> own Cousin German, of one piece, the very same
> impertinent silly flesh and blood with Desdemona.
> Shakespears genius lay for Comedy and Humour.
> In Tragedy he appears quite out of his Element.*

For Rymer, as to some extent for Johnson, the slightest
deviation from tragedy signified comedy.

**In tragedy:** Significantly, Johnson does not say "In his
trage<u>dies</u>".  He seems rather to be thinking of tragic
scenes, moments, or passages in the plays.  But cf.
Hazlitt, *Characters*, *Works*, IV, 314:
> *Much as we like Shakespear's comedies, we can-
> not agree with Dr. Johnson that they are better
> than his tragedies; nor do we like them half
> so well.  If his inclination to comedy some-
> times led him to trifle with the seriousness
> of tragedy, the poetical and impassioned pas-
> sages are the best parts of his comedies.*

**felicity:** I.e. happiness.

PAGE 13.

**congenial to his nature:** Johnson was not of the opinion that
what a writer liked doing best was always in fact his
best work.  Of Pope's *Imitations of Horace*, he noted that
they were written as *relaxations of his genius* . . . *but
what is easy is seldom excellent* (Pope, *Lives*, III, 346-
47).

Johnson's general feeling about Shakespeare's disposition
to comedy was supported by particular judgements in the
notes.  Parolles, in *All's Well that Ends Well*, seemed,
he claimed, *the character which Shakespeare delighted to
draw*, while in *Troilus and Cressida, The comic characters
seem to have been the favourites of the writer*.  The
nurse, in *Romeo and Juliet*, was likewise *one of the characters in which the author delighted*.  However, of a stroke
of wit in *The Comedy of Errors* Johnson wrote that Shakespeare
*takes too much delight* (See *Shakespeare*, IV, 113; IX, 166;
X, 166; II, 207).

**tragick scenes:** Johnson writes of the *tragick scenes of*
Henry IV *and* V in notes.  The *grave scenes* of *Measure for
Measure* have *more labour than elegance* (See *Shakespeare*,
VI, 563; II, 161).

**comedy pleases more by the thoughts and the language:** In
his notes, Johnson wrote of *The Two Gentlemen of Verona*
that *few* (plays) *have more lines or passages which, singly
considered, are eminently beautiful* (*Shakespeare*, I, 123).

**skill:** Used with a meaning nearer to "knowledge".  Not "skill"
in the sense of mere technical expertise.  In his notes,
Johnson wrote of *Henry IV Part II* that *the characters
(are) diversified with the utmost nicety of discernment,
and the profoundest skill in the nature of man*.  *Othello*,
meanwhile, *shows such proofs of Shakespeare's skill in
human nature, as* . . . *it is vain to seek in any modern
writer*.  In his general observation on *The Tempest*,
Johnson praised the play as having *many characters, diversified with boundless invention, and preserved with
profound skill in nature, extensive knowledge of opinions,
and accurate observation of life* (See *Shakespeare*, V, 611;
X, 628; I, 117).

Johnson is describing the disposition congenial to
Shakespeare's nature, not preferring comedy to tragedy.
But cf. *The Critical Review*, XX (Nov. 1765), 328.
*Shakespeare's tragedy, says Mr. Johnson, seems
to be skill, and his comedy to be instinct.  Let
the next of kin to Shakespeare's poetry lodge an
appeal at the tribunal of human feeling against
the first part of this partial sentence.  We*

> *imagine we see the public indignation backing*
> *the appeal, and bringing all the great char-*
> *acters in Shakespeare's tragedies as evidences*
> *in its support.* Our limits will not admit our
> *expatiating on this head, yet we think we can*
> *safely leave Shakespeare's cause to the ver-*
> *dict of any man, who has not read himself out*
> *of a true taste for nature, and who has not*
> *studied himself into a desregard of human*
> *passions.* Such a reader smothers the glow
> *of passion under the embers of learning.*

**his comedy to be instinct:** Perhaps an answer to Dennis,
*On the Genius and Writings of Shakespear: Tho'* Shakespear
*succeeded very well in Comedy, yet his principal Talent*
*and his chief Delight was Tragedy* (See *Critical Works,*
II, 13).
   Cf. also Joseph Warton's note on this comment by Johnson
in Malone's *Shakespeare,* I, 71: *. . . the opinion, which I*
*am sorry to perceive gains ground, that Shakespeare's*
*chief and predominant talent lay in comedy, tends to less-*
*en the unrivalled excellence of our divine bard.*

**very little modified by particular forms:** Johnson is referring to passion independent of the considerations of
particular states of life, and the rules and customs of
individual societies or cultures.

**durable:** Cf. Wordsworth, Preface to the *Lyrical Ballads*
(1800 and 1850): *. . . the manners of rural life germinate*
*from those elementary feelings, and, from the necessary*
*character of rural occupations, are more easily compre-*
*hended, and are more durable* (Prose Works, I, 125).

**the colours of nature:** Cf. Rapin, *Comparison of Thucydides*
*and Livy* (Oxford, 1694), pp.32-33, for similar arresting
language:
> *Perhaps there was never* Historian *more en-*
> *gaging* [*than Livy*] *by the Talent he had of*
> *Expressing Nature to the Life, and giving*
> *her a* different *Face, as became her* several
> *Conditions, painting her always in her*
> proper *Colours, making every Passion speak*
> *its* Genuine *Language that it might have its*
> *effect upon the Mind.* Hence it is he's so
> *incomparable at* painting *the* manners, *that*
> *his* Portraictures *are so like, that he* ex-
> presses *every thing in the* features *that*
> *become it, never* confounding *those Beauties*
> *which Nature has distinguisht.*

**perish with the body that exhibits them:** In his *Life of Butler*, Johnson wrote of *Hudibras* that: . . . *those modifications of life, and peculiarities of practice, which are the progeny of error and perverseness, or at best some accidental influence or transient persuasion, must perish with their parents (Lives, I, 214).*

**heterogeneous modes:** In the *Dictionary*, Johnson defined "heterogeneous" as *Not kindred; opposite or dissimilar in nature.* For "mode" he gave *Form; external variety; accidental discrimination; accident.* In his *Life of Cowley*, Johnson was later to write of the wit of the metaphysical poets as *heterogeneous ideas . . . yoked by violence together (Cowley, Lives, I, 20).*

**suffers decay:** Cf. *Rasselas*, Ch. XLVIII:
  *Of immateriality, said Imlac, our ideas are negative, and therefore obscure. Immateriality seems to imply a natural power of perpetual duration, as a consequence of exemption from all causes of decay: whatever perishes is destroyed by the solution of its contexture, and separation of its parts; nor can we conceive how that which has no parts, and therefore admits no solution, can be naturally corrupted or impaired.*

**stream of time:** In the proof sheets of the *Preface* (1765) Johnson's sentence appears thus: *The stream of time, which is continually shattering the frail cement of other poets, passes without injury by the adamant of* Shakespeare.

**dissoluble:** Means the opposite of what it should mean. Here it means soluble, able to be dissolved.

**fabricks:** I.e. buildings, edifices. In the *Dictionary* Johnson defined "fabrick" as: *any body formed by the conjunction of dissimilar parts.*

**without injury:** I.e. without causing injury.

**adamant of Shakespeare:** In his *Dictionary*, Johnson defined "adamant" as *A stone, imagined by writers, of impenetrable hardness.*


PAGE 14


**analogy:** Since, in his *Dictionary*, Johnson mentions its use by grammarians to signify *the agreement of several words*

*in one common mode; as, from* love *is formed* loved, *from*
hate, hated, *from* grieve, grieved, he seems here to be
referring to the system of relationship between words
in a language, especially the principle by which words
are formed one from another.

the common intercourse of life: Ordinary everyday conversational exchange.

uniform simplicity: Cf. *The Rambler*, No. 36: . . . *poetry
has to do rather with the passions of men, which are uniform, than their customs, which are changeable.* Cf. also
*The Rambler*, No. 125: *Reason and nature are uniform and
inflexible.*
     Of Cowley, Johnson wrote in connection with his
*Anacreontics*: *Real mirth must be always natural, and nature
is uniform. Men have been wise in very different modes;
but they have always laughed the same way* (Cowley, *Lives*,
I, 39-40). In general, however, the "metaphysical" poets
had no regard to that uniformity of sentiment which en-
ables us to conceive and to excite the pains and pleasures
of other minds (Cowley, *Lives*, I, 20).
     In a note on Act IV, scene i of *Coriolanus*, Johnson ex-
plained the lines: *Fortune's blows, / When most struck
home, / Being gentle wounded, craves / A noble cunning.*
He remarked: *Perhaps the first emotions of nature are
nearly uniform, and one man differs from another in the
power of endurance, as he is better regulated by precept
and instruction* (Shakespeare, VII, 438-39).

primitive qualities: Dryden, wrote Johnson, seems not much
acquainted with *the simple and elemental passions as they
spring separate in the mind* (Dryden, *Lives*, I, 457).
     Wordsworth seems to have been looking for something
similar in poetry when he wrote in his Preface to the
*Lyrical Ballads* (1800 and 1850) of *tracing . . . truly
though not ostentatiously, the primary laws of our nature*
(*Prose Works*, I, 123).
     With Johnson's emphasis here on the permanence of passion,
cf. also Matthew Arnold, Preface to the First Edition of
*Poems* (1853):
          *The Poet, then, has in the first place to select
          an excellent action; and what actions are the
          most excellent? Those, certainly, which most
          powerfully appeal to the great primary human
          affections: to those elementary feelings which
          subsist permanently in the race, and which are
          independent of time. These feelings are per-
          manent and the same; that which interests them
          is permanent and the same also . . . To the
          elementary part of our nature, to our passions,
          that which is great and passionate is eternally
          interesting. A great human action of a thousand*

> *years ago is more interesting to it than a*
> *smaller human action of today, even though*
> *upon the representation of this last the*
> *most consummate skill may have been expended,*
> *and though it has the advantage of appealing*
> *by its modern language, familiar manners, and*
> *contemporary allusions, to all our transient*
> *feelings and interests . . . Poetical works*
> *belong to the domain of our permanent pas-*
> *sions: let them interest these, and the voice*
> *of all subordinate claims upon them is at*
> *once silenced* (See *The Poetical Works of*
> *Matthew Arnold* (1909; repr. London: Oxford
> University Press, 1945), p.4).

**propriety:** What is fitting, or right for the occasion; as
opposed to that which is dressed up, or artificially
elevated.

**comick dialogue:** Not perhaps the same thing as his humorous
dialogue, but any dialogue not obviously tragic.  Cf. Rymer/
Rapin, *Reflections on Aristotle*, pp.126-27:
> *'Tis the great Art of* Comedy *to keep close*
> *to* Nature, *and never leave it; to have com-*
> *mon thoughts and expressions fitted to the*
> *capacity of all the world.  For it is the*
> *most certainly true, that the most gross*
> *strokes of* Nature, *whatever they be, please*
> *alwayes more, than the most delicate, that*
> *are not Natural: nevertheless base and vul-*
> *gar terms are not to be permitted on the*
> *Theatre unless supported by some kind of*
> *wit.  The* proverbs *and* wise sayings *of the*
> *People ought not to be suffered, unless they*
> *have some pleasant meaning and unless they*
> *are Natural.  This is the most general prin-*
> *ciple of* Comedy; *by which, whatever is repre-*
> *sented, cannot fail to please; but without it,*
> *nothing.*

**original masters of our language:** Johnson's criteria are
similar to those of Wordsworth in his Appendix to the
*Lyrical Ballads*:
> *The earliest poets of all nations generally*
> *wrote from passion excited by real events;*
> *they wrote naturally, and as men; feeling*
> *powerfully as they did, their language was*
> *daring, and figurative.  In succeeding times,*
> *Poets, and Men ambitious of the fame of Poets,*
> *perceiving the influence of such language, and*
> *desirous of producing the same effect without*
> *being animated by the same passion, set them-*
> *selves to a mechanical adoption of these*

> *figures of speech, and made use of them,*
> *sometimes with propriety, but much more*
> *frequently applied them to feelings and*
> *thoughts with which they had no natural*
> *connection whatsoever. A language was*
> *thus insensibly produced, differing mat-*
> *erially from the real language of men in*
> *any situation . . .*
>
> *Poets, it is probable, who had before*
> *contented themselves for the most part*
> *with misapplying only expressions which*
> *at first had been dictated by real pas-*
> *sion, carried the abuse still further,*
> *and introduced phrases composed apparent-*
> *ly in the spirit of the original figur-*
> *ative language of passion, yet altogether*
> *of their own invention, and characterised*
> *by various degrees of wanton deviation*
> *from good sense and nature* (*Prose Works,*
> I, 160-61).

**unexceptionably:** Without exception.

**ambition of elegance:** Apropos the *Anacreontics* of Cowley,
Johnson wrote that:

> *The familiar part of language continues long*
> *the same: the dialogue of comedy, when it is*
> *transcribed from popular manners and real*
> *life, is read from age to age with equal*
> *pleasure. The artifice of inversion, by*
> *which the established order of words or*
> *meanings of words are introduced, is prac-*
> *tised, not by those who talk to be under-*
> *stood, but by those who write to be admired*
> (*Cowley, Lives,* I, 40).

The criteria expressed in this part of the *Preface* are
closely associated with those which can be found in the
definition of "Easy poetry" from *The Idler,* No. 77 (1759):

> *It is the prerogative of easy poetry to be*
> *understood as long as the language lasts;*
> *but modes of speech which owe their pre-*
> *valence only to modish folly, or to the*
> *eminence of those that use them, die away*
> *with their inventors, and their meaning in*
> *a few years, is no longer known.*

The ideal is defined by an account of the various abuses
of expression:

> *Easy poetry is that in which natural thoughts*
> *are expressed without violence to the language.*
> *The discriminating character of ease consists*
> *in the diction; for all true poetry requires*
> *that the sentiments be natural. Language*
> *suffers violence by harsh or by daring figures,*

*by transpositions, by unusual acceptations*
*of words, and by any licence, which would*
*be avoided by a writer of prose. Where any*
*artifice appears in the structure of the*
*verse, that verse is no longer easy. Any*
*epithet which can be rejected without dim-*
*inution of the sense, any curious iteration*
*of the same word, and all unusual, though*
*not ungrammatical structure of speech, des-*
*troys the grace of easy poetry.*
Johnson's confidence in the mean to be observed between
ornament on the one hand, and grossness on the other, seems
to have been strengthened by his enjoyment of Shakespeare's
natural expression. Milton's expression was *removed from*
*common use,* while Addison *sometimes descends too much to*
*the language of conversation.* Before the time of Dryden
there was *no poetical diction, no system of words at once*
*refined from the grossness of domestick use* . . . (See
*Milton, Addison* and *Dryden, Lives,* I, 190; II, 149; I,
420).

**finding or making better:** Johnson discovered *the native ef-*
*fusion of untaught affection* in *The Tempest,* presumably
in the speeches of Miranda (*Shakespeare,* I, 117).

**distinction:** difference.

**vulgar:** Common or customary, without any derogatory implication; as Johnson says in the next clause, *above grossness.*
He defined "vulgar" in his *Dictionary* as: *suiting to the*
*common people; practised among the common people.*

**seems to write without any moral purpose:** Without any evident
moral direction. The key word here is "seems". According
to Johnson's notes, Shakespeare frequently does write with
moral purpose. *Timon of Athens,* for example, *affords a very*
*powerful warning against that ostentatious liberality; which*
*scatters bounty, but confers no benefits, and buys flattery,*
*but not friendship.* In *Macbeth, The passions are directed*
*to their true end. Lady Macbeth is merely detested; and*
*though the courage of Macbeth preserves some esteem, yet*
*every reader rejoices at his fall.* In *Troilus and Cressida*
likewise Shakespeare's *vicious characters sometimes disgust,*
*but cannot corrupt, for both Cressida and Pandarus are*
*detested and contemned* (See *Shakespeare,* VIII, 458; IV,
611; IX, 566).
On occasion in the notes, Johnson says where he thinks
Shakespeare has taken pains to enforce his moral. In *King*
*Lear,* according to Johnson, Shakespeare sacrificed a
regular plot by inserting the figure of Edmund, who gave
him *the opportunity* . . . *of combining perfidy with perfidy,*
*and connecting the wicked son with the wicked daughters,*

*to impress this important moral, that villainy is never
at a stop, that crimes lead to crimes, and at last ter-
minate in ruin (Shakespeare, IX, 566).*

**must think morally:** I.e. not necessarily like a moralist.
Johnson defined "moral" in his *Dictionary* as: *Relating
to the practice of men towards each other, as it may be
virtuous or criminal; good or bad.*

**no just distribution of good or evil:** Cf. Johnson's criticism of *Hamlet:*
> *The apparition left the regions of the dead to
> little purpose; the revenge which he demands
> is not obtained but by the death of him that
> was required to take it; and the gratification
> which would arise from the destruction of an
> usurper and a murderer, is abated by the un-
> timely death of Ophelia, the young, the
> beautiful, the harmless, and the pious* (See
> Shakespeare, X, 416).

**nor is always careful to shew in the virtuous a disapprobation
of the wicked:** Johnson wrote of Angelo in a note to Act
V, scene i of *Measure for Measure (Shakespeare, II, 156)*
that he believed *every reader feels some indignation when
he finds him spared.*
    Cf. also Johnson's note on *All's Well that Ends Well
(Shakespeare, 134): Decency required that Bertram's double
crime of cruelty and disobedience, joined likewise with
some hypocrisy, should raise more resentment, and that
though his mother might easily forgive him, his king
should more pertinaciously vindicate his own authority
and Helen's merit.*

**indifferently:** *Dict.: In a neutral state, without wish or
aversion.* Cf. A.C. Bradley, *Shakespearean Tragedy* (1904;
London, 1969), p.58: *Most of the defects in his writings
must be due to indifference or want of care.*

**familiar dialogue:** As between friends.

**ruggedness:** Harshness; but also, lack of clarity; awkward-
ness, distortion.

PAGE 15.

**Shakespeare . . . has likewise faults:** The following account
of the faults of Shakespeare is one of the most notorious
parts of the *Preface.* Nichol Smith cites the justification
for the passage in Johnson's letter of 16th October 1765,

to Charles Burney: *We must confess the faults of our
favourite, to gain credit to our praise of his excellencies.  He that claims either for himself or for
another the honours of perfection, will surely injure
the reputation which he designs to assist* (See *Letters
of Johnson*, ed. R.W. Chapman (Oxford: Clarendon Press,
1952), II, 178).

any other merit: Anyone with merits other than those of
Shakespeare.

innocently discussed: Discussed without offending anyone
else; harmlessly; disinterestedly.

that bigotry which sets candour higher than truth: The
bigotry that comes from trying to avoid giving offence
to admirers of Shakespeare.  "Candour" here means kind-
liness or generosity of the wrong sort; not impartiality
or freedom from bias.

sacrifices virtue to convenience: Cf. Johnson's comments on
Shakespeare's treatment of Falstaff in *Henry IV Part II*:
  *I do not see why Falstaff is carried to the
  Fleet.  We have never lost sight of him since
  his dismission from the king; he has committed
  no new fault, and therefore incurred no punish-
  ment; but the different agitations of fear,
  anger and surprise in him and his company,
  made a good scene to the eye; and our author,
  who wanted them no longer on the stage, was
  glad to find this method of sweeping them
  away* (See note to Act V, scene v, *Shakespeare*,
  V, 610).

cannot extenuate: Possibly an answer to Pope, *Preface to
Shakespeare* (1725): *We shall hereby extenuate many faults
which are his and clear him from the imputation of many
which are not* (*Shakespeare*, I, 110).
  Cf. also Dennis, *On the Genius and Writings of Shakespear,
Critical Works*, II, 4: *And what makes the brightest Glory
of his Character, those Beauties were entirely his own,
and owing to the Force of his own Nature; whereas his
Faults were owing to his Education, and to the Age that he
liv'd in.*

make the world better: Cf. Wordsworth to John Wilson, 7 June
1802, Letter 170, *The Letters of William and Dorothy
Wordsworth*, ed. E. de Selincourt, 2nd. ed. rev. C.L. Shaver
(Oxford: Clarendon Press, 1967-69), I, 355:
  *You have given me praise for having reflected
  faithfully in my poems the feelings of human
  nature I would fain hope that I have done so.*

> *But a great Poet ought to do more than
> this he ought to a certain degree to rec-
> tify men's feelings, to give them new com-
> positions of feeling more sane pure and
> permanent, in short, more consonant to
> nature, that is, to eternal nature, and the
> great moving spirit of things.*

See also, *Letters*, I, 358:

> [It] *is not enough for me as a poet, to
> delineate merely such feelings as all men
> do sympathise with but, it is also highly
> desirable to add to these others, such as
> all men* may *sympathize with, and such as
> there is reason to believe they would be
> better and more moral beings if they did
> sympathize with.*

justice: In a general sense; not specifically poetical justice.  It is noteworthy that Johnson does not use the term
"poetical justice", a favourite critical term of his age,
anywhere in the *Preface*.  But cf. Dennis, *On the Genius
and Writings of Shakespear, Critical Works*, II, 7:

> *. . . indeed* Shakespear *has been wanting
> in the exact distribution of Poetical Jus-
> tice not only in his* Coriolanus, *but in most
> of his best Tragedies, in which the Guilty
> and the Innocent perish promiscuously; as*
> Duncan *and* Banquo *in* Mackbeth, *as likewise
> Lady* Macduffe *and her Children;* Desdemona
> *in* Othello; *Cordelia, Kent and King* Lear,
> *in the Tragedy that bears his Name; Brutus
> and* Porcia *in* Julius Caesar, *and young*
> Hamlet *in the Tragedy of* Hamlet.

Johnson seems to be employing the term "justice" more in
the sense of "natural ideas of justice" as he had used this
phrase in his following note on *King Lear*:

> *. . . Shakespeare has suffered the virtue of
> Cordelia to perish in a just cause, contrary
> to the natural ideas of justice, to the hope
> of the reader, and, what is yet more strange,
> to the faith of chronicles.  Yet this conduct
> is justified by* The Spectator, *who blames Tate
> for giving Cordelia success and happiness in
> his alteration, and declares, that, in his
> opinion, the tragedy has lost half its beauty.
> Dennis has remarked, whether justly or not,
> that, to secure the favourable reception of
> Cato, the town was poisoned with much false
> and abominable criticism, and that endeavours
> had been used to discredit and decry poetical
> justice.  A play in which the wicked prosper,
> and the virtuous miscarry, may doubtless be
> good, because it is a just representation of*

the common events of human life; but
since all reasonable beings naturally
love justice, I cannot easily be persuade-
ed that the observation of justice makes
a play worse; or, that if other excel-
lences are equal, the audience will not
always rise better pleased from the final
triumph of persecuted virtue (See Shakespeare, IX, 566).

**very slight consideration:** Cf. Johnson's note on *Henry V*:
The great defect of this play is the emptiness and narrow-
ness of the last act, which a very little diligence might
have easily avoided (*Shakespeare*, VI, 171).

**opportunities of instructing:** Opportunities not only of stat-
ing, but also showing moral truth by example.  E.g. the
conclusion of *As You Like It*, where:
By hastening to the end of his work,
Shakespeare suppressed the dialogue between the usurper and the hermit, and lost
an opportunity of exhibiting a moral lesson
in which he might have found matter worthy
of his highest powers (*Shakespeare*, III, 338).

**or delighting:** E.g. the unmuffling of Claudio, *Measure for
Measure*, Act V, scene i: It is somewhat strange, that
Isabel is not made to express either gratitude, wonder,
or joy at the sight of her brother (*Shakespeare*, II, 158).

**. . . more easy:** Cf. Johnson's note on *All's Well that Ends
Well*, Act V, scene iii:
Dia. He knows himself, my bed he hath defil'd;
And at that time he got his wife with child;
Dead though she be, she feels her young one kick;
So there's my riddle, One, that's dead, is quick.
And now behold the meaning.
Johnson commented:
This dialogue is too long, since the audience
already knew the whole transaction; nor is
there any reason for puzzling the king and
playing with his passions; but it was much
easier than to make a pathetical interview
between Helen and her husband, her mother,
and the king (*Shakespeare*, IV, 148).

**age:** In *King Lear*, Johnson said, Shakespeare *neglects and
confounds the characters of ages, by mingling customs
ancient and modern, English and foreign* (*Shakespeare*, IX,
565).

**nation:** Cf. Johnson's note on *All's Well that Ends Well*

Act I, scene i, *in ward*:
> *Under his particular care, as my guardian,*
> *till I come to age. It is now almost for-*
> *gotten in England, that the heirs of great*
> *fortunes were the king's* wards. *Whether the*
> *same practice prevailed in France, it is of*
> *no great use to enquire, for Shakespeare*
> *gives to all nations the manners of England*
> (*Shakespeare*, IV, 4).

    In a note to *Timon of Athens*, Act III, scene iv, *Enter Servilius*, Johnson remarked that: *It may be observed that Shakespeare has unskilfully filled his Greek story with Roman names* (*Shakespeare*, VIII, 383).

**opinions of another:** Religious opinion was an area of special sensitivity for Johnson: cf. his remarks on the reconciliation scene in *King Lear*, Act V, scene iii:
> *Our author by negligence gives his heathens*
> *the sentiments and practices of Christianity.*
> In Hamlet *there is the same solemn and final*
> *reconciliation, but with exact propriety,*
> *for the personages are Christians* (*Shakespeare*,
> IX, 555).

**of possibility:** Sometimes to the destruction of credibility. See Johnson's note on *Cymbeline*, where he complains of the general confusion and unreality in this play:
> *To remark the folly of the fiction, the absurd-*
> *ity of the conduct, the confusion of the names,*
> *and manners of different times, and the impos-*
> *sibility of the events in any system of life,*
> *were to waste criticism upon unresisting im-*
> *becility, upon faults too evident for detection,*
> *and too gross for aggravation* (See *Shakespeare*,
> IX, 344).

PAGE 16

**in many of his plays:** I.e. the fault described is a frequent but not universal characteristic of Shakespeare.

**shortened the labour to snatch the profit:** In his notes on *Henry IV Part II*, Johnson wrote of Shakespeare's loss of the character of Poins, *by heedlessness, in the multiplicity of his characters, the variety of his action, and his eagerness to end the play.* He fancied that *every reader when he ends this play, cries with Desdomona, O most lame and impotent conclusion* (*Shakespeare*, V, 608 and 610).
    Cf. also Johnson's note on *Henry V*, Act V, scene ii:

> *I know not why Shakespeare now gives the*
> *king nearly such a character as he made him*
> *formally ridicule in Percy . . . The truth*
> *is, that the Poet's matter failed him in the*
> *fifth act, and he was glad to fill it up*
> *with whatever he could get* (Shakespeare, VI,
> 161).

**remits:** For "remit" Johnson gives in his *Dictionary: to*
*give up, to resign.*

**most vigorously exert them:** Cf. Hazlitt, *Lectures on the*
*English Poets, Works,* V, 56: *The natural ease and indif-*
*ference of his temper made him sometimes less scrupulous*
*than he might have been.* He is relaxed and careless in
*critical places; he is earnest throughout only in Timon,*
*Macbeth, and Lear.*

**catastrophe:** I.e. the resolution (of a play).

**time or place:** As shown, for example, in the many references
to pistols in *Henry IV.*

**imagined interpolators:** Cf. Pope, *Preface to Shakespeare:*
*As I believe that what I have mentioned gave*
*rise to the opinion of Shakespeare's want of*
*learning; so what has continued it down to*
*us may have been the many blunders and il-*
*literacies of the first publishers of his*
*works.* In these editions their ignorance
*shines in almost every page; nothing is more*
*common than* Actus tertia. Exit omnes. Enter
three Witches solus. *Their French is as bad*
*as their Latin, both in construction and*
*spelling: their Welsh is as false*
(Shakespeare, I, 117).

**We need not wonder:** There is, perhaps, a hint of resigned
amusement in the following remarks.

**Hector quoting Aristotle:** See *Troilus and Cressida,* Act II,
scene ii (*Shakespeare,* IX, 58):
Hect. *Paris and Troilus, you have both said well;*
*And on the cause and question now in hand*
*Have gloz'd, but superficially; not much*
*Unlike young men, whom Aristotle thought*
*Unfit to hear moral philosophy.*
This seems to have been a famous example of Shakespeare's
neglect of chronology. It is mentioned by Dennis, *On the*
*Genius and Writings of Shakespear, Critical Works,* II,
8:

> *Our Business is here to shew, that* Shakespear
> *had no familiar Acquaintance with the* Graecian
> *and* Roman *Authors . . . How comes he to have*
> *been guilty of the grossest Faults in Chron-*
> *ology, and how come we to find out those Faults?*
> *In his Tragedy of* Troylus *and* Cressida, *he in-*
> *troduces* Hector *speaking of* Aristotle, *who was*
> *born a thousand Years after the Death of*
> Hector.

And by Pope, *Preface* (Shakespeare, I, 117):
> *Nothing is more likely than that those pal-*
> *pable blunders of Hector's quoting Aristotle,*
> *with others of that gross kind, sprung from*
> *the same root: it not being at all credible*
> *that these could be the errors of any man*
> *who had the least tincture of a school, or*
> *the least conversation with such as had.*

mythology: Cf. Johnson's note on *As You Like It*, Act III,
scene i, *Atalanta's better part: Shakespeare was no des-*
*picable mythologist, yet he seems here to have mistaken*
*some other character for that of Atalanta* (Shakespeare,
III, 322).

Arcadia: In his notes on *King Lear*, Johnson suggests that
Act IV, scene vi, where Gloucester enters with Edgar,
dressed as a peasant, together with *the stratagem by*
*which Gloucester is cured of his desperation . . . are*
*wholly borrowed from Sidney's* Arcadia (Shakespeare, IX,
516). In his final note to the play, Johnson stated that
he believed the episode of Edmund had been drawn from
Sidney. Sir Philip Sidney (1554-1586) composed the *Arcadia*
in the years 1577-80.

confounded the pastoral with the feudal times: By pastoral
times, Johnson means the times commonly referred to in
pastoral writings, such as the classical pastoral poetry
of Theocritus and Virgil. By feudal times, Johnson means
what we would call the middle ages.

the days of innocence, quiet, and security: In *The Rambler*,
No. 36, Johnson wrote of the value of pastoral poetry that
*It exhibits a life, to which we have been always accustomed*
*to associate peace, leisure, and innocence.*

. . . adventure: Further notes on this fault can be found
in the edition. See *Shakespeare*, V, 160; 213; 482.

In his comick scenes: In this, and in the following three
paragraphs, Johnson is describing faults typical of certain particular aspects of Shakespeare's art.

**reciprocations of smartness and contests of sarcasm:** On Congreve's comedies, Johnson wrote that *the contest of smartness is never intermitted* (*Congreve, Lives*, II, 228).

**jests are commonly gross:** Cf. Johnson's note on Act V, scene ii of *Henry V*:

> Burg. *Pardon the frankness of my mirth, if I answer you for that. If you would conjure in her, you must make a circle: if conjure up love in her in his true likeness, he must appear naked, and blind: Can you blame her then, being a maid yet rosy'd over with the virgin crimson of modesty, if she deny the appearance of a naked blind boy in her naked seeing self? It were, my Lord, a hard condition for a man to consign to.*

Johnson comments: *We have here but a mean dialogue for princes; the merriment is very gross, and the sentiments are very worthless* (See *Shakespeare*, VI, 167).

**effusions of passion:** Cf. Johnson's note on *Cymbeline*, Act V, scene i, the speech beginning *Yea, bloody cloth . . . .*: *This is a soliloquy of nature, uttered when the effervescence of a mind agitated and perturbed spontaneously and inadvertently discharges itself in words. The speech, throughout all its tenor, if the last conceit be excepted, seems to issue warm from the heart* (*Shakespeare*, IX, 303).

**exigence:** The need of the moment; necessity. Cf. Johnson's note on Act IV, scene ii of *King John*:

> K. John. *Hadst thou but shook thy head, or made a pause, When I spake darkly what I purposed; Or turn'd an eye of doubt upon my face; Or bid me tell my tale in express words; Deep shame had struck me dumb, made me break off, And those thy fears might have wrought fears in me.*

Johnson commented: *These reproaches vented against Hubert are not the words of art of policy, but the eruptions of a mind swelling with consciousness of a crime, and desirous of discharging its misery on another.* (*Shakespeare*, V, 97).

**have much delicacy:** Not only in sexual matters.

PAGE 17.


**clowns:** I.e. rustics.  In the *Folio* many characters are
actually referred to as clowns.

**appearance of refined manners:** On the standard for refinement in comedy, see Boileau, *Art of Poetry*, tr. Dryden
and Soame, lines 832-34: *Yet may he not, as on a Market-
place, / With Baudy Jests amuse the Populace: / With well-
bred Conversation you must Please* . . . .

**not very elegant:** Cf. Johnson's note on *Romeo and Juliet*:
*Here is one of the few attempts of Shakespeare to exhibit
the conversation of gentlemen, to represent the airy
sprightliness of juvenile elegance* (Shakespeare, X, 166).

**some modes of gaiety preferable to others:** Rymer/Rapin,
*Reflections on Aristotle*, pp.125-26, distinguished as a
requisite of comedy: . . . *that* gayetie *which can sustain
the delicacy of his* (the personage's) *character, without
falling into* coldness, *nor into* buffoonery: *that* fine
raillery, *which is the flower of wit, is the Talent which*
Comedy *demands.*
For "gaiety" Johnson gave in his *Dictionary*: *Cheerful-
ness; airiness; merriment; acts of juvenile pleasure.*
Johnson admired writers who exhibited modes of gaiety.
See, for example, *Life of Cowley*, *Lives*, I, 37: *Such
gaiety of fancy . . . and such a dance of words, it is
vain to expect except from Cowley.*

**chuse the best:** In *As You Like It*, Johnson noted: *The comick
dialogue is very sprightly, with less mixture of low buffoonery than in some other plays* (Shakespeare, III, 388).

**striking and energetick:** E.g. the speech of Leontes, *The
Winter's Tale*, Act III, scene ii:
> *The vehement retraction of Leontes, ac-
> companied with the confession of more crimes
> than he was suspected of, is agreeable to our
> daily experience of the vicissitudes of vio-
> lent tempers, and the eruptions of minds op-
> pressed with guilt* (Johnson, *Shakespeare*,
> IV, 350).

**solicits his invention:** For "solicits" Johnson gave in his
*Dictionary*: *To disturb; to disquiet.*

**strains his faculties:** Cf. Joseph Warton, *The Adventurer*,
No. 122, on *King Lear*: . . . *some passages that are too
turgid and full of strained metaphors; are faults which
the warmest admirers of Shakespeare will find it difficult
to excise.*

**throes:** Violent convulsions or struggles preceding or accompanying the birth or bringing forth. Johnson has just been describing the faults of negligence. He comes now to the faults produced by an excess of effort.

**tumour:** Johnson defined this word in his *Dictionary* as: *Affected pomp; false magnificence, puffy grandeur; swelling mien; unsubstantiated greatness.* Cf. Johnson's remark on *Antony and Cleopatra* that *the most tumid speech in the play is that which Caesar makes to Octavia.* Johnson probably means the following speech from Act III, scene vi:

> The wife of Antony
> Should have an army for an usher, and
> The neighs of horse to tell of her approach,
> Long ere she did appear: the trees by the way,
> Should have borne men; and expectation fainted,
> Longing for what it had not: nay, the dust
> Should have ascended to the roof of heaven,
> Rais'd by your populous troops: But you are come
> A market-maid to Rome; and have prevented
> The ostentation of our love, which, left unshewn,
> Is often left unlov'd: we should have met you
> By sea, and land; supplying every stage
> With an augmented greeting . . .
>          . . . He hath give his empire
> Up to a whore; who now are levying
> The kings o'the earth for war: he hath assembled
> Bocchus, the king of Libya; Archelaus,
> Of Cappadocia; Philadelphos, king
> Of Paphlagonia; the Thracian king, Adallas;
> King Malchus of Arabia; king of Pont;
> Herod of Jewry; Mithridates, king
> Of Comagene; Polemon and Amintas,
> The kings of Mede, and Lycaonia,
> With a more larger list of scepters.

**meanness:** *Love's Labour's Lost*, Johnson notes, has *many passages mean, childish, and vulgar.* An example of Shakespeare having produced meanness where he intended dignity can, according to Johnson, be found in the Prologue to *Henry V*:

> Nothing shews more evidently the power of custom over language, than that the frequent use of calling a circle an "O" could so much hide the meanness of the metaphor from Shakespeare, that he has used it many times where he makes his most eager attempts at dignity of stile (See *Shakespeare*, III, 522; VI, iv).

**tediousness:** According to Johnson *the most fatal of all faults*:

> . . . *negligencies or errors are single and local, but tediousness pervades the whole; other faults are censured and forgotten, but the power of tediousness propagates itself. He that is weary the first hour, is more weary the second; as bodies forced into motion, contrary to their tendency, pass more and more slowly through every successive interval of space* (Prior, *Lives*, II, 206).

Of Othello's declaration of marriage to Desdemona, Rymer had complained: *Never, sure, was* form of pleading *so tedious and so heavy, as this whole Scene, and midnight entertainment* (See *Short View on Tragedy*, Ch. VII, *Critical Works*, pp.138-39).

**. . . and obscurity:** Johnson's main effort as an editor of the plays was dedicated to untangling obscure phrases, lines, and speeches.

**narration:** E.g. the beginning of *Henry IV Part II*; the reconciliation of Perdita in *The Winter's Tale*; the last Act of *Cymbeline*; the players' narrative of Hecuba in *Hamlet*; the Prologue to *Troilus and Cressida*; Othello's account of his old campaigns. See *Shakespeare*, V, 441-52; IV 423-28; IX, 303ff.; X, 263-66; IX, 3-5; X, 457-61.

**disproportionate:** Johnson wrote of the Friar's long narrative in Act V, scene iii of *Romeo and Juliet*: *It is much to be lamented, that the poet did not conclude the dialogue with the action, and avoid a narrative of events which the audience already knew* (*Shakespeare*, X, 163).

**declamations:** Johnson glossed "declamation" in his *Dictionary* as: *A discourse addressed to the passions; an harangue; a set speech; a piece of rhetoric.*

**set speeches:** See, for example, the famous speech of Ulysses in Act I, scene iii of *Troilus and Cressida*; the speeches of Bolingbroke in Act I, scene i of *Richard II*; the last speech in *Macbeth*, by Malcolm. See *Shakespeare*, IX, 32-35; V, 133ff.; IV, 610.

**weak:** Cf. *A Word with Dr. Johnson*, *Hood's Magazine*, VI (1846), 117:

> *The speech of Brutus to the people, which precedes that of Antony, has been censured by many as "puerile and weak"; (if our memory serve us rightly, it is so characterized by Godwin) and it is very probable that Johnson might have had this*

> *particular speech in view, when he object-*
> *ed to the declamations that they "are*
> *commonly cold and weak".*

## PAGE 18

**instead of inquiring what the occasion demanded:** What
was really required, instead of declamation, at that
moment in the play. In his *Lives*, Johnson wrote that the
metaphysical poets *never enquired what, on any occasion,*
*they should have said or done.* The great excellence of
Milton, he claimed, was amplitude, *and he expands the*
*adventitious image beyond the dimensions which the*
*occasion required.* Of Addison, Johnson wrote that
*The abundance of his own mind left him little indeed*
*of adventitious sentiments; his wit always could suggest*
*what the occasion demanded.* Johnson's comment on the
*Old Bachelor* of Congreve was that *The dialogue is one*
*constant reciprocation of conceits, or clash of wit,*
*in which nothing flows necessarily from the occasion,*
*or is dictated by nature* (Cowley, Milton, Addison,
Congreve, *Lives*, I, 20 and 179; II, 121 and 216).

**resentment of his reader:** Now and again in his notes,
Johnson drew attention to speeches where Shakespeare
had seized on opportunities of unnecessary amplification.
See, for example, his comment on a speech by King Henry
in Act IV, scene iii of *Henry V: This speech, like many*
*others of the declamatory kind, is too long. Had it*
*been contracted to about half the number of lines, it*
*might have gained force, and lost none of the sentiments*
(*Shakespeare*, VI, 125).
　　A case of Shakespeare, in Johnson's opinion, failing
sufficiently to enquire what the occasion demanded can
be found in Act III, scene iv of *Macbeth*, in the speech
of Lady Macbeth:
> 　　　　　　　　　　*O proper stuff!*
> *This is the very painting of your fear:*
> *This is the air-drawn-dagger, which, you said,*
> *Led you to Duncan. Oh, these flaws, and starts,*
> *(Impostors to true fear), would well become*
> *A woman's story, at a winter's fire,*
> *Authoriz'd by her grandam. Shame itself!*
> *Why do you make such faces? When all's done,*
> *You look but on a stool.*

In Johnson's view: *This speech is rather too long for the*
*circumstances in which it is spoken. It had begun better*
*at, "Shame itself!"* (See *Shakespeare*, IV, 540-41).

sentiment: A thought or expression of feeling. Cf.
Johnson's comment on the poet Prior, who had *no careless
lines, or entangled sentiments; his words are nicely
selected, and his thoughts fully expanded.* In Pomfret's
*Choice: the mind is not oppressed with ponderous or
entangled with intricate sentiment* (*Prior, Pomfret,
Lives*, II, 208; I, 302).

if it continues stubborn: Perhaps by analogy with the task
of the blacksmith. Commenting on Dryden's verses on
Clarendon, Johnson, after quoting some lines, remarked
that *after this he did not often bring upon his anvil
such stubborn and unmalleable thoughts* (*Dryden, Lives,*
I, 429).

evolved: For "evolve" Johnson gave in his *Dictionary*:
*To unfold; to disentangle.* An example of an "unweildy
sentiment" having been "evolved" by Johnson occurs in
his note to the speech of Troilus to Hector in *Troilus
and Cressida,* Act II, scene i, where the two heroes are
debating the return of Helen:
> *If you'll avouch, 'twas wisdom Paris went,*
> *(As you must needs, for you all cry'd - Go, go)*
> *If you'll confess, he brought home noble prize,*
> *(As you must need, for you all clapp'd your hands,*
> *and cry'd - Inestimable!) why do you now*
> *The issue of your proper wisdoms rate;*
> *And do a deed that fortune never did*

Johnson commented:
> *If I understand this passage, the meaning
> is: 'Why do you, by assuming the determina-
> tion of your wisdoms, degrade Helen, whom
> fortune has not yet deprived of her value,
> or against whom, as the wife of Paris, for-
> tune has not in this war so declared, as to
> make us value her less?' This is very harsh,
> and much strained* (*Shakespeare*, IX, 55).

those who have more leisure to bestow on it: I.e. the
readers, especially the editors, of the plays. Johnson
is thinking of his own efforts to "evolve" and disentangle
Shakespeare's unwieldy sentiments in the course of editing the plays.
The Yale editor cites John Upton, *Critical Observations
on Shakespear*, 2nd ed. (1748), p.128:
> *Shakespeare labouring with a multiplicity of
> sublime ideas often gives himself not time
> to be delivered of them by the rules of* slow-
> *endeavouring-art: hence he crowds various
> figures together, and metaphor upon metaphor;
> and runs the hazard of far-fetched expressions,
> whilst intent on nobler ideas he condescends
> not to grammatical niceties: here the audience*

*are to accompany the poet in his con-*
*ceptions, and to supply what he has*
*sketched out for them.*
As an example, Upton cited Hamlet speaking to his
father's ghost: *Oh! answer me, / Let me not burst in*
*ignorance; but tell / Why thy canoniz'd bones, hearsed*
*in death, / Have burst their cearments.*

**language is intricate:** Cf. Johnson's note on *Cymbeline,*
Act I, scene v, Postumus: *rather shunned to go even*
*with what I heard, &c.:*
   *This is expressed with a kind of fantastical*
   *perplexity. He means, I was then willing to*
   *take for my direction the experience of others,*
   *more than such intelligence as I had gathered*
   *for myself* (Shakespeare, IX, 191).

**great:** Sublime or noble, in the sense of "great" employed
by Johnson in his *Life of Cowley*: *Sublimity is produced*
*by aggregation, and littleness by dispersion. Great*
*thoughts are always general . . .* (Cowley, Lives, I,
21).

**trivial sentiments and vulgar ideas:** Cf. Johnson's note
on *Much Ado About Nothing,* Act I, scene i: *to tell us,*
*Cupid is a good hare-finder, &c.:*
   *I know not whether I conceive the jest here*
   *intended. Claudio hints his love of Hero.*
   *Benedick asks whether he is serious, or*
   *whether he only means to jest, and tell them*
   *that* Cupid is a good hare-finder, and Vulcan
   a rare carpenter. *A man praising a pretty*
   *lady in jest, may shew the quick sight of*
   *Cupid, but what has it to do with the car-*
   *pentry of Vulcan? Perhaps the thought lies*
   *no deeper than this,* Do you mean to tell us
   as new what we all know already? (Shakespeare,
   II, 262).

**disappoint the attention:** Cf. Johnson's note on *Love's*
*Labour's Lost,* Act I, scene i, Biron: *Doth falsly*
*blind: The whole sense of this gingling declamation is*
*only this, that* a man by too close study may read himself blind, *which might have been told with less obscur-*
*ity in fewer words* (Shakespeare, II, 379).

**sonorous:** Cf. Johnson's note on *The Winter's Tale,* Act I,
scene ii, Camillo: *Whereof the execution did cry out /*
*Against the non-performance,* where he comments: *This*
*is one of the expressions by which Shakespeare too fre-*
*quently clouds his meaning. This sounding phrase means,*

*I think, no more than* a thing necessary to be done
(*Shakespeare*, IV, 307).
       Cf. also, on *Romeo and Juliet*, Act I, scene ii, Capulet:
*do lusty young men feel*, where he notes: *To say, and to
say in pompous words, that a* young man shall feel *as much
in an assembly of beauties,* as young men feel in the
month of April, *is surely to waste sound upon a very
poor sentiment* (*Shakespeare* , X, 21).

tender emotions: Johnson criticized Juliet's equivocations
    in Act II, scene v of *Romeo and Juliet* as *rather too art-
    ful for a mind disturbed by the loss of a new lover*:
       La. Cap. (*within*) *Ho, daughter! Are you up?*
       Jul. *Who is't that calls- is it my lady mother?*
       *Is she not down so late, or up so early?*
       *What unaccustom'd cause procures her hither?*

                (Enter Lady Capulet)

       La. Cap. *Why, how now, Juliet?*
       Jul. *Madam, I am not well.*
       La. Cap. *Evermore weeping for your cousin's death?*
       *What, wilt thou wash him from his grave with tears?*
       *And if thou could'st, thou could'st not make him live;*
       *Therefore, have done: Some grief shews much of love;*
       *But much of grief shews still some want of wit.*
       Jul. *Yet let me weep for such a feeling loss.*
       La. Cap. *So shall you feel the loss, but not the friend
       Which you weep for.*
       Jul.                 *Feeling so the loss,
       I cannot choose but ever weep the friend.*
       La. Cap. *Well, girl, thou weep'st not so much for his
                                               death,*
       *As that the villain lives which slaughter'd him.*
       Jul. *What villain, madam?*
       La. Cap. *That same villain, Romeo.*
       Jul. *Villain and he are many miles asunder.
       God pardon him! I do, with all my heart;
       And yet no man, like he, doth grieve my heart.*

fall of greatness: Cf. Johnson's note on a speech by King
    Richard in Act III, scene iii of *Richard II*:
       *Or shall we play the wantons with our woes,
       And make some pretty match with shedding tears?
       As thus:- To drop them still upon one place,
       'Till they have fretted us a pair of graves
       Within the earth; and therein laid,* There lies
       Two kinsmen, digg'd their graves with weeping eyes?
       *Would not this ill do well?*
    Johnson commented:
       *Shakespeare is very apt to deviate from the
       pathetic to the* ridiculous. *Had the speech
       of Richard ended at this line* (i.e. 14 lines
       earlier) *it had exhibited the natural language*

> *of submissive misery, conforming its in-*
> *tention to the present fortune, and calmly*
> *ending its purposes in death* (See *Shakespeare*,
> V, 204).

crosses: In his *Dictionary*, Johnson gives: *Any thing*
*that thwarts or obstructs; misfortune; hindrance; vex-*
*ation; opposition; misadventure; trial of patience.*

pathetick: Inspiring pathos: Dryden, wrote Johnson, *is*
*. . . with all his variety of excellence, not often*
*pathetick.* In *Paradise Lost*, meanwhile, *there is . . .*
*little opportunity for the pathetick* (*Dryden, Milton,*
*Lives*, I, 458 and 180).
    Quoting Dryden's *Preface to Fables* (1700) in his final
note to *Romeo and Juliet*, Johnson complained of this
play that Shakespeare's *pathetic strains are always*
*polluted with some unexpected depravations. His persons,*
*however distressed,* have a conceit left them in their
misery, a miserable conceit (*Shakespeare*, X, 166).

contemptible: Cf. Johnson's note on *Romeo and Juliet*, Act
II, scene iv, where Mercutio's speech is censured as
*a series of quibbles unworthy of explanation, which he*
*who does not understand, needs not lament his ignorance*
(*Shakespeare*, X, 74).

equivocation: Using a word in more than one sense; a pun.
Hazlitt, (*Characters, Works*, IV, 277) wrote that *Shakes-*
*peare's fondness for the ludicrous sometimes led to*
*faults in his tragedies,* but that he has *made us amends*
by the character of Falstaff.

he counteracts himself: Cf. *The Rambler*, No. 156:
*Perhaps the effects even of Shakespeare's*
*poetry might have been yet greater, had he*
*not counter-acted himself; and we might*
*have been more interested in the distresses*
*of his heroes had we not been so fre-*
*quently diverted by the jokes of his buffoons.*

terror and pity: The emotions Aristotle said were the products of tragedy.

blasted: Blighted, made to wither.

sudden frigidity: Cf. Johnson's comments on Cowley's poem
on the death of Hervey: *. . . when he wishes to make us*
*weep, he forgets to weep himself, and diverts his sorrow*
*by imagining how his crown of bays, if he had it, would*
*crackle in the fire* (*Cowley, Lives*, I, 37).

PAGE 19


A quibble: *Dict.*: *A low conceit depending on the sound.*

luminous vapours: Ground fog which glows in the dark,
   particularly common over marshy, or boggy, ground.

dignity: Cf. Johnson's note on Enobarbus's: *Throw my
   heart / Against the flint and hardness of my fault; /
   Which, being dried with grief, will break to powder, /
   And finish all foul thoughts.* He writes: *The pathetick
   of Shakespeare too often ends in the ridiculous. It is
   painful to find the gloomy dignity of this noble scene
   destroyed by the intrusion of a conceit so far-fetched
   and unaffecting* (Shakespeare, VIII, 260).

amusing attention . . . or enchaining it . . .: Occupying
   attention. Johnson wrote that Milton was indebted to
   Homer's epic for *all the stratagems that surprise and
   enchain attention* (*Milton, Lives*, I, 194).

golden apple: A reference to the story of Atalanta and
   Hippomenes. Hippomenes raced with Atalanta for her
   hand in marriage, and beat her by dropping golden apples
   in her path.

career: *Dict.*: *Full speed; swift motion.*

such delight: Cf. *ante*, p.12, where Johnson is writing
   of Shakespeare's "disposition" for comedy.

purchase it: Cf. Johnson's note on *Much Ado About Nothing*,
   Act II, scene i, Leonata: *Well then, &c.*:
      *Of the next two speeches Dr. Warburton says,
      All this impious nonsense thrown to the bot-
      tom, is the players', and foisted in without
      rhyme or reason. He therefore puts them in
      the margin. They do not deserve indeed so
      honourable a place, yet I am afraid they are
      too much in the manner of our authour, who
      is sometimes trying to purchase merriment
      at too dear a rate* (Shakespeare, II, 274).

lost the world: Dryden's version of *Antony and Cleopatra*
   was entitled *All for Love, or the World Well Lost* (1678).

content to lose it: George Colman, *The St. James's
   Chronicle* (Oct. 1765), objected thus:
      *Has not Mr. J. been as culpably fond of
      writing upon Quibble, as Shakespeare in
      persuing it? and is not this laboured*

> *Paragraph upon Quibble as puerile as a*
> *Remnant of a School-boy's Declamation?*
> *Besides, was it not a Vice common to*
> *all the Writers of that Age?*

  For further examples of Johnson's censure of quibbles
  see his comments on *Othello*, Act V, scene ii; *Cymbeline*,
  Act V, scene iv; *Richard III*, Act V, scene iii; *Macbeth*,
  Act II, scene ii; *Henry VIII*, Act III, scene i. (See
  *Shakespeare*, X, 603; IX, 314; VII, 154; IV, 504; VII,
  253).

**his neglect of the unities:** The topic of the unities had
  been discussed many times by predecessors of Johnson.
  Early protests against the unities had been made by
  Howard, Preface to *The Duke of Lerma* (1668); Sir William
  Temple, *Of Poetry*, 1690.  Nichol Smith cites Farquhar,
  *A Discourse upon Poetry* (1702); *Some Remarks on the
  Tragedy of Hamlet* (1736); Upton, *Critical Observations
  on Shakespeare* (1746, 1748), I, sect. ix; Fielding, *Tom
  Jones* prefatory Ch. of Bk. v; Kames, *Elements of Crit-
  icism* (1762), III, Ch. XXIII, *The Three Unities*.  Smith
  mentions that Hurd had defended Gothic "unity of design"
  in his *Letters on Chivalry and Romance* (1762), Letter
  VIII (in connection with Spenser's *Fairy Queen*).

**poets:** E.g. Sydney, Ben Jonson, Corneille, Dryden.


**PAGE 20.**


**any of their laws:** Cf. Thomas Percy's *we ought not to try
  Shakespear's Histories by the general laws of Tragedy
  or Comedy* (*Reliques of Ancient English Poetry* (1765), I,
  127).

**unity of action:** Johnson thought that Shakespeare had well
  enough preserved the unity of action in two plays with
  double plots, *The Taming of the Shrew* and *The Merchant
  of Venice* (See *Shakespeare*, III, 536 and 256).

**regularly unravelled:** Cf. Rymer/Rapin, *Reflections on
  Aristotle*, pp.127-28, on comedy:

> *But the most ordinary weakness of our Comedies
> is in the* unravelling; *scarce ever any succeed
> well in that, by the difficulty there is in
> untying happily that knot which had been tyed.
> It is easie to* wind up an intrigue, *'tis only
> the work of fancy; but the* unravelling *is the
> pure and perfect work of the judgement.  'Tis
> this that makes the success difficult, and if*

> *one would thereon make a little reflection,*
> *he might find that the most universal fault*
> *of* Comedies, *is, that the* Catastrophe *of it*
> *is not* Natural.
> Cf. also, Boileau, *Art of Poetry*, tr. Dryden and Soame,
> lines 835-37: . . . *your Intrigue unravel'd be with*
> *ease: / Your Action still should Reason's Rules obey, /*
> *Nor in an empty Scene may lose its way.*

**only to discover it:** I.e. Shakespeare does not generally
keep the true nature of characters and their motivations
deliberately concealed only to reveal them at the last
moment. A possible exception is *The Comedy of Errors*.

**what Aristotle requires:** Cf. Thomas Twining's commentary
on the *Poetics* of Aristotle (1789), pp.226-30:
> *Every one, who knows how much stress has been*
> *laid by modern criticks on the* three dramatic
> unities, *and happens not to be well acquainted*
> *with Aristotle's treatise on Poetry, would,*
> *I suppose, naturally take it for granted,*
> *that they are all explicitly laid down, and*
> *enforced by him, as essential and indispensable*
> *laws, in that famous code of dramatic criticism,*
> *But the fact is, that, of these three rules, the*
> *only one that can be called important - that of*
> *the* unity *of* action *- is, indeed, clearly laid*
> *down and explained, and, with great reason, con-*
> *sidered by him as indispensable . . .*
> *It would be inexcusable to quit this subject*
> *without reminding the reader, that the unities*
> *of time and place, were long ago powerfully,*
> *and, in my opinion, unanswerable combated, as*
> *far as their* principles *are concerned, by Dr.*
> *Johnson, in his preface to Shakespeare.*

**concatenated:** Chained together.

**no regard:** In *The Tempest*, the observation of the unities
of time and place was agreed by Johnson to be *an accident-*
*al effect of the story, not intended or regarded by our*
author. Of *Measure for Measure*, Johnson writes on this
subject only that *the unities of action and place are*
*sufficiently preserved.* In this play: *The time of the*
*action is indefinite* (See *Shakespeare*, I, 117; II, 161).

**time of Corneille:** See Corneille's *Discours de la Tragédie*
and *Discours des Trois Unités* (1660) for his arguments
in favour of the unities.

PAGE 21

The necessity of observing . . .: A literal translation
of this passage was made by Stendhal as part of a
defence of the freedom of romanticism.  See *Oeuvres
Complètes de Stendhal*, texte établi et annoté par
Pierre Martino (Paris: Champion, 1925), *Racine et
Shakspeare* (1823), I, 1-23.   The passage begins:
*La nécessité d'observer les unités de temps et de* lieu
*découle de la prétendue nécessité de rendre le drama
croyable* (*The necessity of observing the unities of time
and place follows from the alleged necessity of making
the drama credible*).

levied: Enlisted, enrolled.

The mind revolts from evident falsehood: A principle that
Johnson would in general support.  Here it is part of
the false logic that Johnson has set himself to oppose.

. . . reality: Most of the events mentioned in this paragraph (except, perhaps, the last), can be found in
Shakespeare.

necessarily: Johnson is following through in this paragraph the reasoning of the critics whose views he aims
ultimately to resist.

dragons of Medea: Medea's chariot was drawn by dragons.
Both Euripides and Seneca have plays on Medea.

Thebes . . . Persepolis: Not, apparently, a reference to
anything in Shakespeare, but settings for ancient plays:
e.g. Thebes for Sophocles' *Oedipus* and *Antigone*, Persepolis
for Aeschylus' *Persae*.

false: I.e. the critic's own arguments expose the falsity
of his assumptions.


PAGE 22

materiality: Representation upon the stage in material or
physical form, with actors, and the paraphernalia of
scenery and props.  Johnson's point is that no one who
sees the painted background of, say, a garden, on stage,
really believes that a garden is there.

credible: I.e. literally credible; does not mean "plausible".

The objection: In this paragraph, Johnson is describing
the state of delusion presupposed by a demand for unity
of time and place. He is not saying that we do not
respond imaginatively to what we see.

Delusion, if delusion be admitted; has no certain limitation: Johnson had touched on the same subject, though
with perhaps less confidence in his position, in *The
Rambler*, No. 156. There he had said that delusion
*must* be admitted:
> *Probability requires that the time of action
> should approach somewhat nearly to that of
> exhibition, and those plays will always be
> thought most happily conducted which croud
> the greatest variety in the least space. But
> since it will frequently happen that some de-
> lusion must be admitted, I know not where the
> limits of imagination can be fixed. It is
> rarely observed that minds not prepossessed
> by mechanical criticism feel any offence from
> the extension of the intervals between the
> acts; nor can I conceive it absurd or im-
> possible, that he who can multiply three hours
> into twelve or twenty-four, might image with
> equal ease a greater number.*

old acquaintance: In *The Rambler*, No. 200, which is supposed
to be a satire on Garrick, Asper, the imaginary corres-
pondent, describes a visit to his "old acquaintance"
Prospero. In *Henry IV Part I*, Prince Hal calls Falstaff
his "old acquaintance" when standing over what he believes
to be his dead body (Act V, scene iv; see *Shakespeare*,
V, 420).

room illuminated with candles: Presumably, Johnson is
thinking of the whole theatre illuminated with candles,
not just that part behind the proscenium arch.

bank of Granicus: The Yale editor points out that Alexander
fought a famous battle near the river Granicus, and
that Johnson may have been thinking of any play about
Alexander or Pompey; *Lee's* Rival Queens *mentions the
Granicus, and Chapman's* Wars of Caesar and Pompey *has
one scene on the plain of Pharsalia.*

of empyrean poetry: The highest heavenly sphere of poetry.

exstasy: Here meaning insensibility to surrounding objects.

count the clock: Tell the time. Johnson's point is that
having once assumed a delusion, the critics cannot at the
same moment insist that there is also a rigid attention
to time.

calenture: *Dict.*: *A distemper peculiar to sailors in*
  *hot climates; wherein they imagine the sea to be green*
  *fields, and will throw themselves into it, if not*
  *restrained.*

players are only players: In the 1803 *Shakespeare*, I,
  269. George Steevens compares Dryden in the Epistle
  Dedicatory to *Love Triumphant* (1693-94). See *The*
  *Works of John Dryden*, ed. Walter Scott, rev. G. Saintsbury
  (Edinburgh, 1884), VIII, 375:
  > *. . . it is an original absurdity for the*
  > *audience to suppose themselves to be in any*
  > *other place than in the very theatre in which*
  > *they sit, which is neither chamber, nor gar-*
  > *den, nor yet a public place of any business,*
  > *but that of the representation.*

recited: Spoken, or acted. Johnson is not referring to
  "recitation" in the modern sense of the term.


PAGE 23


supposition: A term from scholastic logic; something held
  to be true and taken as the basis of an argument.

real and poetical duration: The time elapsed during the
  actual events represented by the lines and the time
  taken to play or speak the lines on stage.


PAGE 24


evils to which we ourselves may be exposed: The remarks
  in this paragraph represent a refinement of the following
  comments from *The Rambler*, No. 60:
  > *All joy and sorrow for the happiness or*
  > *calamities of others is produced by an act*
  > *of the imagination that realises the event*
  > *however fictitious, or approximates it how-*
  > *ever remote, by placing us, for a time, in*
  > *the condition of him whose fortune we con-*
  > *template; so that we feel, while the dec-*
  > *eption lasts, whatever motions would be*
  > *excited by the same good or evil happening*
  > *to ourselves.*
  > *Our passions are therefore more strongly*
  > *moved, in proportion as we can more readily*

> *adopt the pains or pleasures proposed to*
> *our minds, by recognizing them as once our*
> *own, or considering them as naturally in-*
> *cident to our state of life.*

**as a mother weeps over her babe:** Is Johnson
thinking of the story of the last parting of Hector
and Andromache from the sixth book of the *Iliad* of
Homer?

**delight of tragedy proceeds from our consciousness of**
**fiction:** Cf. Dryden, *Essay on Dramatick Poesy*:
*When we see death represented, we are*
*convinced it is but fiction; but when we*
*hear it related, our eyes (the strongest*
*witnesses) are wanting, which might have*
*undeceived us, and we are willing to fav-*
*our the sleight when the poet does not too*
*grossly impose on us* (*Essays*, I, 51).

**recreated:** Refreshed, or, perhaps, relieved. In the
*Dictionary*, Johnson gave *To delight; to gratify.*

**agitated:** In his *Dictionary*, Johnson gave for "to agitate":
*To effect with perturbation; as, the mind of man is*
agitated *by various passions.*

**concomitants:** Attendant circumstances, scenery, props,
etc.

**Mithridates and Lucullus are before us:** The Yale editor
suggests that this may be an imperfect recollection of
Lee's *Mithridates* (1667/8), or, that Johnson may have
another play in mind.

**obsequious to :** I.e. compliant with. Now a very strong
word, used with pejorative implication, but neutral
in Johnson.

**the imagination:** For Johnson, "imagination" was necessary
both to the production and to the enjoyment of great
poetry. In his *Life of Milton* he wrote that: *Poetry*
*is the art of uniting pleasure with truth, by calling*
*imagination to the help of reason* (*Lives*, I, 170). In
*The Rambler*, No. 125, he defined "imagination" as *a*
*licentious and vagrant faculty, unsusceptible of limit-*
*ation, and impatient of restraint.* Ch. XLIV of *Rasselas*,
however, is devoted to *The Dangerous Prevalence of*
*Imagination.*

**. . . we only see their imitation:** Of Rowe, Johnson wrote
that:
> *In the construction of his dramas, there is*

*not much art; he is not a nice observer of
the Unities. He extends time and varies place
as his convenience requires. To vary place
is not in my opinion any violation of Nature,
if the change be made between the acts; for
it is no less easy for the spectator to suppose himself at Athens in the second act, than
at Thebes in the first; but to change the scene,
as is done by Rowe, in the middle of an act, is
to add more acts to the play, since an act is so
much of the business as is transacted without
interruption   (Rowe, Lives, II, 75-76).*
Johnson replied as follows to Dennis's complaints concerning the action and plan of Addison's *Cato*:
*Every critical reader must remark, that
Addison has, with a scrupulosity almost unexampled on the English stage, confined
himself in time to a single day, and in
place to rigorous unity. The scene never
changes, and the whole action of the play
passes in the great hall of Cato's house
at Utica. Much therefore is done in the
hall, for which any other place had been
more fit; and this impropriety affords
Dennis many hints of merriment, and opportunities of triumph (Addison, Lives,
II, 136).*

**Familiar comedy:** E.g. *The Merry Wives of Windsor.* The
language in this play Johnson described as *distorted
and depraved by provincial or foreign pronunciation* so
that *its success must be derived almost wholly from the
players, but its power in a skilful mouth, even he that
despises it, is unable to resist* (Shakespeare, I, 372).

**on the theatre:** Cf. Johnson's note to *Henry V*, Act III,
scene vi, on the persistent joke over Bardolph's red
face: *The conception is very cold to the solitary
reader, though it may be somewhat invigorated by the
exhibition on the stage. This poet is always more careful about the present than the future, about his audience
than his readers* (Shakespeare, VI, 90-91).

**in the page:** I.e. on the page.

**imperial tragedy:** The Yale editor cites a letter to Mrs.
Thrale: *The passions rise higher at domestick than at
imperial tragedies.* George Colman, *The St. James's
Chronicle* (Oct. 1765), noted that:
*Imperial Tragedy, such at least as is attend-
ed with these Effects, is of all the coldest;
and that Tragick Writer has but very ill
effected the Purposes of the Species of*

> *Drama, whose Productions are more power-*
> *ful in the Page, than on the Theatre.*
> *Cato, perhaps, may possess more Dignity*
> *and Force in the Closet; but we know*
> *that Richard, Lear, Othello, &c. have*
> *most Power on the Stage.*

**always less:** Perhaps because "imperial tragedy" depends
less upon the "concomitants" of the stage. By "imperial
tragedy" Johnson perhaps means tragedy concerned with
the rise and fall of empires, where the speeches, or
some of them, have the quality of declamations.

**The humour of Petruchio:** In *The Taming of the Shrew.*

**grimace:** Cf. Johnson's note on *Henry V*, Act III, scene
iv: *The scene is indeed mean enough, when it is read;*
*but the grimaces of the two French women, and the odd*
*accent with which they uttered the English, made it*
*divert upon the stage* (Shakespeare, VI, 77).

**what voice or gesture:** Cf. Charles Lamb, *On the Tragedies*
*of Shakespeare, considered with reference to their Fitness*
*for Stage Representation, Theatralia,* No. 1 (1812),
*Works*, ed. P. Fitzgerald (London: Moxon, 1876), IV,
205-06, on *King Lear*:
> *. . . the Lear of Shakespeare cannot be*
> *acted. The contemptible machinery by which*
> *they mimic the storm which he goes out in,*
> *is not more inadequate to represent the*
> *horrors of the real elements, than any actor*
> *can be to represent Lear . . . The greatness*
> *of Lear is not in corporal dimension, but*
> *in intellectual . . . On the stage we see*
> *nothing but corporal infirmities and weak-*
> *ness, the impotence of rage. While we read*
> *it, we see not Lear, but we are Lear . . .*
> *What have looks, or tones, to do with that*
> *sublime identification of his age with that*
> *of the* heavens *themselves, when, in his re-*
> *proaches to them for conniving at the injus-*
> *tice of his children, he reminds them that*
> *'they themselves are old?' What gesture shall*
> *we appropriate to this? What has the voice*
> *or the eye to do with such things?.*

**soliloquy:** Addison's *Cato*, Act V, scene i. In *The Idler*,
No. 77 (1759), Johnson had earlier described it as *at*
*once easy and sublime* and he quoted lines 7-9 and 15-
18:
> *'Tis the Divinity that stirs within us;*
> *'Tis heav'n itself that points out an hereafter,*
> *And intimates eternity to man.*
> *. . . If there's a pow'r above us,*
> *And that there is all nature cries aloud*

> *Thro' all her works, he must delight in virtue,*
> *And that which he delights in must be happy.*


## PAGE 25


**A play read, affects the mind like a play acted:** Johnson
is saying that a play affects the mind like all other
imaginative literature, and obeys the same general
laws, with or without a performance on the stage.

**revolutions:** Turns of fortune, not as in The French
Revolution.

**rules merely positive:** Rules arbitrarily or artificially
instituted. In the Introduction to his *Cursory Remarks
on Tragedy* (1772), Edward Taylor attacked fiercely
Johnson's account of Shakespeare's attitude to the
unities of time and place, and asserted what was in his
opinion the value of rules. Taylor complained that
Johnson's criticism was at variance with the injunctions
of Boileau, and of Pope, who he cited, and his attempt
to refute Johnson recalls Rymer/Rapin: *Nor are we to
suppose that rules are an unnecessary prescription, or
that they reduce Nature into method more than is con-
venient or fit.* Rymer/Rapin, *Reflections on Aristotle*,
p.16, had written that though rules were necessary,
they were made *only to reduce Nature into Method.* This
remark was cited approvingly by Dryden, *Essays*, I, 260,
and adapted by Pope, *Essay on Criticism*, ll. 88-89: *Those
RULES of old* discover'd, *not* devis'd, */ Are* Nature
*still, but* Nature Methodiz'd.

**tolli:** Lucan, *Pharsalia*, III, 138-40. Nicholas Rowe's
*Pharsalia*, a translation much admired by Johnson, had
the following: *Nor time, nor chance breed such con-
fusions yet, / Nor are the mean so rais'd, nor sunk
the great; / But laws themselves would rather chuse
to be / Suppress'd by Caesar, than preserved by thee.*


## PAGE 26


**slightly:** I.e. slightingly.

**mere authority:** By authority alone. For "mere", Johnson
gave in his *Dictionary*: *This only.*

**orders of architecture:** There are five orders or types
in architecture, e.g. Doric. The point here is that
some of them will be too frail in a building designed
for defence.

**instruct life:** I.e. display life. To "instruct" here has
underlying it the Latin *instruere*, meaning to "draw
up" as a general draws up his troops for inspection
or for battle.

**deliberately:** With careful consideration. The first
edition of the *Preface* (1765) has *deliberatively
written*. Johnson's phrase was quoted by F.R. Leavis
as a motto to his *Great Tradition*.

**. . . empire:** The Yale editor points out that Johnson was
promptly taken to task for these remarks on dramatic
illusion by William Kenrick, *Monthly Review*, XXXIII
(1765), 298-301.
    However, the passage on the unities has been widely
admired. Hazlitt, *Lectures on the Comic Writers*, *Works*,
VI, 89, wrote of *all that Dr. Johnson has urged so
unanswerably on the subject*, *in his preface to Shakespeare*. Joseph Warton (Warton's *Pope*, IX, 433) also
described Johnson's account as *unanswerable*. Joseph
Towers, *An Essay on the Life, Character, and Writings
of Dr. Samuel Johnson* (1786), p.44 called Johnson's
comments *original, acute, and rational*. See also the
praise by Elizabeth Montague, *An Essay on the Writings
and Genius of Shakespear* (1769), p.15:
>    *Mr. Johnson, whose genius and learning
>    render him superior to a servile awe of
>    pedantic institutions, in his ingenious
>    preface to his edition of Shakespear has
>    greatly obviated all that can be objected
>    to our author's neglect of the unities of
>    time and place.*

For modern opinion on Johnson's passage on the unities,
see T.M. Raysor, *The Downfall of the Three Unities*, *MLN*,
62 (Jan. 1927), 1-9; J.H. Adler, *Johnson's "He that
Imagines This"*, *Shakespeare Quarterly*, 11 (Spring, 1960),
225-28; W.B. Fleischmann, *Shakespeare, Johnson and the
Unities*, *SP*, Extra Ser. No. 4 (Jan. 1967), 128-34.

**did not want:** I.e. did not lack.

**Venice . . . Cyprus:** A reference to *Othello*. Cf. Johnson's
note on this play: *Had the scene opened in Cyprus, and
the preceding incidents been occasionally related, there
had been little wanting to a drama of the most exact and
scrupulous regularity* (*Shakespeare*, X, 629).

Rymer had criticised Shakespeare for his shift of
scene in his *Short View of Tragedy*, Ch. VII.  Cf.
also Dennis, *To Judas Iscariot, Esq.*, *On the Degeneracy of the Publick Taste*, *Critical Works*, II, 168-
69:

> If a Modern Poet in one of his Tragedies
> should shew any Thing like Shakespear's
> Rambles, should introduce a Tragedy upon the
> Stage, which should begin in Europe and end
> in Asia, like the Moor of Venice, that Play
> would be exploded and damn'd with very great
> Damnation. But the Modern Spectators of
> Tragedies greatly esteem and are fond of
> those, in which the Unity of Place is
> preserv'd sometimes by whimsical comick
> Absurdities, and sometimes by dreadful and
> prodigious Extravagances.

Voltaire: See *Appel à toutes les nations*, *Oeuvres*, XXIV,
*Mélanges*, III, 208: *Avec quel plaisir nous aurions vu
la première scène à Venise, et la dernière en Chypre!*
(*With what pleasure would we have seen the first scene
at Venice and the last in Cyprus!*).  Voltaire is being
sarcastic, of course.

frighted: I.e. frightened.

those that maintain the contrary opinion: I.e. innumerable English and European critics from the time
of the Renaissance.


PAGE 27


heading the besiegers: *Aeneid*, II, 610-15.  Cf. Dryden's
translation, Bk. II, lines 837-39: *See* Jove *new Courage
to the foe supplies, / And Arms against the Town, the
partial Deities. / Haste hence, my Son; this fruitless
Labour end . . .*

rightly estimated: Cf. Johnson's note on *Macbeth*, Act I,
scene i: *In order to make a true estimate of the abilities and merit of a writer, it is always necessary to
examine the genius of his age, and the opinions of
his contemporaries* (*Shakespeare*, IV, 441).

state of the age in which he lived: In his *Life of Pope*,
Johnson wrote in connection with Homer that: *Time and
place will always enforce regard* (*Lives*, III, 238).  Cf.
also Pope, *Essay on Criticism*, lines 118-23:
> You *then whose Judgment the right Course would steer,*

> *Know well each ANCIENT'S proper* Character,
> *His* Fable, Subject, Scope, *in ev'ry Page,*
> Religion, Country, Genius *of his* Age:
> *Without all these at once before your Eyes,*
> Cavil *you may, but never* Criticize.

**particular opportunities:** Cf. *Life of Dryden,* where
Johnson claimed that: *To judge rightly of an author,*
*we must transport ourselves to his time, and examine*
*the wants of his contemporaries, and what were his*
*means of supplying them* (*Lives,* I, 411).

**silent reference of human works to human abilities:** I.e.
the reader cannot help but think on the author, and on
his particular circumstances, when reading the book.

**rate his native force:** In his *Dictionary,* Johnson defines "to rate" as: *To value at a certain price.* The
thought here is to do with how far great works assist
us in receiving an enlarged idea of human potential.

**without the use of iron:** Perhaps without the use of iron
implements to hew the stone; or Johnson may mean without the use of iron tie-rods, or braces, to strengthen
the structure.

**barbarity:** Barbarism, here with special reference to bar-
arity, or impurity, of speech. Cf. Johnson's defence
of Pope against the charge that his translation of
Homer was not Homeric:
> *There is a time when nations emerging from*
> *barbarity, and falling into regular sub-*
> *ordination, gain leisure to grow wise,*
> *and feel the shame of ignorance and the*
> *craving pain of unsatisfied curiosity.*
> *To this hunger of the mind plain sense*
> *is grateful; that which fills the void*
> *removes uneasiness, and to be free from*
> *pain for a while is pleasure; but repletion*
> *generates fastidiousness; a saturated in-*
> *tellect soon becomes luxurious, and know-*
> *ledge finds no willing reception till it*
> *is recommended by artificial diction* (*Life*
> *of Pope, Lives,* III, 239).

PAGE 28

**Lilly:** William Lilly, or Lily (1468?-1522), a famous
grammarian and one of the earliest Greek scholars in

England; he was on intimate terms with More, and a
friend of Linacre. Lilley's main contribution to the
cultivation of the learned languages was a Latin
grammar, designed as a standard work. This was issued
in 1542, and Shakespeare quotes from it in his plays.
Johnson refers to the publication in the notes on
*Twelfth Night*, *The Taming of the Shrew* and *Much Ado
About Nothing*, and calls it "the *Accidence*". See
*Shakespeare*, IV, 264; III, 422; II, 330.

**Linacre:** Thomas Linacre (1460?-1524), physician and
classical scholar, made scholarly expeditions to
Europe and returned to teach Greek at Oxford. He was
admired by Erasmus and is famous for his translation of
Greek texts into Latin.

**More:** Sir Thomas More (1478-1535), a one-time pupil of
Linacre, was appointed Lord Chancellor. His greatest
literary work was the *Utopia*, written in Latin and
completed in 1516.

**Pole:** Reginald Pole (1500-1558), a statesman, cardinal
and Archbishop of Canterbury. He was a pupil of Linacre
at Oxford and became Chancellor of Cambridge University.

**Cheke:** Sir John Cheke (1514-1557), Secretary of State
and one of the principal restorers of Greek learning
in England. He lectured in Greek at Cambridge and
became professor in 1540. He was a translator and
imitator of the classical authors and was responsible
for the reform of the Greek pronunciation in England.

**Gardiner:** Stephen Gardiner (1483-1555), became Bishop of
Winchester and Master of Trinity Hall, Cambridge: a
scholar and a statesman.

**Smith:** Sir Thomas Smith (1513-1577), a statesman, scholar
and author. A friend of Cheke, he lectured at Cambridge
and wrote tracts on the reform of the Greek and English
language.

**Clerk:** John Clerk (d. 1541), became Bishop of Bath and
Wells. He was Wolsey's chaplain and Dean of the King's
Chapel.

**Haddon:** Walter Haddon (1516-1572), attended Smith's Greek
lectures at Cambridge. A friend of Ascham, he became
Master of Trinity Hall and worked with Cheke on translations.

**Ascham:** Roger Ascham (1515-1568), a pupil of Cheke at
Cambridge, was a friend of Haddon and author of *The
Scholemaster, a plaine and perfite way of teaching
children to understand, write, and speake in Latin*

*tong* (1570). The work was edited by James Upton in
1711 and reissued in 1743. Johnson's *Life of Ascham*
was prefixed to James Bennet's 1771 edition of
Ascham's *English Works*. Boswell describes one of
Johnson's unfulfilled ambitions as being to write a:
...*History of the Revival of Learning in*
*Europe, containing an account of what-*
*ever contributed to the restoration of*
*literature; such as controversies, print-*
*ing, and destruction of the Greek empire,*
*the encouragement of great men, with the*
*lives of the most eminent patrons and most*
*eminent early professors of all kinds of*
*learning in different countries* (*Lives*,
IV, 382).

**Italian:** E.g. Petrarch, Ariosto and Tasso. Ariosto's
*Orlando Furioso* was published in English translation
by Sir John Harington in 1591. Tasso's *Gerusalemme*
*Liberata* was translated by Richard Carew in 1594 and by
Edward Fairfax in 1600.

**Spanish:** E.g. Lopez de Vega.

**valued for its rarity:** The accuracy of these general
comments is difficult to ascertain.

**proposed as its resemblance:** Since people could not,
at this time, understand the nature of things, they
could not judge of the truth to nature of a work of
literary art.

**The Death of Arthur:** Perhaps one of the *barbarous romances*
referred to by Johnson on page 7. Johnson is no doubt
thinking of several works in which the death of Arthur
is described, but he may have especially in mind the
*Morte D'arthur* of Sir Thomas Malory.

**Palmerin:** *Palmerin d'Oliva* and *Palmerin of England* were
prose romances translated from Spanish. Boswell, *Life*,
III, 2, records that in 1776 Johnson read *Il Palmerino*
*d'Inghilterra*, a romance praised by Cervantes; but did
*not like it much. He said he read it for the language*
*by way of preparation for his Italian expedition.*

**Guy of Warwick:** Written ca. fourteenth century.

PAGE 29

**unskilful:** I.e. ignorant.  See *ante*, p.105, note on "skill".

**novels:** Not in the modern sense, but as in the *novelle* of Boccaccio and Cinthio.  In his *Dictionary*, Johnson defined "nouvelle" as: *A small tale, generally of love.*

**supposed to be copied:** John Upton, Preface, *Critical Observations on Shakespeare*, 2nd ed., xvii, noted that: *'Tis well known that the* Coke's Tale of Gamelyn *was the original of the play called* As You Like It. Zachary Grey, *Critical, Historical, and Explanatory Notes on Shakespeare* (1754), I, 156-89 makes long quotations from the *Coke's Tale of Gamelyn in Chaucer* as a source of *As You Like It*.

**Chaucer's Gamelyn:** *Gamelyn* was commonly ascribed wrongly to Chaucer, as it was included in several manuscripts and printed versions of the *Canterbury Tales*.  In a note to Act I, scene i of *As You Like It*, Richard Farmer suggests that a source of the tale was *Lodge's Rosalynd*, or *Eupheus' Golden Legacye* (1590), (*Shakespeare*, III, 263).  It is reasonable therefore to assume that Johnson was aware of the mistaken ascription.

**old Mr. Cibber:** Colley Cibber (1671-1757).  The Yale editor notes that Cibber must have seen a later edition of, or variation on, the prose *History of Hamlet*, first published in 1608.

**English ballads:** The ballad of King Leire is quoted by Johnson in his edition.  The Yale editor records that Johnson's attention had been drawn to the ballad of King Liere by Mrs Lennox's *Shakespear Illustrated* (1753), III, 303-08, and that it continued to be printed in editions of Shakespeare by Steevens and Malone.

**dilated:** For "dilate" Johnson gave in his *Dictionary*: *To tell diffusely and copiously.*

**North:** Sir Thomas North's translation (from the French translation of Plutarch's Greek) was first published in 1579.

**fabulous:** Drawn from fables.

**attention:** Johnson defined "attention" in his *Dictionary* as *The act of attending or heeding; the act of bending the mind upon any thing.*  "Attention" is one of the key terms of Johnson's criticism.  In Butler's *Hudibras*, he

finds that *the scenes are too seldom changed, and the
attention is tired by long conversation.* Prior's
*Solomon,* too, *wanted that without which all others*
(excellencies) *are of small avail, the power of engaging attention and alluring curiosity.* The *Samson
Agonistes* of Milton *wants that power of attracting
attention which a well-connected plan produces;* while
in *Comus,* *the language is poetical and the sentiments are generous, but there is something wanting
to allure attention.* In his *Life of Dryden,* Johnson
stressed the importance of his standard: *Works of
imagination excel by their allurement and delight; by
their power of attracting and detaining attention*
(*Butler, Prior, Milton, Dryden, Lives,* I, 211; II, 206;
I, 189; I, 169 and 454).

Johnson discriminated between works which fixed the
attention, and those which relieved it. Replying to
the charge that Pope's poetry was too uniformly musical, he wrote that:
> *I suspect this objection to be cant of those
> who judge by principles rather than perception;
> and who would even themselves have less pleasure
> in his works if he had tried to relieve atten-
> tion by studied discords, or affected to break
> his lines and vary his pauses* (*Pope, Lives,*
> III, 248).

Of Cowley's *Davideis,* Johnson wrote that: *Attention
has no relief; the affections are never moved* (*Cowley,
Lives,* I, 55).

**rude:** Ignorant; raw; untaught.

**sentiment or argumentation:** Cf. Boileau, *Art of Poetry,*
tr. Dryden and Soame, Canto III, lines 445-454:
> *In all you Write, observe with Care and Art
> To move the Passions, and incline the Heart,
> If, in a labour'd Act, the pleasing Rage
> Cannot our Hopes and Fears by turns ingage,
> Nor in our Mind a feeling Pity raise;
> In vain with Learned Scenes you fill your Plays:
> Your cold Discourse can never move the mind
> Of a stern Critic, naturally unkind;
> Who, justly tir'd with your Pedantic flight,
> Or falls asleep, or censures all you Write,
> The Secret is, Attention first to gain;
> To move our Minds, and then to entertain.*

**marvellous:** A critical term in Johnson's day; usually
opposed to "the probable" and meaning all that excites
wonder, astonishment or surprise in a work of art.

those who despise it: That Johnson was himself a des-
piser of the "marvellous" we may gather from his note
on *Henry VIII*, Act IV, scene ii (*Shakespeare*, VII,
283). See *ante*, p.87: *hyperbolical joy and outrageous
sorrow*.


PAGE 30


strongly seized by the tragedies of Shakespeare: *Timon
of Athens*, wrote Johnson *strongly fastens on the attention of the reader*. In his notes on *King Lear* he
commented that: *There is no play which keeps the
attention so strongly fixed; which so much agitates
our passions and interests our curiosity* (See
*Shakespeare*, VIII, 458; IX, 565).

particular speeches: In his *Life of Butler*, Johnson
wrote of *Hudibras* that: *It is indeed much more easy to
form dialogues than to contrive adventures* (*Lives*,
I, 211).

anxious for the event: In his *Dictionary*, Johnson defined "event" as: *The consequence of an action; the
conclusion; the upshot*.

unquenchable curiosity: Johnson's pleasure in the curiosity excited by the best plays is apparent from his
note on *Coriolanus*, where, *the various revolutions of
the hero's fortune fill the mind with anxious curiosity*.
*Antony and Cleopatra*, he reported: . . . *keeps curiosity always busy, and the passions always interested.
The continual hurry of the action, the variety of incidents, and the quick succession of one personage to
another, call the mind forward without intermission
from the first act to the last* (*Shakespeare*, VII, 500;
VIII, 312).

read it through: Johnson is notorious for abandoning books
half way through.

shows: I.e. pageantry. A "show" is defined in the *Dictionary* as: *pomp; magnificent spectacle*.

of men: Cf. Wordsworth, Preface to *Lyrical Ballads* (1850),
*Prose Works*, 137, 132. See note on "selection" (*ante*, p.86).
Cf. Johnson's comparison between the language of poets
and the language of men with Hazlitt, *Lectures on the
English Poets*, *Works*, V, 50: *His characters are real
beings of flesh and blood; they speak like men, not like
authors*.

we see nothing that acquaints us . . . : Cf. Horace,
*Ars Poetica*, lines 180-87: *segnius irritant animos
demissa per aurem / quam quae sunt oculis subiecta fidel-
ibus et quae / ipse sibi tradit spectator* (*The mind is
stirred less by what enters through the ears than by
what lies before its faithful eyes, and by what the
spectator sees for himself*).
    Cf. also Rapin, *Comparison of Thucydides and Livy*:
    *'Tis by this Art he* (Thucydides) *engages
    and fixes the mind of his Reader upon the*
    action *he describes by so dazling Colours
    and lively Images representing to his Eyes,
    as it were, rather than his Understanding
    the things he speaks of, moving his Passion,
    raising his Attention, and filling him full
    of the matter he's expressing whilst the
    Mind* dragg'd *along with a pleasing kind of
    violence, lets go its hold, and is willing-
    ly carried away by the* Impetus *of the current
    for the better attending to the Impression.*
Hazlitt, *Lectures on the English Poets*, Works, V, 48,
had written of Shakespeare that: *In reading this author,
you do not merely learn what his characters say, - you
see their persons.*

propagates: *Dict.*: To spread by generation.


PAGE 31


genius: William Guthrie, *An Essay upon English Tragedy*
(1747), pp.25-26, contrasted the soliloquys of Cato and
Hamlet in terms similar to those in Johnson's comparison
of *Cato* and *Othello*:
    *For a particular instance of the difference
    betwixt the poet and the genius, let us go
    to two speeches upon the very same subject
    by those two famous soliloquys of Cato and
    Hamlet. The speech of the first is that of
    a scholar, a philosopher, and a man of vir-
    tue: all the sentiments of such a speech are
    to be acquired by instruction, by reading, by
    conversation; Cato talks the language of the
    porch and academy. Hamlet, on the other hand,
    speaks that of the human heart ready to enter
    upon a deep, a dreadful, a decisive act. His
    is the real language of mankind, of its high-
    est to its lowest order, from the king to the
    cottager; from the philosopher to the peasant.
    It is a language which a man may speak with-*

*cut learning; yet no learning can improve,*
*nor philosophy mend it. This cannot be said*
*of Cato's speech. It is dictated from the*
*head rather than the heart; by courage rather*
*than nature. It is the speech of pre-determined*
*resolution, and not of human infirmity; it is*
*the language of doubting; but of such doubts*
*as the speaker is prepared to cut asunder if*
*he cannot resolve them. The words of Cato are*
*not like those of Hamlet, the emanations of*
*the soul; they are therefore improper for a*
*soliloquy, where the discourse is supposed to*
*be held with the heart, that fountain of*
*truth.*

artificial: Cf. Joseph Warton, *The Enthusiast, or The*
*Lover of Nature: What are the lays of artful Addison, /*
*Coldly correct, to Shakespeare's warblings wild?*
(*Shakespeare*, I, 230).

sentiments: In his *Life of Addison*, Johnson called *Cato*
*rather a poem in dialogue than a drama, rather a suc-*
*cession of just sentiments in elegant language, than a*
*representation of natural affections, or any state*
*probable or possible in human life* (*Lives*, II, 132).

elevated: George Steevens cited Twining's commentary on
Aristotle's *Poetics* in a note to this passage of the
*Preface* printed in Malone's *Shakespeare*, I, 84:
    *What he has here said of the recent*
    *Tragedies of his time, may perhaps be*
    *said, in general, of our modern Trag-*
    *edies, compared with those of Shakespeare.*
    *The truth, I believe, is that the Tragedy*
    *of a refined and polished age will always*
    *have less ἦθος than that of ruder times,*
    *because it will have more dignity; more*
    *of the uniform and level elevation, which*
    *excludes strong traits of character, and*
    *the simple, unvarnished delineation of*
    *the manners.*

vibration to the heart: Rymer/Rapin, *Reflections on*
*Aristotle*, pp.118-19, wrote of Euripides: . . . *he*
*is not enough a religious observer of the decencies;*
*and by a too great affectation to be moral and sentent-*
*ious, he is not so ardent and passionate as he ought to*
*be; for this reason he goes not to the heart.*
    Of Otway's *Orphan*, Johnson wrote: . . . *if the heart*
*is not interested, many other beauties may be wanting,*
*yet not missed* (*Otway*, *Lives*, I, 245).

**refers** us only to the writer:  In Cowley's *Mistress*,
Johnson wrote, the compositions *turn the mind only on
the writer* (*Cowley, Lives*, I, 42).

**think on Addison:** Johnson's main inspiration for his
comparison may have been Pope's comparison of Homer
and Virgil in the Preface to his translation of the
*Iliad* (1715):

> It is to the strength of this amazing in-
> vention we are to attribute that unequalled
> fire and rapture, which is so forcible in
> Homer, that no man of a true poetical spirit
> is master of himself while he reads him.
> What he writes is of the most animated nat-
> ure imaginable; every thing moves, every
> thing lives, and is put in action. If a
> council be called, or a battle fought, you
> are not coldly informed of what was said or
> done as from a third person; the reader is
> hurried out of himself by the force of the poet's
> imagination, and turns in one place to a hearer,
> in another to a spectator. . . . Exact dis-
> position, just thought, correct elocution,
> polished numbers, may have been found in a
> thousand; but this poetical fire, this Vivida
> vis animi, in a very few.
> As there is more variety of characters in the
> Iliad, so there is of speeches, than in any
> other poem.  Every thing in it has manners
> (as Aristotle expresses it); that is, every
> thing is acted or spoken.  It is hardly cred-
> ible in a work of such length, how small a
> number of lines are employed in the narration.
> In Virgil the dramatic part is less in pro-
> portion to the narrative; and the speeches
> often consist of general reflections or
> thoughts, which might be equally just in
> any person's mouth upon the same occasion.
> As many of his persons have no apparent char-
> acters, so many of his speeches escape being
> applied, and judged by the rule of propriety.
> We oftener think of the author himself when
> we read Virgil, than when we are engaged in
> Homer: all which are the effects of a colder
> invention, that interests us less in the action
> described. Homer makes us hearers, and Virgil
> leaves us readers.

Johnson seems also to have had parts of Pope's comparison
in mind when he composed his comparison between Dryden,
and Pope himself, in his *Life of Pope, Lives*, III, 222.

Cato: See *Appel à toutes les nations*, p.201: . . . *comment on a pu élever son âme jusqu'à voir ces pièces avec transport, et comment elles sont encore suivies dans un siècle qui a produit le* Caton *d'Addison?* ( . . . *in what way can the mind be raised, or carried away, at the sight of these works, and how is it that they are still taken as models in a century which has produced the* Cato *of Addison?*).

*Cato* is discussed in *Lettres Philosophiques, Oeuvres,* XX, *Mélanges,* I, 154-156. Voltaire's comments on the faults of *Cato* in the following extract suggest that he was not perhaps in total disagreement with Johnson:

*Le premier Anglais qui ait fait une pièce raisonable et écrite d'un bout à l'autre avec élégance est l'illustre M. Addison. Son* Caton d'Utique *est un chef-d'oeuvre pour la diction et pour la beauté des vers. Le rôle de Caton est à mon gré fort au-dessus de celui de Cornélie dans le* Pompée de *Corneille; car Caton est grand sans enflure, et Cornélie, qui d'ailleurs n'est pas un personnage nécessaire, vise quelquefois au galimatias.  Le Caton de M. Addison ne paraît le plus beau personnage qui soit sur aucun théâtre, mais les autres rôles de la piece n'y répondent pas, et cet ouvrage si bien écrit est défiguré par une intrigue froide d'amour, qui répand sur la pièce une langueur qui la tue.* (Addison is the first Englishman to have created a work of Reason, a work elegantly composed from first to last. In its diction and in the beauty of its verse, his *Cato* is a masterpiece. The part of Cato is in my view superior to that of Cornelius in Corneille's *Pompey*. Cato is great without being turgid; Cornelius - who is in addition not an essential personage in the play - tends sometimes towards the obscure. Addison's Cato seems to me the most successful personage who could appear on any stage, but the other parts in the play fall short by comparison, and this work, so well written though it is, is disfigured by a frigid love intrigue. The sense of langour conferred on the play by this kills the drama).

language of poets: Though Shakespeare also used the language of poets. See, for example, Johnson's comments in *The Rambler*, No. 168 on the speech beginning *Come, thick night!* from Act I, scene v of *Macbeth: In this passage is exerted all the force of poetry, that force which calls new powers into being, which embodies sentiment, and animates matter* . . . In his notes to the same

play, Johnson commented that the image in the following
speech by Macbeth is *perhaps the most striking that
poetry can produce* (Shakespeare, IV, 496):
>                  *Now o'er the one half world
>        Nature seems dead, and wicked dreams abuse
>        The curtain'd sleep; now witchcraft celebrates
>        Pale Hecate's offerings*
See also, note to *Cymbeline*, Act I, scene vii: *To
vomit emptiness is in the language of poetry . . . .;*
*Henry V*, Act IV, scene i: *To sweat in the eye of*
Phoebus, *and* to sleep in Elysium, *are expressions
very poetical;* Richard III, Act I, scene i: *War* capers.
*This is poetical, though a little harsh;* King John, Act
II, scene ii: You men of Angiers, &c. *This speech is
very poetical and smooth, and except the conceit of the*
widow's husband *embracing* the earth, *is just and beautiful.* See *Shakespeare*, IX, 205; VI, 115; VII, 5; V,
36.

**skill in:** Familiarity with.

**we still find:** In his use of "we" Johnson may again be
thinking of his own efforts as the author of *Irene*.

**something must be done as well as said:** In his *Life of
Butler*, Johnson wrote that *every reader . . . complains
that in the poem of Hudibras, as in the history of
Thucydides, there is more said than done.* Johnson himself complained of Addison's *Cato*: *Of the agents we have
no care; we consider not what they are doing, or what
they are suffering; we wish only to know what they have
to say (Butler, Addison, Lives,* I, 211; II, 132).

**very coldly heard:** As was reported of Johnson's *Irene*.
Throughout his criticism, Johnson came down strongly
against *inactive declamation*. It was, for him, a main
defect of his century's drama.

**Voltaire:** On Johnson's reply to Voltaire, the *Edinburgh
Review*, XC (July, 1849), p.55, commented as follows:
> *Dr. Johnson has been applauded for his answer
> to Voltaire, who expressed his wonder that
> Shakespeare's extravagances should be endured
> by a nation which had seen Cato: Let him be
> answered that Addison speaks the language of
> poets, and Shakespeare of men. But this ep-
> igram has really neither sense nor truth in it .
> Shakespeare did not speak the language of men,
> but of poets; it was because his language, as
> poetry, was so superior to that of Addison that
> the effect it produced was so much greater.
> The secret of Shakespeare's success is, that
> his representations of nature are more vivid*

*and lifelike than those of Addison; and
from what does this vividness arise, but
from the intensity of poetic power and the
brightness of the medium through which it
passes? That medium is style. Had Shakespeare spoken only the language of men, as
distinguished from that of poets, he would
never have delighted thousands upon thousands of all ranks and characters.*

myrtles: A "myrtle" is defined in the *Dictionary* as: *A
fragrant tree sacred to Venus.*

awful: Awe-inspiring.

endless diversity: This may be set alongside Johnson's
later comparison of Pope and Dryden in his *Life of Pope*:
*Dryden's page is a natural field, rising into in-
equalities, and diversified by the varied exuberance
of abundant vegetation; Pope's is a velvet lawn, shaven
by the scythe, and levelled by the roller (Lives,* III,
222). Nichol Smith points out that the garden and
forest comparison had already appeared in a versified
form in *The Connoisseur*, No. 125, June, 1756, and suggests comparison with Mrs. Piozzi's *Anecdotes of Johnson*
(1786), p.59: *Corneille is to Shakespeare . . . as a
clipped hedge is to a forest.*
    But see also Voltaire, *Lettres Philosophiques, Oeuvres,*
XX, *Mélanges,* I, 456:
*Les monstres brillants de Shakespeare plaisent
mille fois plus que la sagesse moderne. Le
génie poétique des Anglais ressemble, jusqu'à
présent, à un arbre touffu planté par la
nature, jetant au hasard mille rameaux, et
croissant inégalement avec force. (Shakespeare's brilliant monstrosities please a
thousand times more than today's prudent
dramas. Up to now, English poetic genius
resembles a bushy tree planted by nature,
haphazardly sprouting a thousand branches,
an uneven but vigorous growth.*

cabinets: A "cabinet" was a girl's private jewel box.

common: I.e. usual(in Johnson's day).

science: I.e. knowledge, as in the Latin: *scientia*.


PAGE 32


wanted: I.e. lacked.

. . . **learning:** The question of Shakespeare's learning had been much debated by previous eighteenth-century editors of the plays.

**regular education:** Perhaps education in the traditional areas of learning rather than unbroken, or systematic, education.    In his *Dictionary* Johnson defined "regular" as: *Instituted or initiated according to established forms or discipline: as, a regular doctor; regular troops.*

**Johnson:** In his poem to the memory of Shakespeare, quoted in the prefatory matter to (Samuel) Johnson's edition.

**Some have imagined:** E.g. John Upton and Zachary Grey. Johnson refers to specific works by these men later in the *Preface*.

**I prae, sequar:** Zachary Grey, *Critical, Historical, and Explanatory Notes on Shakespeare,* II, 53 suggests that Richard of Gloucester's *Go you before, and I will follow you,* from *Richard III,* Act I, scene i, is in imitation of Terence: *I prae, sequar.*   Terence's line is from *The Fair Andrian (Andria),* 171.

**Anacreon:** Read "to dream".   Nichol Smith says that the spurious eighth ode was usually called *The Dream.*

## PAGE 33

**in English:** Shakespeare's use of WW's translation of Plautus' *Menaechmi* (1595) has been doubted.

**assistance:** Cf. note to *Henry V,* Act IV, scene iv: *If the pronunciation of the French language be not changed since Shakespeare's time, which is not unlikely, it may be suspected some other man wrote the French scenes (Shakespeare,* VI, 131).

**easy perusal of the Roman authors:** I.e. he could read a wide variety of Latin authors with ease, without using a dictionary, glossary or crib.   Cf. Dennis, *Essay on the Genius and Writings of Shakespear,* Critical Works, II, 13: *I believe he was able to do what Pedants call construe, but that he was able to read Plautus without pain and difficulty I can never believe.*

**only such fables as he found translated:** See Mrs. Lennox's *Shakespear Illustrated,* I, 90, on the source of *Romeo and Juliet:*

> *Had* Shakespear *ever seen the original*
> *Novel in* Bandello, *he would have been*
> *sensible that the Translation of it is*
> *extremely bad: That he did not see it,*
> *must be owing to nothing else than his*
> *not understanding* Italian; *for can it be*
> *supposed, that having resolved to write*
> *a Tragedy upon the Subject of an* Italian
> *Story, he would rather chuse to copy from*
> *a bad Translation of that Story, than fol-*
> *low the Original.*

by Pope: In his *Preface to Shakespeare*, Pope wrote: . . . *it*
  *is plain he had much reading at least, if they will not*
  *call it learning.* He goes on to enumerate the various areas
  of this reading (*Shakespeare*, I, 114).


PAGE 34


closet: Study.

shop: Workshop?

indigent: Wanting, lacking.

some of the Greek: A list of *Ancient Translations from Classic*
  *Authors* was drawn up and printed in the edition of 1778.
  The list first appeared in the edition of 1773.

but success: Perhaps Johnson is thinking of Spenser, as he
  mentions him with high praise later in the *Preface* (p.39).

rudeness: Rudimentariness.

essays: I.e. attempts at tragedy and comedy, not essays
  on them.

Neither character nor dialogue . . . .: Neither the arts of
  creating character nor representing dialogue were yet understood. The Yale editor says that Johnson's scanty knowledge of Elizabethan drama is evident here, and a few
  paragraphs further on. Dryden, Rowe, Hanmer and Upton
  held similar views of Shakespeare's learning.

happier: More successful.

chronology of his works is yet unsettled: When the first
  edition of Johnson's *Shakespeare* came out in 1765 the
  chronology was completely unsettled. The edition of 1778
  makes considerable concessions to George Steevens' work
  on chronology. But even today precise dating of the plays
  rests on the most tenuous evidence.

PAGE 35


**were the best:** Quoted from memory, with some alterations,
from Rowe's *Some Account of the Life of . . . Shakespeare*
(*Shakespeare*, I, 177).

**combining or applying them:** Compare this with Johnson's comment in his *Life of Butler* that: *Imagination is useless*
*without knowledge: nature gives in vain the power of com-*
*bination, unless study and observation supply materials*
*to be combined.* In his *Life of Pope*, he wrote of that
energy *which collects, combines, amplifies, and animates*
(*Lives*, I, 212; III, 222).
  Cf. also Dryden, *The Grounds of Criticism in Tragedy*
(1679):
    *A poet must be born with this quality* (of
    genius)*; yet, unless he helps himself by an*
    *acquired knowledge of the passions, what they*
    *are in their own nature, and by what springs*
    *they are to be moved, he will be subject either*
    *to raise them where they ought not to be raised,*
    *or not to raise them by the just degrees of*
    *nature, or to amplify them beyond the natural*
    *bounds, or not to observe the crisis and turns*
    *of them, in their cooling and decay: all which*
    *errors proceed from want of judgement in the*
    *poet, and from being unskilled in the principles*
    *of moral philosophy. Nothing is more frequent*
    *in a fanciful writer than to foil himself by*
    *not managing his strength . . .* (*Essays*, I, 254).
  Cf. this with Pope on witty writers, who, besides their
wit, *yet want as much again to manage it* (*Essay on Criti-*
*cism* (1711), lines 80-81).

**like other mortals:** A sign of Johnson's disinclination towards the bardolatry exhibited by later critics.

**. . . amply instructed:** Johnson is correcting the exagger-
ations of Rowe in this paragraph.

**books and precepts cannot confer:** Milton, on the other hand,
*. . . would not have excelled in dramatick writing; he knew*
*human nature only in the gross, and had never studied the*
*shades of character, nor the combinations of concurring,*
*or the perplexity of contending passions. He had read much,*
*and knew what books could teach; but he had mingled little*
*in the world, and was deficient in the knowledge which*
*experience must confer* (*Milton, Lives*, I, 189).

**native excellence:** I.e. inborn excellence. Johnson has just
been talking about the combination of natural and acquired
powers in a writer.

perspicacity: *Dict.*: *Quickness of sight.*

accidental appendages of present manners: Modern fashions
of speech and social custom.  Again, Johnson uses "manners"
in contrast to "nature".  "Manners", while giving expression
to "nature", changed from generation to generation.  "Nature" did not.

the characters of Chaucer: One of the few references to
Chaucer in Johnson's writings, though he had proposed
an edition of Chaucer in his early career.  Interest in
the poems of Chaucer, in the original language, was growing at the time of the publication of the *Preface*.  Early
eighteenth-century interest in Chaucer had been stimulated
particularly by Dryden's translations in *Fables* (1700).

not much indebted: I.e. he may well be a little indebted, as
in, for example, *A Midsummer Night's Dream*.


PAGE 36


original benevolence: E.g. David Hume, *Of goodness and benevolence, A Treatise of Human Nature* (London, 1740), III.

seminal principles: Seeds.

motives of action: A similar point was made by Johnson in
his Dedication to *Shakespear Illustrated* (*Yale*, VII, 49):
   *He lived in an age when the books of chivalry*
   *were yet popular, and when therefore the minds*
   *of his auditors were not accustomed to balance*
   *probabilities, or to examine nicely the pro-*
   *portion between causes and effects.  It was*
   *sufficient to recommend a story, that it was*
   *far removed from common life, that its changes*
   *were frequent, and its close pathetic.*
   Cf. Rapin, *Comparison of Thucydides and Livy*, pp.28-29:
   *But after all, this* great Man *seems to be nothing*
   *worthier of Admiration, than in his Treating of*
   *the* manners *of Men, as one that excellently under-*
   stood Mankind, *and had all the* penetration *re-*
   *quisite to* unfold the most intricate *doublings*
   *of the* Heart: *'Twas from this profound knowledge,*
   *he could so well discover the* springs *and* motives
   *of the nicest Interests, and the most imperceptible*
   movements *of the secretest Passions that set Man-*
   *kind on work.*

All those enquiries . . . human nature: Including perhaps
   David Hume's *Treatise of Human Nature*, first published in

1736-40. The first part, recast as the *Enquiry concerning the Human Understanding* appeared in 1748, the
second, as the *Enquiry concerning the Principles of
Morals* in 1751.

The tales: I.e. the tales that Shakespeare could in his time
have encountered. Johnson's argument is that because learning was in its infancy in Shakespeare's time, the dramatist,
to acquire his materials, must search them out in the world.

omitted the causes: Perhaps a reference to the philosophical
essays of John Locke.

remarks: Johnson defined "remark" in his *Dictionary* as:
*Observation.*

proper combinations: Cf. *Rasselas*, Ch. X:
> *But the knowledge of nature is only half the
> task of a poet; he must be acquainted likewise
> with all the modes of life.  His character re-
> quires that he estimate the happiness and
> misery of every condition; observe the power
> of all the passions in all their combinations,
> and trace the changes of the human mind . . .*

maxims of theoretical knowledge: In his *Dictionary*, Johnson
defined a "maxim" as: *An axiom; a general principle; a
leading truth*, and quoted Shakespeare: *This* maxim *out of
love I teach.* The quotation comes from *Troilus and Cressida*,
Act II, scene ii, where Cressida is reciting a list of
maxims, including: . . . *Women are angels, wooing; /
Things won are done, joy's soul lies in the doing: /
That she belov'd knows nought, that knows not this, - /
Men prize the thing ungain'd more than it is* (Shakespeare,
IX, 27). Johnson frequently makes a point of drawing
attention to maxims and rules in his notes to the plays.

an exact surveyor of the inanimate world: As this passage
suggests, Johnson's term "general nature" includes both
human and inanimate nature.

peculiarities: Distinguishing marks.

really exist: Cf. *Pope, Lives*, III, 225: *If by nature is
meant, what is commonly called* nature *by the criticks, a
just representation of things really existing, and actions
really performed, nature cannot be properly opposed to* art;
nature *being, in this sense, only the best effect of art.*

from knowledge: I.e. from knowledge of nature. Cf. *Rasselas*,
Ch. X:
> . . . *whether, as the province of poetry is to
> describe Nature and Passion, which are always
> the same, the first writers took possession of*

> *the most striking objects for description, and*
> *the most probable occurences for fiction, and*
> *left nothing to those that followed them, but*
> *transcription of the same events, and new*
> *combinations of the same images . . .*

**Boyle:** See Thomas Birch, *Life of Robert Boyle* (1744), p.19:
> *. . . to a person, that affected so much an*
> *universal knowledge, and arbitrary vicissitudes*
> *of quiet and employments, it could not be un-*
> *welcome to be of a quality, that was a hand-*
> *som stirrup to preferment, without an obli-*
> *gation to court it, and which might at once*
> *both protect his higher pretensions from guilt*
> *of ambition, and secure his retiredness from*
> *contempt.*

**mean employments:** In *An Addition to Rowe's Account of Shakespeare* (1765), Johnson hands on the story that Shakespeare held horses outside the theatre.

**. . . enquiry:** Similar general observations were made by Johnson of Richard Savage in his *Life of Savage.*

**depressed:** Cf. Johnson's *London* (1738), line 177: *SLOW RISES WORTH, BY POVERTY DEPRESS'D.* Johnson is allying himself with Shakespeare in this paragraph.

**conversation:** Perhaps in the wider eighteenth-century sense, meaning commerce with society.

PAGE 37

**as dew drops from a lion's mane:** The words are those of Patroclus to Achilles, urging him to fight (*Troilus and Cressida*, Act III, scene iii; *Shakespeare*, IX, 95-96):
> *To this effect, Achilles, have I moved you:*
> *A woman impudent and mannish grown*
> *Is not more loath'd, than an effeminate man*
> *In time of action. I stand condemn'd on this;*
> *They think, my little stomach to the war,*
> *And your great love to me, restrains you thus:*
> *Sweet, rouse yourself; and the weak wanton Cupid*
> *Shall from your neck unloose his amorous fold,*
> *And, like a dew-drop from the lion's mane,*
> *Be shook to air.*

The heroic endurance of a writer in adversity was one of Johnson's favourite topics.

**dispositions:** Cf. *ante* (p.12) the remark that his *disposition . . . led him to comedy.* In his *Dictionary*, Johnson defined "disposition" as: *Temper of mind.* The word was a common Shakespearean usage.

**just:** *Dict.*: *Exact; proper; accurate.*

**their fame:** I.e. the fame of the previous writers.


PAGE 38


**capricious and casual:** Cf. the opening of *The Rambler*, No 38: *. . . the imitator treads a beaten walk, and with all his diligence can only hope to find a few flowers or branches untouched by his predecessor, the refuse of contempt, or the omission of neglect.*

**with his own eyes:** Thomson, wrote Johnson *looks round on Nature and on Life, with the eye which Nature bestows only on a poet; the eye that distinguishes, in every thing presented to its view, whatever there is on which imagination can delight to be detained.* Of Milton, on the other hand, he wrote: *his images and descriptions of the scenes or operations of Nature do not seem to be always copied from original form, nor to have the freshness, raciness, and energy of immediate observation. He saw Nature, as Dryden expresses it, "through the spectacles of books"* (Thomson, Milton, *Lives*, III, 298-99; I, 178).
    In a note on Act III, scene i of *Midsummer Night's Dream*, Johnson commented on the Queen's *And, for night-tapers, crop their waxen thighs, / And light them at the fiery glow-worm's eyes,* as follows: *I know not how Shakespeare, who commonly derived his knowledge of nature from his own observations, happened to place the glow-worm's light in his eyes, which is only in his tail* (Shakespeare, III, 65).

**any other mind:** Cf. Dryden, in the passage from the *Essay on Dramatic Poesy* quoted at the conclusion of the *Preface* (p.66): *he needed not the spectacles of books to read nature.*

**. . . complete:** The substance of this paragraph has affinities with remarks by Wordsworth on the later ages of poetry. See Appendix to the *Lyrical Ballads, Prose Works*, I, 161-62 on the corruption of language by succeeding generations of poets.

**invented:** In his Dedication to *Shakespear Illustrated*, Johnson had written: *Among the powers that must conduce to constitute a poet, the first and most valuable is invention* (Yale, VII, 47). *The essence of poetry is invention* he affirmed in his

*Life of Waller* (*Lives*, I, 291).

**as Shakespeare:** The Yale editor notes that this comparison was already conventional in Shakespeare criticism, and refers the reader to Arthur Sherbo, *Samuel Johnson, Editor of Shakespeare* (Illinois, Urbana, 1956), p.127 for a list of earlier comments.

**effused:** Poured out.

**dissyllable:** In his *Dictionary*, Johnson defined the noun "dissyllable" as: *A word of two syllables.*

**trisyllable:** *Dict.*: as a noun: *A word consisting of three syllables.* Writers of Pope's day (and of Johnson's) preferred monosyllabic terminations, or rhyme words.

**in common conversation:** *On the Genius and Writings of Shakespear, Critical Works*, II, 4-5. George Steevens compares Dryden in the Epistle Dedicatory to *The Rival Ladies* (1664): *Shakespeare (who, with some errors not to be avoided in that age, had undoubtedly a larger soul of poesy than ever any of our nation) was the first who, to shun the pains of continual rhyming, invented that kind of writing which we call blank verse . . .*
    Of Fenton's *Mariamne*, Johnson noted that it *is written in lines of ten syllables, with few of those redundant terminations which the drama not only admits but requires, as more nearly approaching to real dialogue* (Fenton, *Lives*, II, 260).

**before our author:** By T. Norton and T. Sackville (1562). There was a reprint of the play in 1736.

**not certain:** A reference to Thomas Kyd's *Spanish Tragedy* (ca. 1592).


PAGE 39


**. . . much esteemed:** The 1778 edition of Johnson's *Shakespeare* is rich in references to old plays. Steevens' additions had Johnson's approval. Hazlitt, *Lectures on the Age of Elizabeth, Works*, VI, 179 complained thus:
    *Dr. Johnson said of these writers generally that "they were sought after because they were scarce, and would not have been scarce had they been much esteemed". His decision is neither true history nor sound criticism. They were esteemed, and they deserved to be so.*

**Spenser:** It is sometimes thought that Johnson's interest in English poetry began with Cowley, the first author considered in his *Lives of the Poets.*

**smoothness:** *Dict.*: *Sweetness or softness of numbers.* For "smooth" Johnson gave: *Flowing; soft; not harsh.*

**could be softened:** Of the three parts of *Henry VI*, Johnson wrote in his notes that: *If we take these plays from Shakespeare, to whom shall they be given? What author of that age had the same easiness of expression and fluency of numbers (Shakespeare, VI, 563).*

**delicacy of Rowe:** The Yale editor mentions Johnson's fondness for Rowe's "she tragedies" and his references to *The Fair Penitent* and *Jane Shore* in the notes. In his *Life of Rowe*, Johnson said of *The Fair Penitent* that it *is one of the most pleasing tragedies on the stage . . . for there is scarcely any work of any poet at once so interesting by the fable, and so delightful by the language.* Of *Jane Shore*, he wrote: *this play, consisting chiefly of domestick scenes and private distresses, lays hold upon the heart (Rowe, Lives, II, 67, 69).*

**sooth by softness:** See, for example, the songs in *Cymbeline,* Act III, scene ii (*Shakespeare*, IX, 220-21) and Act IV, scene ii (*Shakespeare*, IX, 291-92).

**veneration:** *Dict.*: *Awful respect.*

**endured:** I.e. endured in silence.

**excuse us:** I.e. excuse us from having to face the charge of not protesting loudly enough at Shakespeare's deformities.

**some modern critick:** John Upton, *Critical Observations on Shakespeare* (1746), pp.284-328, gives the following series of "Rules" by which Shakespeare's language was to be understood:
> RULE I.   *Shakespeare alters proper names according to the English pronunciation . . .*
> RULE II. *He makes Latin words English, and uses them according to their original idiom and latitude . . .*
> RULE III. *He sometimes omits the primary and proper sense, and uses words in their secondary and improper signification . . .*
> RULE IV. *He uses one part of speech for another . . .*
> RULE V. *He uses the active participle passively . . .*
> RULE VII. *He often adds to adjectives in their comparative and superlative degrees, the signs marking the degrees . . .*
> RULE VIII. *He frequently omits the auxiliary verb,*

> *am, is, are &c. and likewise several particles,*
> *as to, that, as &c. . . .*
> *RULE IX. He uses, But, for otherwise than: Or, for*
> *before: Once, once for all, peremptorily: From, on*
> *account of: Not, for not only: Nor do two negatives*
> *allways make an affirmative, but deny more strongly,*
> *as is well known from the Greek, and modern French*
> *languages.*
> *RULE X. He uses the abstract for the concrete.*
> *RULE XI. To complete the construction, there is,*
> *in the latter part of the sentence sometimes to*
> *be supplied some word, or phrase from the former*
> *part, either expressed, or tacitly signified.*
> *RULE XII. He uses the nominative case absolute;*
> *or rather elliptical.*
> *RULE XIII. He makes a sudden transition from the*
> *plural number to the singular.*
> *RULE XIV. He shortens words by striking off the*
> *first or last syllable: and sometimes lengthens*
> *them by adding a Latin termination.*

**mode of depravation:** Something of what Johnson meant by depravation of language may be gathered from his notes. On Edgar's *Poor pelting villages* from Act II, scene iii of *King Lear*, he wrote that *Pelting is . . . only an accidental depravation of* petty. *Shakespeare uses it in* Midsummer-Night's Dream *of* small brooks (*Shakespeare*, IX, 427). In his *Dictionary*, Johnson defined "depravation" as *The act of making anything bad; the act of corrupting; corruption.*


## PAGE 40


**heard to the conclusion:** Cf. Rowe, *Account of the Life of . . . Shakespeare: When one considers, that there is not one play before him of a reputation good enough to entitle it to an appearance on the present stage, it cannot but be a matter of great wonder that he should advance dramatick poetry so far as he did* (*Shakespeare*, I, 186-7).

**ideas of perfection:** Cf. Johnson on Dryden:
> *Dryden was no rigid judge of his own pages;*
> *he seldom struggled after supreme excellence*
> *but snatched in haste what was within his*
> *reach. He did not keep present to his*
> *mind an idea of pure perfection; nor compare*
> *his works such as they were, with what they*
> *might be made* (*Dryden, Lives*, I, 464).

**encomiasts:** Writers of formal praise.

**contending with themselves:** Dryden, according to Johnson:
*. . . standing . . . in the highest place . . . had no
care to rise by contending with himself; but while there
was no name above his own, was willing to enjoy fame on
the easiest terms (Dryden, Lives, I, 465).*

**worthy of posterity:** Cf. Hazlitt, *On Shakespeare and Milton,
Works,* V, 56:
> *The natural ease and indifference of his temper
> made him sometimes less scrupulous than he might
> have been. He is relaxed and careless in
> critical places; he is earnest throughout only
> in Timon, Macbeth, and Lear . . . he had no
> models of acknowledged excellence constantly in
> view to stimulate his efforts, and by all that
> appears, no love of fame. He wrote for the
> "great vulgar and the small", in his time, not
> for posterity.*

**levy any ideal tribute:** I.e. to exact a tribute from future
times as Rome exacted money from its tributary states.
In his *Dictionary,* Johnson defined "ideal" as: *Intellectual.*

**same jests in many dialogues:** In a note on *Henry VI Part III,*
Act III, scene i, Johnson wrote that: *It is common in these
plays to find the same images, whether jocular or serious,
frequently recurring (Shakespeare,* VI, 490). The immediate
occasion of the remark is the play on *Thy balm wash'd off*
. . .

**Congreve's four comedies:** I.e. *The Old Batchelor* (1693),
*The Double Dealer* (1694), *Love for Love* (1695) and *The Way
of the World* (1700).

**marriage in a mask:** *The Old Batchelor* and *Love for Love.*

**knot of perplexity:** I.e. device of mistaken identity.

**declined into the vale of years:** From *Othello,* Act III,
scene iii; see *Shakespeare,* X, 534.

**. . . be disgusted with fatigue:** I.e. have lost his literary
and critical taste because of fatigue.


PAGE 41


**depravations:** Corruptions. See *ante,* p.161: mode of depravation

**publishers:** Some publishers refused to print their name, or
gave false information.

revisers: I.e. editors: Rowe, Pope, Theobald and Warburton.

temerity: Overboldness.

tear what we cannot loose: We now tear out what has not of
   its own accord got lost.

ungrammatical, perplexed, and obscure: Cf. Johnson's note
   on Postumus' lines in *Cymbeline*, Act I, scene v (*ante*,
   p.125: language is intricate).


PAGE 42


without correction of the press: Without proof correction.

unregarded: See Warburton, *Preface to Shakespeare*:
   *Shakespear's works, when they escaped the players,*
   *did not fall into much better hands when they*
   *came amongst printers and booksellers: who, to*
   *say the truth, had at first but small encourage-*
   *ment for putting him into a better condition.*
   *The stubborn nonsense, with which he was in-*
   *crusted, occasioned his lying long neglected*
   *amongst the common lumber of the stage. And*
   *when that resistless splendor, which now shoots*
   *all around him, had, by degrees, broke thro'*
   *the shell of those impurities, his dazzled*
   *admirers became as suddenly insensible to the*
   *extraneous scurf that still stuck upon him, as*
   *they had been before to the native beauties*
   *that lay under it. So that, as then he was*
   *thought not to deserve a cure, he was now sup-*
   *posed not to need any* (Shakespeare, I, 151-52).

to modern languages: Before this time the skills of editors
   had been almost exclusively applied to texts of classical
   and religious literature.

by Rowe: Of Rowe's edition, Johnson wrote in his *Rowe, Lives,*
   II, 70-71:
   *As his studies necessarily made him acquainted*
   *with Shakespeare, and acquaintance produced*
   *veneration, he undertook (1709) an edition of*
   *his works, from which he neither received much*
   *praise nor seems to have expected it; yet, I*
   *believe, those who compare it with former copies*
   *will find that he has done more than he promised,*
   *and that, without the pomp of notes or boasts of*
   *criticism, many passages are happily restored.*
   *He prefixed a life of the author, such as tradition,*

> *then almost expiring, could supply, and a preface*
> *which cannot be said to discover much profundity*
> *or penetration.* He at least contributed to the
> *popularity of his author.*

published: I.e. edited *and* published.

by a poet: In his *Preface*, Warburton had complained:
> *His growing eminence . . . required that he*
> *should be used with ceremony: and he soon had*
> *his appointment of an editor in form. But the*
> *bookseller, whose dealing was with wits, having*
> *learnt of them, I know not what silly maxim,*
> *that* none but a poet should presume to meddle
> with a poet, *engaged the ingenious Mr Rowe to*
> *undertake this employment* (*Shakespeare*, I, 152).
Warburton is presumably thinking of Ben Jonson's *To judge*
*of Poets is only the facultie of Poets.* See *Timber or*
*Dicoveries, Works of Jonson*, ed. C.H. Herford and P. and
E. Simpson, Vol. VIII, *The Poems, the Prose Works* (Oxford,
1947), p.642.

did not undertake: By Theobald and Warburton, the latter
complaining in his *Preface*:
> *A wit indeed he was; but so utterly unacquainted*
> *with the whole business of criticism, that he did*
> *not even collate or consult the first editions of*
> *the work he undertook to publish; but contented*
> *himself with giving us a meagre account of the*
> *author's life, interlarded with some common-place*
> *scraps from his writings* (*Shakespeare*, I, 152).

## PAGE 43

I have preserved the prefaces: Johnson reprinted the Prefaces
of Rowe, Pope, Theobald and Hanmer.

the author's life: The Yale editor points out that the version
of Rowe's *Account of the Life of . . . Shakespeare*, reprinted in Vol. I of Johnson's edition, is actually Pope's
revision of the original.

for many years: Rowe's edition appeared in 1709, Pope's in
1725. Not, perhaps, a very long interval, except by comparison with the short periods between editions after Pope's.

compendious criticism: For "compendious", Johnson's *Dictionary*
gives *Short; summary; abridged; direct; comprehensive;*
*holding much in a narrow space; near; by which time is saved,*
*and circuition cut off.*

**amputation than of cure:** He ejected rather than amended what he disliked. In his *Life of Pope*, Johnson wrote that Pope:

> . . . hoped to persuade the world that he mis-
> carried in this undertaking only by having a
> mind too great for such minute employment.
>   Pope in his edition undoubtedly did many
> things wrong, and left many things undone; but
> let him not be defrauded of his due praise: he
> was the first that knew, at least the first
> that told, by what helps the text might be
> improved. If he inspected the early editions
> negligently, he taught others to be more
> accurate. In his Preface he expanded with
> great skill and elegance the character which had
> been given of Shakespeare by Dryden; and he drew
> publick attention upon his works, which though
> often mentioned, had been little read (*Lives*,
> III, 138-39).

**spurious plays:** See Warburton, *Preface*:

> He separated the genuine from the spurious
> plays: and, with equal judgment, though not
> always with the same success, attempted to
> clear the genuine plays from the interpolated
> scenes: he then consulted the old editions;
> and, by a careful collation of them, rectified
> the faulty, and supplied the imperfect reading
> in a great number of places: and lastly, in an
> admirable preface, hath drawn a general, but
> very lively sketch of Shakespear's poetick
> character: and, in the corrected text, marked
> out those peculiar strokes of genius which were
> most proper to support and illustrate that
> character. Thus far Mr Pope. And although
> much more was to be done before Shakespeare
> could be restored to himself (such as amending
> the corrupted text where the printed books afford
> no assistance; explaining his licentious phrase-
> eology and obscure allusion; and illustrating
> the beauties of his poetry) yet, with great
> modesty and prudence, our illustrious editor left
> this to the critick by profession (*Shakespeare*,
> I, 152).

**Hemings and Condel:** Friends of Shakespeare who issued the first Folio in 1623.

**licentiousness of the press:** Referring to the lax enforcement of copyright.

**omitted by his friends:** I.e. by Hemings and Condel.

**1664:** The spurious plays were added to the third Folio in
1664. The seven plays *Never before Printed in Folio* were
*Pericles, The London Prodigal, The History of Thomas, Lord
Cromwell, Sir John Oldcastle, The Puritan Widow, A York-
shire Tragedy* and *The Tragedy of Locrine.*

**editor:** See Pope, *Preface to Shakespeare: I have discharged
the dull duty of an editor, to my best judgment, with more
labour than I expect thanks, with a religious abhorrence of
all innovation, and without any indulgence to my private
sense of conjecture* (*Shakespeare,* I, 121-22).

## PAGE 44

**modes of language prevailing in every age:** Cf. Johnson's
comment in his *Proposals* that *Mr. Rowe and Mr. Pope were
very ignorant of the ancient English literature* (*Yale,*
VII, 56).

**dull duty of an editor:** dulness of an editor's duty.

**their powers are universal:** In his *Proposals* of 1756, Johnson
wrote of the *observation of faults and beauties* by previous
editors that *For this part of his task, and for this only,
was Mr. Pope eminently and indisputable qualified* (*Yale,*
VII, 57).

**expectations:** Of praise.

**I have retained all his notes:** The Yale editor points out that
Johnson, though he may have intended to do so, actually did
not include everything.

## PAGE 45

**insertion:** Mrs. Thrale notes that: *Of Pope as a writer he
has the highest opinion, and once when a lady at our house
talked of his preface to Shakespeare as superior to Pope's
I fear not, Madam (said he), the little fellow has done
wonders* (See *Johnsonian Miscellanies,* I, 184-85).

**Theobald:** His edition appeared in 1733 and was frequently
reprinted. The Yale editor points out that Johnson used
some plays in the 1757 edition as printer's copy for his
own.

**small acquisitions:** Cf. Johnson's estimate of Theobald in his

*Life of Pope* as *a man of heavy diligence, with very slender powers, who first, in a book called* Shakespeare Restored, *and then in a formal edition, detected his deficiencies with all the insolence of victory* (*Lives*, III, 138).

**artificial:** I.e. acquired by application and study.

**indefinitely:** I.e. without numerical precision.

**will produce:** George Steevens, in his Prolegomena to the 1773 edition also asserts that only the first Folio is authoritative; but in the 1778 edition he says the second Folio of 1632 *is not without value.*

**used only the first:** Differences between the Folios are merely printers' errors.

**minute:** *Dict.: Small in consequence.* Johnson means that these notes were too concerned with philological niceties.


PAGE 46


**exuberant excrescence of his diction:** I.e. in his verbosity. Johnson defined "excresecence" in his *Dictionary* as: *Somewhat growing out of another without use, contrary to the common order of production.*

**inflated emptiness of some notes:** See perhaps Theobald's long note on Pope's objection to the reading *Good morrow Alexander* in Act I, scene ii of *Troilus and Cressida*, where Alexander (or Paris) is supposed not to be on the stage. Theobald sets out to excuse the inclusion of the name Alexander, and ends with the jibe: *And why might not* Alexander *be the name of Cressid's man? Paris had no patent, I suppose, for engrossing it to himself. But the late* editor, *perhaps, because we have had* Alexander *the Great,* Pope Alexander *and* Alexander *Pope, would have so eminent a name prostituted to a common* varlet (*Shakespeare*, IX, 17).

**Pope for his enemy:** Theobald was anathematized in *The Dunciad* for the criticisms he had made of Pope's edition in his *Shakespeare Restored* (1726). See *The Dunciad in Four Books* (1742), Book I, lines 133-34: *There hapless Shakespear, yet of Tibbald sore, / Wish'd he had blotted for himself before.* Of *The Dunciad*, Johnson wrote in his *Life of Pope* that:

> . . . *the first motive was the desire of revenging the contempt with which Theobald had treated his* Shakespeare, *and regaining the honour which he had*

> *lost, by crushing his opponent. Theobald*
> *was not of bulk enough to fill a poem, and*
> *therefore it was necessary to find other*
> *enemies with other names, at whose expence*
> *he might divert the publick (Pope, Lives,*
> *III, 241).*

**no man can envy:** This is by and large a harsher account
of Theobald's weaknesses than Johnson had given in his
*Miscellaneous Observations on Macbeth*, in 1745 (*Yale*, VII,
8): *There are among Mr. Theobald's alterations others*
*which I do not approve, though I do not always censure*
*them; for some of his amendments are so excellent, that,*
*even when he has failed, he ought to be treated with in-*
*dulgence and respect.*

**the Oxford editor:** Johnson is more generous to Hanmer's
edition here than he had been in 1745 in his *Miscellaneous*
*Observations on Macbeth* (*Yale*, VII, 43-45). There he had
written that, from the little that he had seen of it, he
thought it *not dangerous to declare that . . . its pomp*
*recommends it more than its accuracy:*
> *There is no distinction made between the*
> *ancient reading, and the innovations of the*
> *editor; there is no reason given for any of*
> *the alterations which are made; the emend-*
> *ations of former criticks are adopted with-*
> *out any acknowledgment, and few of the dif-*
> *ficulties are removed which have hitherto em-*
> *barrassed the readers of Shakespeare.*

Johnson is supposed to have been the author of a translation of a Latin Epitaph on Hanmer published in *The Gentle-*
*man's Magazine* (May 1747), pp.239-40, which testifies to
his respect for this scholar.

**. . . would have found:** He makes emendations where a little
more attention would have enabled him to find the meaning.

**solicitous to reduce to grammar:** Commenting upon the lines
spoken by the First Gentleman in Act IV, scene i of *Henry*
*VIII*: *. . . 'tis the list / Of those, that claim their*
*offices this day, / By custom of the coronation.* Johnson
pointed out that Hanmer had read *these days* for *this day*,
adding that *Shakespeare meant* such a day as this, *a coro-*
*nation day. And such is the English idiom, which our*
*authour commonly prefers to grammatical nicety* (*Shakespeare*,
VII, 278).


PAGE 47


**more the series of ideas than of words:** This view was contin-

ually reiterated by Johnson.  Unlike previous editors
he did not go to great lengths in his emendations to
make Shakespeare grammatical.  The Duke's *We have with
a leaven'd and prepared choice / Proceeded to you* in Act
I, scene i of *Measure for Measure* had prompted Warburton
to amend "*leaven'd*" to "*level'd*".  Johnson responded:
> *No emendation is necessary.  Leaven'd choice
> is one of Shakespeare's harsh metaphors.  His
> train of ideas seems to be this.  I have pro-
> ceeded to you with choice mature, concocted,
> fermented,* leavened.  *When bread is* leavened,
> *it is left to ferment: a* leavened *choice is
> therefore a choice not hasty, but considerate,
> not declared as soon as it fell into the imag-
> ination, but suffered to work long in the mind.
> Thus explained, it suits better with* prepared
> *than* levelled (*Shakespeare*, II, 11).

reader's desk: Johnson thought that in *Richard II*, Carlisle's
"Yet best beseeming me to speak the truth" might "be read
more grammatically" as "*Yet best* beseems it *me to speak
the truth*" but added: *I do not think it is printed other-
wise than as Shakespeare wrote it.*  He noted that "imaginary" had been used for "imaginative" in the lines from
the Chorus in the Prologue to *Henry V*: *And let us, cyphers
to this great accompt, / On your imaginary forces work*
because "Active and passive words are by this author frequently confounded" (See *Shakespeare*, V, 216; VI, iv).

conveyed his meaning: Johnson was particularly sensitive to
Shakespeare's *train of ideas*, accepting, frequently, that
the text must remain ungrammatical.  Aeneas' "Valour and
pride excel themselves in Hector" in Act IV, scene v of
*Troilus and Cressida* had been called *high absurdity* by
Warburton, who emended "excel" to "*parcell*".  Johnson
wrote:
> *I would not petulantly object, that "excellence"
> may as well be "little" as "absurdity" be "high",
> but to direct the reader's attention rather to
> sense than words.  Shakespeare's thought is not
> exactly deduced.  Nicety of expression is not
> his character.  The meaning is plain . . .* (See
> *Shakespeare*, IX, 119).
Warburton's note and Johnson's first sentence do not,
however, appear in the edition of 1778.  They were omitted
from 1773 onwards.

. . . audience: Further examples of Johnson's theory and
practice can be found in notes to *Twelfth Night*, Act II,
scene i, *The Winter's Tale* Act IV, scene i and *Henry IV
Part I*, Act I, scene i.  See *Shakespeare*, IV, 184 (on
Shakespeare's confounding of active and passive adjectives);
IV, 361 (where Shakespeare *attends more to his ideas than
to his words*); V, 252 (where Johnson says that *to regard
sense more than grammar, is familiar to our author*).

**violently censured:** By Warburton, *Preface*:
> *How the Oxford editor came to think himself*
> *qualified for this office, from which his whole*
> *course of life had been so remote, is still*
> *more difficult to conceive. For whatever parts*
> *he might have either of genius or erudition, he*
> *was absolutely ignorant of the art of criticism,*
> *as well as of the poetry of that time, and the*
> *language of his author. And so far from a*
> *thought of examining the* first *editions, that*
> *he even neglected to compare Mr. Pope's, from*
> *which he printed his own, with Mr. Theobald's;*
> *whereby he lost the advantage of many fine lines*
> *which the other had recovered from the old quar-*
> *tos. Where he trusts to his own sagacity, in*
> *what affects the sense, his conjectures are*
> *generally absurd and extravagant, and violating*
> *every rule of criticism. Though, in this rage*
> *of correcting, he was not absolutely destitute*
> *of all* art. *For, having a number of my conjectures*
> *before him, he took as many of them as he saw fit,*
> *to work upon; and by changing them to something,*
> *he thought, synonymous or similar, he made them*
> *his own; and so became a* critic *at a cheap ex-*
> *pence (Shakespeare, I, 154).*

**received all his notes:** The Yale editor says that most of
Hanmer's notes are in fact included.


PAGE 48


**the last editor:** Warburton. Johnson's respect for Warburton
was undoubtedly genuine. In the *Life of Pope* he included
the following tribute to his editorial predecessor:
> *He was a man of vigorous faculties, a mind*
> *fervid and vehement, supplied by incessant*
> *and unlimited enquiry, with wonderful extent*
> *and variety of knowledge, which yet had not*
> *oppressed his imagination nor clouded his*
> *perspicacity. To every work he brought a*
> *memory full fraught, together with a fancy*
> *fertile of original combination, and at once*
> *exerted the powers of the scholar, the reason-*
> *er, and the wit. But his knowledge was too*
> *multifarious to be always exact, and his pur-*
> *suits were too eager to be always cautious.*
> *His abilities gave him an haughty confidence*
> *which he disdained to conceal or mollify, and*
> *his impatience of opposition disposed him to*

> *treat his adversaries with such contemptuous*
> *superiority as made his readers commonly his*
> *enemies, and excited against the advocate the*
> *wishes of some who favoured the cause . . . when*
> *Theobald published* Shakespeare, *in opposition*
> *to Pope the best notes were supplied by*
> *Warburton* (Lives, III, 165-67).

. . . serious employments: Because, being a man of God, he
had, or should have had, higher matter before him.

precipitation: On Goneril's line from Act I, scene iii of
  *King Lear*: *Old fools are babes again; and must be used /*
  *With checks, as flatteries when they are seen abus'd,*
  Warburton had been convinced that Shakespeare "must have
  wrote": *Old folks are babes again; and must be us'd /*
  *With checks, not flatteries when they're seen abus'd.*
  Johnson, however, preferred the reading of the old quarto,
  giving the following reasons:
> *I am in doubt whether there is any error of*
> *transcription. The sense seems to be this:*
> Old men must be treated with checks, *when as*
> they are seen to be deceived with flatteries:
> *or, when they are weak enough to be seen ab-*
> *used by flatteries, they are then weak enough*
> *to be* used with checks. *There is a play on*
> *the words* used *and* abused. *To abuse is, in*
> *our author, very frequently the same as to*
> deceive. *This construction is harsh and un-*
> *grammatical* . . . (See *Shakespeare*, IX, 384).

consciousness of quick discernment: Cf. note to *Cymbeline*, Act
  I, scene iii, 1st Lord: *She's a good sign, but I have seen*
  *small reflection of her wit.* Warburton had commented:
> *If* sign *be the true reading, the poet means*
> *by it* constellation, *and by* reflection *is*
> *meant* influence. *But I rather think, from*
> *the answer* ("She shines not upon fools, lest
> the reflection should hurt her"), *that he*
> wrote shine. *So, in his* Venus and Adonis:
> *"As if, from thence, they borrowed all their*
> *shine".*
  Johnson, by way of reply, remarked: *There is acuteness*
  *enough in this note, yet I believe the poet meant nothing*
  *by* sign *but* fair outward shew (*Shakespeare*, IX, 185).

perverse interpretations: On Warburton's interpretation of
  the Duke's famous speech on death in Act III, scene i of
  *Measure for Measure*, Johnson remarked: . . . *I think Dr.*
  *Warburton totally mistaken* (*Shakespeare*, II, 75).

where the sense is plain to every other reader: Johnson replied
  to a long note by Warburton on *Hamlet*, Act I, scene iv:

> *The critic, in his zeal for change, writes*
> *with so little consideration, as to say, that*
> *Hamlet cannot call his father* canonized, *be-*
> *cause* we are told he was murdered with all his
> sins fresh upon him. *He was not then told it,*
> *and had so little power of knowing it, that he*
> *was to be told it by an apparition. The long*
> *succession of reasons upon reasons proves*
> *nothing, but what every reader discovers,*
> *that the king had been buried, which is im-*
> *plied by so many adjuncts of burial, that the*
> *direct mention of* earth *is not necessary*
> (*Shakespeare*, X, 211).

**emendations . . . happy and just:** Warburton's justification
    for his reading of Hamlet's: *For if the sun breed maggots*
    *in a dead dog, / Being a god, kissing carrion. / Have you*
    *a daughter?* in place of "a good kissing carrion" in *Hamlet,*
    Act II, scene ii inspired Johnson to remark: *This is a noble*
    *emendation, which almost sets the critic on a level with*
    *the author* (*Shakespeare*, X, 246-47).


PAGE 49


**specious:** Plausible.

**wantonness of insult:** Warburton expressed his anger at this
    passage in private letters. Nichol Smith cites Nichols,
    *Anecdotes*, V, 595 for Johnson's prediction that Warburton
    would not reply directly: *he'll not come out, he'll only*
    *growl in his den.* For an account of Warburton's response,
    the Yale editor refers the reader to A.W. Evans, *Warburton*
    *and the Warburtonians* (1932), pp.163-64, and records that
    Johnson actually softened a number of his notes on War-
    burton's edition.

**revising:** Here meaning Johnson's final looking-over of
    his edition.

**fabricks:** I.e. buildings.

**comments:** Comments on.

**meteors of intelligence:** Cf. *The Vanity of Human Wishes* (1749),
    lines 73-76 (*Yale*, VI, 95):
      *Unnumber'd suppliants croud Preferment's gate,*
      *Athirst for wealth, and burning to be great;*
      *Delusive Fortune hears th'incessant call,*
      *They mount, they shine, evaporate, and fall.*

PAGE 50

**suffered by Achilles:** *Iliad,* XII, 106-13.   See Pope, lines
   115ff:
   *Die then, my Friend! what boots it to deplore?*
   *The great, the good* Patroclus *is no more!*
   *He, far thy Better, was fore-doom'd to die,*
   *"And thou, dost thou, bewail Mortality?"*
   *See'st thou not me, whom Nature's Gifts adorn,*
   *Sprung from a Hero, from a Goddess born;*
   *The Day shall come (which nothing can avert)*
   *When by the Spear, the Arrow, or the Dart,*
   *By Night, or Day, by Force or by Design,*
   *Impending Death and certain Fate are mine.*
   *Die then - He said; and as the Word he spoke*
   *The fainting Stripling sunk, before the Stroke;*
   *His Hand forgot its Grasp, and left the Spear;*
   *While all his trembling Frame contest his Fear.*
   *Sudden,* Achilles *his broad Sword display'd,*
   *And buried in his Neck the reeking Blade.*

**Dr. Warburton:** Only now does Johnson mention Warburton by name.

**The canons of criticism:** *The Canons of Criticism,* by Thomas
   Edwards (1748; 3rd ed. 1750).   Edwards makes fun of Warburton
   by ennumerating various *Canons or Rules for Criticism* ex-
   tracted from Warburton's notes on Shakespeare.   Canon I
   reads: *A Professed Critic has a right to declare, that his*
   *Author wrote whatever he thinks he should have written, with*
   *as much positiveness as if he had been at his elbow.*
      Of Thomas Edwards, Johnson is reported by Boswell to have
   said: *A fly, Sir, may sting a stately horse and make him*
   *winze; but the one is an insect, and the other is a horse*
   *still* (*Life,* I, 263, n.3).

**the revisal of Shakespeare's text:** By Benjamin Heath (1765).

**incendiary:** Arsonist.

**puny battle:** *Coriolanus,* Act IV, scene iv, lines 4-6, a mis-
   quotation: *. . . then know me not; / Lest that their wives*
   *with spits, and boys with stones, / In puny battle slay me*
   (*Shakespeare,* VII, 446).

**kill'd:** *Macbeth,* Act II, scene iv, lines 14-15.   Upton's second
   edition of his work on Shakespeare (1748) included attacks
   on Warburton's edition of the previous year.

PAGE 51

**one is a wit, and one a scholar:** Edwards is the wit, Heath
   the scholar. According to the 'Twickenham Pope', Edwards
   had: *dealt some damaging blows at Warburton's reputation
   as an editor.* Irritated by Edwards' attack, Warburton replied scathingly in notes to his edition of Pope (1751).
   Johnson is concerned to remove the discussion from the
   realm of personal controversy.

**the little which they have been able to perform:** Only very
   occasionally are notes or conjectures of Edwards and Heath
   admitted into Johnson's edition.

**candour:** Indulgence, generosity.

**endeavours of others:** It is characteristic of Johnson to
   show generosity towards other writers, however insignificant.

**skilled in:** Knowledgeable in.

**curious:** *Dict.*: *Accurate; careful not to mistake.*

**licentious confidence of editors:** I.e. the confidence of
   editors in their right to be unrestrained.

**empirick:** One who relies solely upon observation and experiment. In his *Dictionary*, Johnson gave: *A trier or experi-
   menter; such persons as have no true education in, or knowledge of physical practice, but venture upon hearsay and
   observation only.*

**Dr. Grey:** In two volumes (1754). The Yale editor notes that
   on the flyleaf of his copy of Heath's *Revisal*, Johnson wrote:
   *Such critics of Shakespear as Theobald and Gray perceive
   matters that eluded Pope and Warburton. This phenomenon
   is only to be explained by the fact that we editors have
   attempted to restore, that is, emend the text instead of
   explain it.*

PAGE 52

**scholiast:** *Dict.*: *The writer of explanatory notes.*

## PAGE 53

**wit:** Here meaning mind or intelligence.

**mean men proud:** *Henry VI Part II*, Act IV, scene i, line 106: *Small things make base men proud.* One of the "practical axioms" that Johnson mentions earlier in the *Preface* (p.5).

**turbulence:** *Dict.*: *Tumult; confusion.*

**exalt:** *Dict.*: *To heighten; to improve; to refine by fire, as in chemistry.*

## PAGE 54

**merely relative:** I.e. depending entirely on the background, education, etc. of the person responsible for them: relating to the idiosyncrasies of particular readers.

**innocent and rational pleasure:** Cf. Boswell, *Life* (April 1778), III, 292, where Johnson is criticizing "monastick morality": *Pleasure of itself is not a vice. Having a garden, which we all know to be prefectly innocent, is a great pleasure.* When asked if harmless pleasure is not very tame, Johnson replied:
> *Nay, Sir, harmless pleasure is the highest praise. Pleasure is a word of dubious import; pleasure is in general dangerous, and pernicious to virtue; to be able therefore to furnish pleasure that is harmless, pleasure pure and unalloyed, is as great a power as man can possess* (*Life* (April 1779), III, 388).

**consequential:** With logical and mathematical sequence.

**vagrant:** I.e. wandering.

**any single scholiast:** The Yale editor cites Johnson's letter to Thomas Warton (14 April, 1758): *A commentary must arise from the fortuitous discoveries of many men in devious walks of literature.* In the same letter Johnson thanked Warton for his contribution of notes, promising to add an appendix, *so that nothing comes too late.* See *The Letters of Samuel Johnson*, ed. R.W. Chapman, I, 114.

**customs, too minute to attract the notice of law:** Those which do attract this notice can be traced by reference to old law statutes.

**fugitive:** Fleeting rather than hidden.


PAGE 55


**poetical beauties or defects I have not been very diligent to observe:** Cf. Johnson's comments in the *Proposals* where he is criticising Pope and Warburton for giving too much of their attention to the poetical beauties and defects, by using asterisks, commas, and double commas, to mark them.   Of these, he wrote:
> . . . *the only effect is, that they preclude the pleasure of judging for ourselves, teach the young and ignorant to decide without principles; defeat curiosity and discernment, by leaving them less to discover; and at last shew the opinion of the critick, without the reasons on which it was founded, and without affording any light by which it may be examined.*
> *The editor, though he may less delight his own vanity, will probably please his reader more, by supposing him equally able with himself to judge of beauties and  faults, which require no previous acquisition of remote knowledge* (*Yale* , VII, 57).

In the same place, Johnson nevertheless wrote that: *The observation of faults and beauties is one of the duties of an annotator . . .*

**table book:** *Dict.: A book on which any thing is graved or written without ink.*  A table book would be used as we would use a jotting pad.


PAGE 56


**candidate:** I.e. beginner, or tyro.

**affectation of singularity:** I.e. desire to be different for the sake of it.


PAGE 57


**advanced into:** Inserted into.

animadversion: Literally meaning a turning away of one's mind
   from. Johnson defined to "animadvert" in his *Dictionary*
   as: *To pass censure.*

collectors of these rarities: This passage is supposed to
   have been aimed at David Garrick. Joseph Warton wrote
   to his brother on 22 Jan. 1766 that: *Garrick is intirely
   off from Johnson, and cannot, he says, forgive him his
   insinuating that he witheld his old editions, which always
   were open to him.* See Wool, *Biographical Memoirs of
   Joseph Warton* (1806), p.313.

enumeration: Usually below the *Dramatis Personae.*


PAGE 57


publishers: Johnson means "editors".


PAGE 58


measure: I.e. metre.

particle: In the grammatical sense.

primitive diction: I.e. first wording.

perspicuity: Clarity.


PAGE 59


with least violence: With least deviation from the received
   text.

interstice: *Dict.*: *Space between one thing and another.*

Huetius: The French Scholar, Pierre Daniel Huet, *De Inter-
   pretatione Libri Duo* (1661). The Yale editor suggests
   that Johnson is thinking of Book I, Part ix *Ars inter-
   pretandi paucis explicatur.* The book was apparently in
   Johnson's possession.

have no division in the first folio: In a note on Act II, scene
   i of *Troilus and Cressida*, Johnson remarked that: *This play*

*is not divided into acts in any of the original editions*
*(Shakespeare, IX, 46).*

change of place: Johnson defines an act as we might define
a scene.

A pause: On the last line of Act IV, scene i of *Richard III*,
Johnson noted that: *Hither the third act should be extended,*
*and here it very properly ends with a pause of action*
*(Shakespeare, VII, 107).*

accidental and arbitrary: Cf. Johnson's remarks in *The Rambler*,
No. 156:
> *By what accident the number of acts was limited*
> *to five, I know not that any author has informed*
> *us; but certainly it is not determined by any*
> *necessity arising either from the nature of*
> *action or propriety of exhibition.  An act is*
> *only the representation of such a part of the*
> *business of the play as proceeds in an unbroken*
> *tenor, or without intermediate pause.  Nothing*
> *is more evident than that of every real, and by*
> *consequence of every dramatick action the inter-*
> *vals may be more or fewer than five; and in-*
> *deed the rule is upon the English stage every day*
> *broken in effect, without any other mischief than*
> *that which arises from an absurd endeavour to ob-*
> *serve it in appearance.  Whenever the scene is*
> *shifted the act ceases, since some time is*
> *necessarily supposed to elapse while the person-*
> *ages of the drama change their place.*

one unbroken continuity: There are act and scene divisions
in some of the quartos.  Cf. Johnson's comments on Act V,
scene i of *Richard III*:
> *This scene should, in my opinion, be added to*
> *the foregoing act, so the fourth act will have*
> *a more full and striking conclusion, and the*
> *fifth act will comprise the business of the*
> *important day, which put an end to the competi-*
> *tion of York and Lancaster.  Some of the quarto*
> *editions are not divided into acts, and it is*
> *probable, that this and many other plays were*
> *left by the author in one unbroken continuity,*
> *and afterwards distributed by chance, or what*
> *seems to have been a guide very little better,*
> *by the judgment or caprice of the first editors*
> *(Shakespeare, VII, 141).*

PAGE 60

**thousand absurdities:** In a note at the beginning of Act IV,
scene ii of *As You Like It,* Johnson said that:
*The foregoing noisy scene was introduced only
to fill up an interval, which is to represent
two hours. This contraction of the time we
might impute to poor Rosalind's impatience,
but that a few minutes after we find Orlando
sending his excuse. I do not see that by any
probable division of the acts this absurdity
can be obviated (Shakespeare,* III, 360).

**points:** Punctuation marks.

PAGE 61

**margin:** Johnson is thinking of the practice in classical
texts of an earlier generation.   His notes, of course,
appear at the foot of the page.

PAGE 62

**nec feceris:** *When in doubt, don't (Pliny, Letters,* I, xviii).

**wit struggling with its own sophistry:** Cf. Pope, *Dunciad,* Bk.
IV, lines 21-26:
*Beneath his foot-stool,* Science *groans in Chains,
And* Wit *dreads Exile, Penalties and Pains.
There foam'd rebellious* Logic, *gagg'd and bound,
There, stript, fair* Rhet'ric *languish'd on the ground;
His blunted Arms by* Sophistry *are born,
And shameless Billingsgate her Robes adorn.*

**. . . first behind:** *Temple of Fame,* lines 37-40.   The last line
should read *names deface.*

**wonderful:** A source of wonder.

PAGE 63

**Bishop of Aleria:**   Johnson is referring to Joannes Andreas, Bishop
of Aleria, in Corsica.   While at Rome he edited the writings of
various Latin authors.   These were published between 1468 and 1475.

**English Bentley:** Richard Bentley was the famous editor of Milton and published an edition of *Paradise Lost* in 1732.

**regimen:** Prevailing system.

**invariable quantities:** The syllables in Greek and Latin words have fixed lengths, being either long or short. These are an essential element in Greek and Latin verse metres, whose rhythm is based on syllable length rather than on stress.

**Scaliger:** Joseph Justus Scaliger (1540-1609). Sandys, *A History of Classical Scholarship* (Cambridge, 1908), II, 201 says he was *the first to point the way to a sounder method of emendation founded on the genuine tradition of the MSS.*

**Salmasius:** The classical scholar, Claude de Saumaise (1588-1653), received letters from the aged Scaliger. He is famous for his political controversy with the poet Milton.

**. . . codices incidimus:** *Our conjectures make fools of us, putting us to shame, when later we hit upon better MSS.* Joseph Scaliger, *Epistolae* (Leyden, 1627), *Epistola CCXLVIII to Claudius Salmasius*, 14th July, 1608.

**Lipsius:** Justus Lipsius (1547-1606). Sandys, *A History of Classical Scholarship*, III, 309: *the greatest Latin scholar of the Southern Netherlands.* Lipsius was a textual critic and writer of exegeses, famed for his edition of Tacitus, *Ad Annales Cornelii Taciti Liber Commentarius* (Antwerp, 1574). He held posts at Jena, Cologne, Louvain and Leyden.

PAGE 64

**. . . remediis laboratur:** The quotation is from Lipsius's preface *Ad Lectorem* to his *Ad Annales Cornelii Taciti Liber Commentarius* (Antwerp, 1574).

PAGE 65

**highest pleasure that the drama can give:** Johnson is here returning to an encomium on Shakespeare.

**throws away the book:** The "reader" referred to here is Johnson himself. *He had,* writes Boswell, *a peculiar facility in* *seizing at once what was valuable in any book, without submitting to the labour of perusing it from beginning to end (Life, I, 71).*

**. . . whole has been surveyed:** Cf. Pope, *Essay on Criticism,* lines 235-36: *Survey the WHOLE, nor seek slight faults to find.*

**grateful:** I.e. gratifying.

## PAGE 66

**allusions understood:** The 1664 Folio is the worst in every respect.

**comprehensive soul:** "Comprehensive" was the term habitually applied by Johnson to Dryden himself.  On this same passage, Johnson wrote in his *Life of Dryden:*
> *In a few lines is exhibited a character, so extensive in its comprehension, and so curious in its limitations, that nothing can be added, diminished, or reformed; nor can the editors and admirers of Shakespeare, in all their emulation of reverence, boast of much more than of having diffused and paraphrased this epitome of excellence, of having changed Dryden's gold for baser metal, of lower value though of greater bulk* (*Lives,* I, 412)

**greatest of mankind:** Jesus Christ.

**clenches:** Puns.

**. . . cupressi:** From Dryden's *Essay on Dramatic Poesy, Essays,* I, 67.  The Latin is line 25 of Virgil's *Eclogue,* I.  In his translation of The First Pastoral, or Tityrus and Meliboeus, *The Works of Virgil* (1697), lines 34-35, Dryden translated: *But Country Town's, compar'd with her, appear / Like Shrubs, when lofty Cypresses are near.*  Johnson had himself written a verse translation of part of this pastoral as a school exercise in 1726, and had borrowed from Dryden's version.

**use of types:** I.e. use of the printing press.

## PAGE 67

**. . . of truth:** This paragraph was added in the edition of 177'